FAMILIAR ANIMALS
OF AMERICA

.

FAMILIAR ANIMALS

Drawings by CARL BURGER

HARPER & ROW, PUBLISHERS
NEW YORK, EVANSTON, AND LONDON

OF AMERICA

by WILL BARKER

foreword by ALASTAIR MacBAIN

FAMILIAR ANIMALS OF AMERICA

To the Memory of My Mother and Father

CONTENTS

AMPHIBIANS AND REPTILES

FOREWORD

by ALASTAIR MacBAIN

America's history, traditions, and folklore are full of Nature. Early colonists of New England and Virginia had in the wild turkey a tremendously important source of food. Benjamin Franklin wanted the wild turkey as the bird for our national emblem rather than the bald eagle. The rage for beaver hats inaugurated by Beau Brummel in England in 1779 came at a time when the European beaver was practically exterminated. The demand for beaver pelts by European hatters was responsible for the opening up of the far West. From Canada to the Rio Grande, and from the Missouri to California, such mountain men as Kit Carson, Joseph Meek, and Jim Bridger set out on trapping expeditions to supply Europe's tremendous demand for beaver skins.

Thoreau recognized man's need of living close to nature when he wrote in *Walden*:

"We need the tonic of wildness—to wade sometimes in marshes where the bittern and the meadow-hen lurk, and hear the booming of the snipe, to smell the whispering sedge where only some wilder and more solitary fowl builds her nest, and the mink crawls on its belly close to the ground . . . We can never have enough of Nature."

Today our people are still discovering the fascination and pleasure to be found in nature and the wild animals around us. One hundred and sixty million strong, preoccupied by tensions and fears of the Atomic Age, Americans have turned to the out-of-doors for recreation as never before. At least one of every three men, women, and children in this country takes part in some outdoors activity having to do with the almost infinite variety of flora and fauna of our generously endowed land.

I first met Will Barker when he was writing and editing for the U. S. Fish and Wildlife Service. His ever-present curiosity and enthusiasm gave real values to his daily chores; his appreciation at uncovering little-known facts about his favorite animals lent authenticity to his copy. These things also set him on the path from which —many a naturalist will testify—there is no escape once you begin to explore the endless entrancing vistas of nature.

It is a good thing to see, this business of somebody discovering the out-of-doors. Will Barker's never-ending delight at the wonder of it all becomes part of every essay he writes, each animal portrait he makes.

Familiar Animals of America should give you a better understanding of our animal neighbors. And while you are reading it, Will Barker will be out exploring new wild places, making new friends among Nature's varied clan.

PREFACE

North America, with its Arctic areas and subtropical regions, with mountain country East and West, and with arid deserts, fertile plains, and well-watered valleys has almost every possible variation in temperature, precipitation, soil fertility, and plant cover.

As a result our wildlife is diversified: it includes such widely differing species as the Alaska brown bear, the largest land carnivore in the world; the short-tailed shrew, possibly the smallest mammal in the world; and the opossum, which has survived apparently unchanged since it roamed the continent with dinosaurs seventy to one hundred million years ago. Then there is the prairie dog, whose social behavior resembles that of a clannish human community; the beaver, whose impoundment of water is an important contribution to man's economy and wildlife's needs; and the hoptoad, whose consumption of crop and garden pests makes it worth about twenty dollars a year to the agriculturist. All these, and such commonly seen species as rabbits, squirrels, and garter snakes, are but a few of the many animals around us.

The better we become acquainted with the wildlife of the regions in which we live or that in sections of the country we intend to visit, the more enjoyment we have in watching animals. In Colonial times the abundance of animals, particularly big-game species, was almost unbelievable; the American bison, or buffalo, drifted between summer and winter feeding grounds in herds estimated at fifty million; the American elk, or wapiti, was almost as numerous, and in seemingly endless numbers the antelope, or pronghorn, raced across the sage-dotted prairies of the Northwest. Although many of our animals are no longer so abundant and some species have not survived the spread of civilization, there are more than many people realize.

Familiar Animals of America is about many of our present-day mammals and some of our reptiles and amphibians. Most of the well-known species are included and some that are rare or regional have been written about, too. Each sketch gives the life history of the animal, its behavior, its ecological role—that is, its place in the plant and animal community—and its range.

The plan of *Familiar Animals of America* is simple; it is in two sections. Section I is about mammals; Section II is about a few of our reptiles and amphibians. Each sketch, illustrated by Carl Burger's fine drawings, is captioned by the animal's common name or names, and either the scientific name of the family, genus, or species. The choice for the form of the scientific name depended upon whether the sketch was about a single species, several species belonging to the same genus, or an entire family.

For the valuable information furnished me while writing this book, I wish to thank the following Federal agencies: Fish and Wildlife Service and National Park Service, United States Department of the Interior; Forest Service, United States Department of Agriculture; Division of Mammals and Division of Reptiles and Amphibians, United States National Museum; and the National Zoological Park. I also wish to thank the American Red Cross, the Canadian Embassy, and the Pan-American Sanitary Bureau for information they supplied or answers their staffs have given to my questions. And to all those individuals who have given of their time and knowledge to aid me in the writing of this book I am deeply grateful.

If any of the data these organizations or individuals so willingly furnished are misinterpreted, the fault is mine. Any branch of natural history is an ever-changing science; yesterday's theories and observations may be disproved or corroborated by today's findings. Current for many centuries, Aristotle's theory that instead of migrating swallows buried themselves in the mud to hibernate has long since been proved untrue. How little we sometimes know about even a common species like the chimney swift is evident when we realize that until 1944 no one knew where the swift went during the winter. Through the recovery of banded swifts in that year it was learned that some of these birds spend the winter in northeastern Peru.

The Cooperative Wildlife Research Unit Program is conducting long-term research projects that include, among others, studies of deer browsing on plantations and forests, appraisal of damage by small rodents, ecological and life-history studies of deer, and a preliminary sea-otter study to determine the possibilities of restocking this marine mammal in areas of its former range. Studies on the ecology of the muskrat and the nutria in gulf-coast marshes have been made, and one on the biology, habits, and economic importance of the American bobcats is nearing completion.

No doubt when these studies are published and available, new facts about the animals around us will come to light. But as Victor H. Cahalane, formerly a mammologist with National Park Service and now with the Museum of the State of New York, has remarked, "It is impossible to write a book about the lives of mammals that will generalize their actions with invariable accuracy."

I hope that all of you who read *Familiar Animals of America* have as much enjoyment as I did in writing it. If you find an inaccuracy or have some new information about a particular species, I hope you will let me know. And to Richard B. McAdoo, my editor and mentor at Harper & Brothers, I wish to give particular thanks for making this book possible.

W. B.

Washington, D. C.

MAMMALS

OPOSSUM

Didelphis virginiana

O nce the opossum was an animal of the Southeast, but now it has extended its range north into Canada and west as far as Colorado, and has been introduced in California, Oregon, and Washington. Recent scientific studies of this grayish-white animal suggest that the extension of its range, particularly to the north, may derive from a superior ability to adjust to body temperature. If this proves to be true, then it is about the only superior characteristic of the opossum—apparently somewhat of a moron among mammals.

Vernon Bailey, naturalist of the United States Biological Survey (now incorporated into the Fish and Wildlife Service), once measured cranial capacity of several animals, including the opossum, by counting the number of beans it took to fill the brain cases:

Opossum	21	Raccoon	150
Skunk (2)	35, 50	Red fox	198
Arctic hare	46	Coyote	325
Porcupine	70	Gray wolf	438

The opossum belongs to the "Ancient Order of Marsupials or Pouched Mammals," and is something of an anachronism among present-day American mammals. It has changed but little since it roamed the continent with dinosaurs seventy to one hundred million years ago. Most animals have become more and more specialized as they evolved, but not the opossum, which was described by Captain John Smith in 1612 as follows: "An opassom hath an head like a Swine, a taile like a Rat, and is of the bigness of a Cat. Under the belly she hath a bagge wherein she lodgeth, carrieth, and sucketh her young."

The opossum described by Smith is the Virginia opossum, largest of a family that is native only to North, Central, and South America. The animal's generic name stems from two Greek words—"di," meaning two, and "delphys," meaning uterus, and its common name is a derivative of the Algonquin term *apasum*, meaning "white animal." Its color phases also include black, cinnamon, and all white in the case of a true albino.

An opossum, whose individual home range is about fifteen to forty acres, likes woods and water, with swamps and wet bottomlands the favored environment. The animal is not at all particular about living quarters and dens in whatever is at hand—rocky crevice, tree-trunk cavity, hollow log, deserted 'chuck or skunk burrow, or brush pile. Into any of these places it carries dried leaves or grasses, using its prehensile, or grasping, tail to transport nesting material. To place material in its tail, an opossum grasps the object in its mouth, then with the aid of forefeet passes the object back under the arched body to the tail, held crooked beneath the body. Hind feet pack material into the crook of the tail, then the material is carried into the nest.

One litter a year is born in the North, two litters a year in the South. Northern 'possums are born somewhat later than southern animals, which are brought forth during January and February. The young are born in a sparsely lined nest after the shortest gestation period of any North Amercian mammal—only twelve and one-half days. At birth a 'possum, one in a litter of five to sixteen, is little more than an embryo. Hairless and scarcely two-thirds the size of a honeybee, the newborn animal weighs about 1/270 ounce; sixteen to twenty of the tiny creatures fit easily into a tablespoon.

Forefeet are well developed at birth and a young 'possum loses no time in squirming its way to one of the nipples in the mother's fur-lined abdominal pouch. Her nipples usually number thirteen. Once it has found a nipple of its dam, the animated embryo fastens on to the mammary gland, which then becomes so swollen inside the nurser's mouth that the animal cannot be shaken off. In a litter numbering more than thirteen those arriving in the pouch last, die.

After about sixty days a young 'possum develops a coat of fine fur, its eyes open, and it sometimes ventures outside the pouch or travels around with the mother by clinging to the fur of her back. In another thirty days an opossum weighs about eight ounces and forages for itself, and by the following February the animal is mature. A full-grown opossum weighs from four to fourteen pounds and measures twenty-four to thirty-four inches from the tip of its pointed nose to the pinkish-white tip of its twelve-inch tail. The tail is used for balance in climbing, or for assistance in coming down out of trees; and by the young it is often used to hang hindside up. As with many prolific animals, the life span of a 'possum is short—perhaps two years in the wild, seven to eight years in captivity.

The 'possum, a silent, solitary animal except at mating time, when the male grinds its teeth while seeking several mates, sleeps the day away in the home site of its choice. During extremely cold weather, though not a true hibernator, the animal may den up in a torpid state for several days. If abroad during cold weather, an opossum's tail and ears are often frostbitten; sometimes part of a tail may drop off because of frostbite, then the animal has difficulty in climbing.

When the sun has set and the forlorn call of the screech owl echoes through the woods, a 'possum sets forth in search of food on a circuitous trip of two or more miles. On such a quest the animal leaves a distinctive track—due to the big toes on the hind feet that can be moved, like a thumb, at right angles to the other four toes. Hind prints resemble a human hand; smaller fore prints resemble a star or bird track, and when the tail drag shows it looks something like a parenthesis mark.

The animal, really a scavenger, eats flesh, living and dead, and fruits and vegetables. On the long list of other foods in its diet are ants, crickets, and grasshoppers; mice, moles, and other small mammals; lizards, snakes, and skinks; wild birds and their eggs as well as the eggs of domestic poultry and some poultry itself; and blackberries, wild cherries, and mulberries. A 'possum is particularly fond of pokeberries and eats them until its grayish-white coat is stained purple. In the South the opossum, a good climber, goes up persimmon trees to gorge on the fruit when ripe.

Among predators that a young animal has to be on the lookout for are bobcats, coyotes, dogs, foxes, ocelots, and wolves, and hawks and owls. And of course man, who, with almost any kind of dog, "runs 'possums" at night. Its flesh tastes rather like pork and with sweet potatoes makes an esteemed dish in some areas.

Although 'possum fur is of no great value, trappers and farm boys take thousands of the animals each year. Prime pelts bring about fifty cents each; ordinary pelts bring thirty cents or less. Opossum fur is used naturally or dyed to simulate fitch, marten, and skunk, or sheared to resemble beaver and nutria. The fur is seldom made up

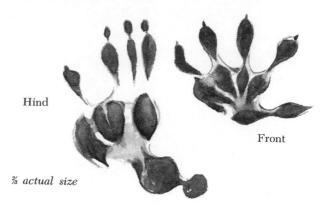

Hind

Front

⅔ actual size

into full-length coats, as the wearing quality is poor. Its durability rating in comparison with some others is as follows:

Rabbit	5	Mink	75
Opossum	37	Raccoon	80
Muskrat	35 to 60	Beaver	85
Striped skunk	50 to 75	Otter	100

Opossums are easily caught, often in traps set for more valuable fur animals like the fox. As pets, the animals are unsatisfactory, due to their stupidity and their repellent odor, caused by the secretion of a musk that is vastly different from the acrid scent of skunk musk. Perhaps the odor of the 'possum is one reason why many other wild, flesh-eating animals bypass it as prey.

Discounting the 'possum's odor, the only way by which the animal can apparently protect itself is to feign death. If you corner the animal, it flops down, shuts its eyes, rolls over on its side, lets its tongue loll out of its mouth, and goes limp all over. Occasionally a gurgle or a hiss precedes this performance. Whether the act is deliberate or an automatic trance induced by shock no one has determined. Playing 'possum may have a survival value for the animal; a dog will leave an inert opossum alone.

Because it has ignored evolution, the animal may be of value in medical research. If a scientist wishes to observe the effects of an injected hormone on embryonic development, a pregnant mammal of any other species has to be cut open. But with the 'possums at hand, the embryonic young in a female's pouch are easily available for scientific experiment. So it looks as if the opossum which has survived unchanged for eons due to its fecundity, may prove to be more than a mere curiosity as North America's only marsupial.

SHREWS

Soricidae

Titian R. Peale, the wildlife artist for whom George Washington once sat for a portrait, accompanied Stephen H. Long on his expedition to the Rocky Mountains during the 1820's. At Engineer Cantonment on the Missouri River, Peale inspected a wolf pitfall to see if a catch had been made. Instead of finding a hundred-pound gray wolf in the bottom of the pit, the artist found one of the smallest mammals in the world. Scurrying back and forth was a mouselike creature, with a tapering muzzle, tiny eyes, almost invisible ears, and a velvety coat of dark-gray fur. The restive animal in the pitfall was a short-tailed shrew, whose greatest weight is no more than one half an ounce. Peale became the first man known to collect a specimen of the short-tailed shrew.

The salivary glands of this shrew contain venom similar to that of such poisonous snakes as the cobra. When the shrew bites a mouse with its thirty-two black-tipped teeth, the venom flows into the wound, causing paralysis. With the victim rendered helpless the shrew then proceeds to devour it. While gobbling down its food, the shrew utters a high-pitched growl and quivers from head to foot. The short-tailed shrew is the only one in North America that has this potent venom.

Among North American shrews the most widely distributed is the common shrew (*Sorex cinereus*), and the smallest is the pigmy shrew (*Microsorex hoyi*), the tiniest mammal on this continent—perhaps in the world. An adult pigmy shrew weighs about as much as a dime—one-fourteenth of an ounce—and its body measures about two inches.

The common shrew lives in damp areas throughout the greater part of the continent. In such places small round holes in the leaf litter near logs or tunnels in the snow are likely signs of shrew activity. As an adult this gray-brown animal weighs about one-third to

Trail of a shrew made by the animal's
body plowing through the snow.

four-fifths of an ounce and measures about three and one-half to six
and one-half inches from tip of nose to tip of tail.

A solitary animal, the common shrew is active at all times. It darts
about, hunting anything that crawls, flies, or runs. Although classed
as an insectivore, the shrew's diet is varied: in part its food consists
of insects and their larvae, various mollusks including snails, earthworms, lizards, salamanders, small birds, and some vegetation. The
animal also eats carrion, in which maggots may have set to work, and
even devours other shrews.

Day in and day out, all year round, the animal hunts. In captivity
its appetite is so voracious that it has been known to eat three times
its weight every twenty-four hours. If the shrew does not eat frequently it starves to death. Its metabolic rate is more than twice that
of a human being's; this accounts for the enormous intake of foods.
The animal needs such amounts to replenish the energy it burns up
during the course of its hectic life—which is anywhere from twelve
to fourteen months.

The shrew begins life in a small, ball-shaped nest of grasses and
leaves, which may be in a hollow stump, under a log, or in a shallow
burrow. During the mating season the nest is shared by the male and
the female, but once the young are born the female drives the male
from the nest. Usually six young shrews are born at a time, though
there may be three or as many as eight. A newly born shrew is

approximately the size of a honey bee, and is naked, pink, and wrinkled. When a week old its starts crawling around in the nest and begins acquiring a coat of fur. By the time the creature is four weeks old it is well furred, and can hear and see. The young shrew and its litter mates are driven from the nest then; for the mother is getting ready for another of the two or three litters she bears each summer.

Although the great-horned owl, the bobcat, and the weasel prey on young and old shrews, there are a great many flesh-eating animals which leave the shrew alone or kill but do not eat it. On each flank there are glands which secrete a strong-smelling musk; this makes a shrew unpalatable to many animals, including house cats and foxes.

Among the thirty-odd American species of shrews there is one that can walk on water. The largest of the long-tailed group, the water shrew lives around lakes, along rocky streams, and in beaver meadows throughout the greater part of Canada, and in the northern United States. Either black or brown, depending upon the species, the water shrew has a hairy fringe on its hind feet. So equipped the animal swims, dives, and actually walks on the water, apparently supported by surface tension.

Like all of its kind the water shrew has a disposition far from amiable, but like all of its kind it is beneficial to man. Its unrelenting appetite, seemingly out of proportion to its size, helps to keep our insect enemies under control.

MOLES

Talpidae

The mole has a velvetlike coat of gray or brown fur which can be brushed either backward or forward, and thus offers no resistance as this burrowing mammal moves in either direction in its tunnel. Most species of moles are characterized by a pointed muzzle, weak eyes which are only capable of distinguishing light from dark, and a lack of external ears. The powerful forelegs terminate in somewhat circular paws that have five large digging claws. Although the mole is seldom seen, most of us are familiar with its ridges in fields, gardens, and lawns.

Only the Rocky Mountain area and arid regions of the Western prairies are excepted from the ranges of our various moles: the western mole, the shrew mole, the hairy-tailed mole, the star-nosed mole, and the common or eastern species.

The common mole (*Scalopus aquaticus*) makes its tunnels in soil throughout the greater part of the East, and as far West as central Minnesota in the North and central Texas in the South. It digs like a swimmer using the breast stroke. The forepaws are brought forward until they touch in front of the nose, then they are thrust outward and backward, pushing the earth to one side and back. Then the mole usually turns around by executing a slow somersault, and pushes the loosened earth to the surface, creating a "molehill."

In this way the mole often digs as much as 15 feet in an hour with stops for rest and food. During a single night the animal may tunnel for a distance of 75 feet. In observing one mole at work the naturalist and wildlife conservation leader, William Temple Hornaday, discovered that the animal had dug 68 feet of main tunnel and 36½ feet of side tunnels—in all 104½ feet of burrows—in about twenty-five hours.

There are two kinds of tunnels: the deep one and the shallow surface tunnel. A deep one may be as much as six feet below the surface of the ground; in such a burrow the animal lives during

Head and forefeet of the star-nosed mole

winter or passes periods of dry weather and heat. During an inactive stage, induced by extremely low temperatures, the mole lies with its head curled under the body. The other type of tunnel is the surface variety which ridges your lawn. It is made to reach such foods as earthworms, ants, centipedes, snails, slowbugs, and slugs which live in the subsoil—the weathered material which underlies the surface soil. Sometimes the mole eats the seeds of field crops, and the larger western species devours iris and tulip bulbs. Like the shrew, to which it is related, the average mole is an enormous feeder; the creature often consumes half its body weight in food each day.

Except at mating time all but the hairy-tailed and the star-nosed species are solitary. During early spring in the North and late winter in the South males seek females. Six weeks later the annual litter of one to five is born in a chamber in the lower tunnel. Measuring about eight inches across and five inches in depth, the chamber may be lined with dried grasses and leaves or it may be unlined. The nest may also be under a boulder, a stump, or the roots of a bush. A newly born mole is naked, but by the time it is ten days old the little creature is covered with a coat of fine gray fur, and by the time it is a month old it is independent.

During the three years of the life of either the common or western mole, each is so seldom above ground that few predators trouble them. Although coyotes, foxes, and skunks kill some, predators often leave their kills untouched, for the mole has a strong musky odor that many animals dislike. Such owls as the barn, barred, and great-horned, and such hawks as the broad-winged and red-tailed prey on moles, and occasionally snakes go into tunnels after them.

The species you are most likely to see aboveground are the hairy-tailed, the shrew-mole, and the star-nosed mole (*Condylura cristata*), an animal distinguished by a fleshy growth on the end of its snout. The growth, or "star," is composed of twenty-two light-pink rays, symmetrically arranged so that there are eleven on each side. This species is sometimes caught by the pike as it swims along, using its forepaws as a seal uses its flippers to push through the water. During winter the star-nosed mole often runs over the surface of hard-crusted snow—a habit of the shrew-mole which is the climbing member of the family; it goes up into small bushes.

Although the tunnelling of our various moles causes a certain amount of damage (and sometimes necessitates control) and they occasionally destroy the tubers of some flowering bulbs, the animals do a useful job by aerating the soil and consuming numbers of such crop-destroying insects as Japanese beetles and cutworms. So, in general, the mole, whose fur is highly valued, is beneficial to man's interest.

LITTLE BROWN BAT

Myotis lucifugus

The Chinese consider the bat a harbinger of good fortune and use likenesses of it in many symbolic motifs. The animal appears in the *Wu-fu* emblem, a design of five bats circling a stylized tree of life. This signifies the five blessings presumably sought by man: virtue, riches, offspring, long life, happy death; and the *Wu-fu* emblem is frequently set above the door of a Chinese home to attract these benefits.

Throughout the world there are nearly two thousand named species of bats. Among this array are the "pipistrelle," our smallest bat, with a wingspread of about five inches, the "flying fox" of the Philippines, with a foxlike muzzle and a wingspread of nearly five feet, and the "vampire bat" of Central and South America, which laps (rather than sucks) the blood of its human or animal victims.

In North America there are three families: the leaf-nosed bats (*Phyllostomidae*), the free-tailed bats (*Molossidae*), and the typical insect-eating bats (*Vespertilionidae*). Most of our bats, including the various little brown bats and several other species, belong to the third family, which gets its name from the Latin *vespertilio*, meaning "the evening ones."

Among the evening ones are the thirteen species that belong in the group known as Myotis bats (Little Brown Bats); in one form or another these flying mammals range over most of forested North America. And in this group the one known as "the little brown bat" has the widest distribution of them all.

This bat is a small mouselike animal, whose fur is generally brown or blackish-brown. The creature has a pug nose, small, forward-pointing ears, and beady black eyes almost hidden in the folds of the wrinkled skin of its hairless face. The leathery wings are membranes stretched between the long bones of the four fingers and extend back along the body from the forelegs to the hind legs and then back to the tail. Thus the entire membrane forms a sort of parachute which encloses all four legs and the tail. These members serve—like the ribs of an opened umbrella—to keep the membrane taut while flying.

The thumbs on the bat's hands, similar to the human hand but with tremendously elongated fingers, are small, clawed, and free of the membrane. The legs are smaller than the arms and the knee joints bend backward, a physical characteristic that makes walking difficult. Apparently the bat's peculiar knee construction is no handicap in the water, as the animal swims well if necessary.

When evening comes the little brown bat leaves its daytime hideaway—cave, garret, or hollow tree—to seek its prey. The animal employs an undulating flight pattern that resembles the progress of a stone skipped over water. In flying a bat guides itself by sonar or echo-location; as it flies it emits a series of squeaks of such high frequency that they cannot be heard by the human ear. The range of these frequencies is anywhere from 30,000 vibrations a second to about 70,000 vibrations a second. This range is well above the limit of human hearing which extends from 16 vibrations a second to about 30,000.

As soon as the bat starts flying it utters these supersonic cries at the rate of about 30 a second. The frequency is increased as the animal approaches an obstacle and the cries are sometimes emitted at the rate of 50 or 60 a second. As the obstacle is passed the frequency of the cries is decreased.

The bat's cries are deflected by objects in the flight path and the resulting echoes bounce back and are intercepted by the animal's extremely sensitive ears. Muscles in the ears momentarily contract while the squeak is uttered so that the animal is enabled to hear the echo which guides it in avoiding obstacles.

Bats whose ears have been plugged are unable to fly a course without hitting obstructions in their paths—evidence that the animals fly more by ear than by eye. A bat's vision is good, however, and aids daytime species in flying.

The little brown bat both feeds and drinks on the wing. As the animal flies to and fro over water, it dips down and scoops up a tiny mouthful of water, doing this time and again until its thirst is slaked. The various insects on which the bat feeds are caught in its mouth or in its tail membrane. The animal drops this tail membrane so that it curves backward behind the tail and acts as a scoop—a sort of "cowcatcher" in reverse.

In relation to its size the bat eats an amazing amount. At one feeding the little creature often consumes one-quarter of its weight—one-seventh to one-third of an ounce depending upon the species—and more than half its weight during an entire evening of feeding. And by the time the animal is ready to hibernate it may have doubled its weight.

Depending upon the species, bats hibernate in such places as caves, hollow trees, abandoned buildings, bell towers, marten houses, under eaves, and behind shutters of unused rooms. During the prehibernation period bats mate; sometimes there is a winter mating, and one may even occur in the spring. After a delayed fertilization of the egg cell, the embryo develops slowly during the fifty or sixty days required for gestation. When the time of the female is at hand, she flies from one section of the cave in which she is hibernating to an area that is apparently reserved for females about to go into labor. Males stay by themselves in "bachelor quarters." At the "maternity center" the female hangs herself up, head down, holding on by her feet and thumbs, and stretches her encircling membrane so that she can catch the new-born bat as it emerges.

One bat to a litter is the rule for most species; however, there may be two or three and sometimes even four. At birth the little animal is blind, almost naked, and helpless. It clings to its mother's breast, helped to stay in place by the partly folded wings of the parent, and nurses at one of the two nipples. At first the mother carries her baby with her when she flies out in the evening; in about two weeks her offspring is too heavy to carry and is left home, where it hangs itself up like an adult bat. When about three weeks old, a young bat starts practice flights and is soon able to catch its own food.

The little brown bat has few enemies to worry it as it flits back and forth like some will-o'-the-wisp on summer evenings in search of insects. Various species of owls probably capture some bats and others are killed by accidents or severe storms. Animals that have been banded to trace migrations—red, hoary, and silver-haired bats among others migrate south for the winter—have lived ten years or more. A few bats have been kept successfully as pets and among some captive Old World fruit bats, individuals have lived about twenty years.

Contrary to popular belief the bat is a clean animal. The little brown bat has been seen to spend half an hour grooming itself. While hanging upside down the animal uses its long, red tongue to sponge every part of its body within reach of the tongue. Parts of the body beyond the tongue's limit are gone over by a moistened hind foot. The ears, which pick up the sounds bouncing back from obstructions, are cleaned painstakingly by a thumb, moistened by licking. The animal twists the thumb around and around in its ears, much as a mother cleans a baby's ear with a cotton swab.

Bats harbor few parasites other than fleas and none of the little brown bats are thought to carry the human bedbug or any human disease. However, the Pan-American Sanitary Bureau has found through the work of various research teams, including one of Army veterinary and medical officers at Fort Sam Houston, Texas, that some species of fruit-eating and insect-eating bats such as the Mexican free-tailed bat (*Tadarida mexicana*), an insect-eater, may be the medium for spreading various diseases, including rabies.

Bats do not deliberately alight in a woman's hair, as is commonly supposed. Occasionally the animal may use a human being for a perch if none other is available. In handling a bat take care that the little flier does not nip you with some of its thirty-eight, needle-sharp teeth. These animals do not take kindly to much handling and in addition to biting, show their annoyance by squeaking at a frequency audible to the human ear.

Objectionable characteristics of the bat are the musky odor of some species, the greasy spot where the animal hangs, and the droppings below. The droppings, guano, are valuable as fertilizer. At one time guano commanded a price of sixty to ninety dollars a ton, and at such prices more than one hundred thousand tons were taken from Carlsbad Caverns in New Mexico, where there is an enormous bat colony. At times the numbers of bats in this colony have been estimated from one to nine millions, but availability of night-flying insects determines the size of the evening flights. When they leave the caverns at sundown the animals look as if unseen hands were unfurling an almost endless banner of some dark material. It takes about twenty minutes for the bats to stream out of the caverns at sundown as they head for the Pecos River valley where they feed.

The largest bat colony known east of the Mississippi River is in an abandoned New Jersey iron pit about thirty miles from Times Square. More than 20,000 bats, including the big brown bat (*Eptesicus fuscus*), the pigmy bat (*M. subulatus*), and the little brown bat hibernate in the shafts and tunnels of this disused iron pit. Singly or in clusters that look like withered leaves on a branch, the animals cling to the mine's ceiling of magnetite.

Bats in this pit are regularly banded to trace the animals' migrations, and to test their homing instinct. Some work has already been done in this field. The animals are usually banded on the ears or arms so that they can be observed while hanging upside down in the caves in which they hibernate.

In 1953 one bat was found that carried a band dated 1938; another banded bat migrated more than 800 miles from New Mexico to Central America; and a bat banded in Wisconsin and released in Minnesota proved that it knew its way home by flying two hundred and fifty miles to reach the point at which it was banded.

Recently bats have been making a contribution to human welfare. They are now frequently used in laboratory experiments instead of rats; the world's only flying mammal is three hundred times more resistant to the effects of radiation than the usual laboratory rats. So in addition to acting as a natural check on injurious insects, it looks as if the bats may aid us in the fight to overcome the effects of atomic radiation. This use should help to dispel the aversion most people have for bats, and might lead to wider adoption of the *Wu-fu*, two of whose symbolic bats signify long life and a happy death.

NINE-BANDED ARMADILLO

Dasypus novemcinctus

In his book about the quadrupeds of North America John James Audubon wrote: "This singular product of nature resembles a small pig with the shell of a turtle."

Audubon's description of the armadillo is well put; about the size of a house cat, the animal has a shell covering over its entire back and tail. This sheath is a mottled dark brown or yellow-white and is ridged by nine bands. The undersides and the base of the tail are not protected by this hard covering, and are almost naked except for a few hairs. The somewhat horse-like looking head has large ears that remind you of those of a mule, the small, lackluster eyes are set in a fringe of long lashes, and the long, slender nose is tipped with pink.

The animal's appearance is not its only odd characteristic. The armadillo gulps air upon entering a good-sized stream or river. The ingested air inflates the intestines so that the animal swims along buoyed up by its internal "waterwings," and with its snout held above the surface like the periscope of a submarine. To cross narrow streams the animal walks along the bottom under water.

A third peculiarity of the armadillo that makes it unique among mammals is the size and the sex of its yearly litter. During February, March, or April, in a nest of grasses in an underground burrow, the female produces four, open-eyed young; these identical quadruplets are either all males or all females. Sometimes a female twins; then there are eight young, all of the same sex.

The animal belongs to an ancient group of mammals, known as the *Edentates*, the toothless ones. The country's only armored mammal, the armadillo is one in a zoological division which includes the aardvark, an ant-eating mammal of Africa; the three-toed sloth, a slow-moving tree-dweller of Central and South America; and the hedgehog, an English animal which rolls itself up into a ball.

About one hundred years ago the armadillo came north from Central America, crossing the Rio Grande into Texas. The three-foot

Hind

Front

Actual size

animal, whose tail accounts for about half its total length, has spread
to New Mexico, Louisiana, and as far north as the Panhandle of
Oklahoma. It will probably go no farther north, as it cannot stand
prolonged cold weather. In Florida where the armadillo was released it has adapted itself to the environment, and increased.

In these areas the armadillo or its birdlike tracks are usually found
in shady places, where native brushy growths are dense. Although
the animal is generally abroad at dusk, a female with young is apt to
be active during the day. As the animal roots in leaf litter or loose
top soil with its long snout, it grunts. In its diet are fire ants, roaches,
scorpions, tarantulas, and many destructive insects including grasshoppers and sugar-cane borers.

As the armadillo seeks its food, sometimes in the company of as
many as fifty or sixty of its kind, it is preyed upon by such flesh-
eating mammals as the cougar, the coyote, and the wolf. Frequently
the peccary, a pig-like animal of the Southwest, eats the armadillo.
Dogs and men hunt it too.

The armadillo's only defense measure is escape. When alarmed
or attacked, the animal sometimes bounces straight up into the air
before racing away. It can usually outdistance a man, and gets away
from most dogs. Once at a safe distance the armadillo burrows into
the soil so rapidly that it is generally out of sight before a man can
dismount from a horse. Even if its long scaly tail is not completely
underground, the animal can seldom be yanked out; its ridged sheath
"locks" it in the ground.

The flesh of the armadillo tastes rather like pork; in eastern Texas
the animal is frequently called "poor man's pig." It is hunted for
its shell, which is used to make baskets, candlesticks, lampshades, and
ash trays.

PIKA OR CONY

Ochotona princeps

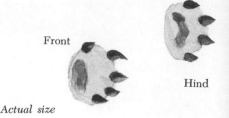

Front

Hind

Actual size

The coloring of a pika, or cony, blends in so well with the gray of the talus-rock piles among which the little mammal lives that to locate one is difficult. And though the pika is a noisy little animal, its peculiar wailing cry is not much help in spotting one, for the cry has an odd, ventriloquial effect. The "Ka-ack! Ka-ack!" sometimes repeated as many as twenty times, first seems to come from a distant rock, when in reality it comes from an animal close at hand, or conversely, it seems to come from nearby when the crier is some distance away.

Eventually you may spot the pika, weighing about seven ounces, atop a broken granite boulder, gray-green with lichens. This animated bit of pale gray fluff looks something like an undersized guinea pig, and has a prominent nose, shoe-button eyes, and large, round ears rimmed with white. Soles of a pika's feet are almost entirely covered with fur, except for a naked pad at the base of each tiny palm and sole which affords traction.

Thus shod a pika can leap from rock to rock without losing its footing. Such leaps often save a pika from a weasel, one of the animal's most relentless predators. Martens, eagles, hawks, and owls are other predators of pikas, which live on mountain crests in western and northwestern North America at altitudes of 8,000 to 13,600 feet. Pikas number about six to an acre and generally dwell in the vicinity of great rock slides at the bases of cliffs, though a few animals live on the valleys and plains between mountain ranges.

A pika does not hibernate, and prepares for winter by laying up a supply of hay like a provident farmer. In gathering its winter food supply, a pika sometimes travels several hundred feet to a mountain meadow. Such expeditions are generally undertaken in the early morning or in the late afternoon. The animal collects many varieties of plants, cutting off short lengths of such herbs as the gentian, the saxifrage, and the yarrow. It climbs into the lower branches of trees like aspens, elders, and chokecherries, and nips off twigs and leaves with its long, chisel-like incisors. With these cuttings and cuttings of thistles, a favorite food, it builds a haystack. Only enough forage is cut each day to make one layer of a stack, the sole property of the pika that racks it up. The stack, often containing as much as a bushel, is always placed so that the sun can cure the vegetation and is generally placed in the lee of some sort of shelter—a fallen tree or a lichen-covered rock. A pika is solicitous of the stack, hauling it underground at the approach of a storm and dragging it out again when the sun is shining.

Even in the fall, when working hardest to gather its winter food supply, a pika quits around noontime to rest. Perched on a rock, dozing in the sun, it looks not unlike a little old Indian chief, hunkered down. Perhaps this was the reason a pika was called "Little Chief Hare" by the Chippewas, who sometimes used pika fur for baby clothes. Upon awakening from its nap, a pika washes its face cat fashion, then goes on with its hay-gathering.

Another name for the pika is rock rabbit, and though related to a rabbit, it does not have rabbit habits. A pika never sits up nor hops, as fore and hind legs are practically the same length, and there is not even the wisp of a tail that is found on a rabbit. In fact, its scientific family name, *Ochotona*, means "short-eared rabbit without a tail."

Though pikas were first discovered on this continent as long ago as 1828 in the Canadian Rockies, scientists have not learned a great deal about their family life. Three to four young are born in any month from late May to early September in a nest under rocks. Weighing about one-third of an ounce at birth, they are weaned early, and then subsist entirely on vegetable matter.

Species closely resembling our pikas live in the Himalayas and the Urals, and the name "pika" comes from an Asiatic tribe in northeastern Siberia. In one form or another the animal makes hay on such high spots as Wheeler Peak, a mountain of 13,600 feet in northern New Mexico. Wheeler Peak is about the southern limit of the pikas' range, which runs north and west to the region of Mount McKinley in Alaska, and on whose snowy slopes the pika makes small tracks that look like those of a miniature snowshoe hare.

VARYING HARE

Lepus americanus

Hares may be differentiated from rabbits by their longer ears and longer hind legs, and the fact that at birth the young have their eyes open and are covered by fur. Among North American hares are the varying or snowshoe hare, the jack rabbit, and the Arctic hare, an animal that is also native to both northern Europe and Asia. And in the East there is the European hare, which was introduced during the early 1900's.

Of these animals the varying hare is the only one with a transcontinental range. A silent forest animal of our northern climates this hare bounds through wooded country from Newfoundland to western Alaska. In the United States the varying hare lives in open woods, brushy areas, and wooded swamps as far south as the mountains of Virginia in the East; in the North-Central states; and in the forests of the Rocky Mountains and those of the Pacific coast.

The varying hare is one of nature's turncoats: in summer the animal is gray-brown, except for the white underside of its short tail; in winter the fur is usually white, except on the rounded ears which are tipped with black. One subspecies (*L. washingtoni*) is distinctive, retaining nearly the same-colored fur the year round.

This seasonal change seems to be associated with survival: in summer the varying hare is barely discernible among the shadows of the woods; in winter the animal becomes such a part of the snowy landscape that it is again difficult to see. Such protective coloring saves many a varying hare from the numerous flesh-eating mammals and predatory birds that hunt it.

Despite these predators and a mortality rate which indicates that less than two animals in one hundred live until they are five years of age, the varying hare maintains itself and reaches peak populations about every ten years. At the height of one of these cycles the animals reached a density of 3,400 in a square mile in Ontario. Three to five litters a season, with each litter containing three or four young, are responsible for the continuing population of varying hares. Sometimes litters are even larger; there may be as many as six or even ten, though the latter number is unusual.

This hare first breeds when it is about a year old. The male, somewhat smaller than the female, starts courting in the northern United States during March. The courtship lasts anywhere from two weeks to a month; during this time the promiscuous male, or buck, chases the equally promiscuous female, or doe, up hill and down dale and back and forth over forest trails.

Sometimes the zigzag course of the chase takes an unexpected turn when the female leaps high into the air, and then upon landing takes off in a new direction. The pursuing male, coming along pellmell, runs beneath the object of his affection, and goes some little distance before he is able to brake, turn, and locate the female. By the time the male spots the female, hightailing off as fast as her strong hind legs can send her, she is well ahead of him. Sometimes a hare in flight builds up a speed to as much as thirty miles an hour.

Often several males pursue one female, and occasionally fights take place; contending males bite and kick out with their large furry hind feet. The catch-me-if-you-can period ends abruptly as the female suddenly becomes docile as a lamb, and mates several times within a few hours.

Some thirty days later the female delivers her young, wherever she happens to be. As soon as a young hare or leveret is born it begins to nurse and continues nursing as the others in the litter are delivered during the next half hour. If danger threatens during the delivery or after they are born, the little hares make gurgling sounds.

Once the young have been fed, the doe leaves them in an inconspicuous spot, then moves off and stations herself some distance away. She feeds her offspring regularly during the next four weeks, even though the young hares can walk and hop within a few hours after birth, and start nibbling green vegetation less than two weeks after their delivery. By the end of the first week, a young hare takes short trips away from the place of its birth, and by the time it is four weeks old the little animal is completely weaned and able to take care of itself.

On a home territory of less than one hundred acres, which the varying hare seems to know as a cartographer knows the area for which he is making a map, the animal feeds in the early morning or during the first part of the night. Through the day a hare remains hunched down in any one of several forms which dot the territory. Forms are depressions in the ground or leaf litter in summer and saucer-like depressions in the snow in winter. Sometimes in winter this hare burrows into the snow for safety or warmth. From time to time the animal rises on tiptoe from its form to look around, though it depends on its keen senses of smell and hearing to detect danger. And during the day a great deal of time is spent in grooming the fur.

The varying hare is inclined to be solitary, but the animal does not drive away other hares on its range; occasionally these hares gather in groups on moonlight nights. Such groups usually converge in clearings, where the animals sit quietly, as if pondering weighty matters. These gatherings are often interrupted when one animal "gets out of order" by chasing another.

On occasion the varying hare eats carrion, but the animal is primarily a vegetarian. During summer it eats herbs, grasses, clover, dandelions, and a great variety of other plants; during winter it feeds on twigs and needles of conifers, and the bark of such trees as the aspen, the birch, the maple, and the willow. The animal strips off the bark with slanting cuts of its four large incisor teeth; behind those on the upper jaw are two additional, small rounded incisors. (The six cutting teeth of hares and rabbits differentiate them from rodents, which have four.) To slake its thirst this hare drinks dew in summer and eats snow in winter.

In its winter feeding the varying hare sometimes competes with deer and moose for browse and also causes damage to conifer plantations. Frequently bark is eaten off to a height of two feet by a feeding hare, standing on its hind legs to pull off the last shred within its reach. This girdling often kills trees and where it is excessive control measures are necessary. The killing of a limited number of seedlings and saplings is probably beneficial, for the remaining trees have additional room to grow.

The varying hare supplies table meat for many people in the North, including Indians, who make sleeping robes of the skins by cutting them into strips and then plaiting them. And for the hunter this hare probably furnishes at least as much sport as all our big-game species put together.

ARCTIC HARE
Lepus arcticus, L. othus

Beyond the limits of the spruce growth the big-footed Arctic hare bounds over the wind-swept slopes of rocky ridges and low mountains. Known by scientists as *L. arcticus* east of the Mackenzie River in the Northwest Territories, and *L. othus* in Alaska, this hare leaves almost deerlike tracks as it travels its range.

In addition to being larger than the varying hare, the Arctic hare is distinguished from the more southerly animal by a tail that is white all year round. Also, in winter the fur of the Arctic hare is white to the base, whereas that of the varying hare is somewhat dark near the body at this season. And of course most Arctic hares have their winter coats for a much longer period than the varying hare. In one area, Ellsmere Island and Greenland, the animals are white the entire year.

The winter coat of the Arctic hare is the clean white of new-fallen snow. Seemingly the animal likes to keep its fur immaculate; if it becomes streaked with dirt, the hare takes a snow bath or rubs against a clump of grass until there is no trace of soil on the fur.

Less solitary than varying hares, the Arctic species will gather in groups of as many as fifty. Such groups often indulge in antics like those of kangaroos. Suddenly the hares may rear up on their hind legs, and hop off in a fashion like people dancing a polka. The animals move along over the frozen ground in a series of springy leaps, with tails sticking out behind like slightly bent whisks, the forelegs extended and bent at the wrists so that the paws dangle, and the black-tipped ears held like the V-shaped victory sign.

Hopping on tiptoe is a habit when this hare senses danger. Although the animal depends primarily on its nose and ears to detect enemies, it often looks over the terrain by rising on tiptoe, then extending itself to its greatest height. Balancing like a ballet dancer on her points, with forelegs held either out from or close to the densely furred body, the animal usually hops over to and up the nearest rocky, snow-powdered ridge.

At a good lookout point the hare pauses to survey the surrounding countryside. For minutes at a time the animal stands upright, maintaining perfect balance even in strong wind. As it scans the countryside like a sentry at a remote outpost, the hare's three- to four-inch ears twist first one way and then another and its nose quivers so that the animal, apparently not trusting entirely to its vision, can hear or scent danger.

If it discovers that a brown or grizzly bear or a lynx, wolf, wolverine, or weasel is approaching, the animal drops to all fours. Then it starts uphill, gaining speed as it bounces along, and continuing its flight until it has outdistanced a pursuer. If the predator is a snowy owl or gyrfalcon, the hare tries to reach the base of a cliff or dodge in among broken rocks, where it is safe from the swooping attacks of these birds.

On the southern part of its range the Arctic hare is ready to mate about the first of April, but farther north the breeding season begins a month later. In June or July a single litter of four to eight is born at a time when the female is wearing her brown or brownish-gray summer coat.

Young Arctic hares have wooly coats that are similar in color to those of their parents and rather like those of lambs in texture. The little animals develop much more slowly than the young of varying hares. Even when this hare is half-grown it cannot outrun an Eskimo child. But by the time it reaches adult weight, anywhere from six to twelve pounds—perhaps even as much as fifteen pounds on the Alaska peninsula—the Arctic hare is as fleet of foot as a greyhound.

As the hare moves over the trails of its territory it looks for food in spots from which the wind has blown the snow. Willow is its mainstay; the animal eats this winter and summer, consuming the buds, the leaves, the twigs, the bark and even the roots, which it grubs out of the ground with its long incisors. During winter the incisors are used to break through hard-crusted snow to get at various plants. At this time of year some carrion and dried grasses and mosses are a part of the diet. In summer the animal eats a variety of dwarf Arctic plants which grow suddenly and profusely during the long hours of sunlight. And hares living on the tundra bordering the sea or ocean feed on kelp and other marine vegetation brought in by the tides.

Except during severe weather a feeding hare is abroad in the morning and evening. But when the wind drives the snow across the frozen waste of its habitat the animal huddles close to a sheltering rock or tunnels into a drift.

As a prey species and as a source of meat for the Eskimos the Arctic hare is valuable. Eskimos prepare the meat by boiling it and make robes by braiding strips of the pelt of this, the largest species of hare in North America.

JACK RABBITS

Lepus townsendii, L. californicus, L. alleni, L. gaillardi

Close relatives of the varying hare are the four species of jack rabbits. For the most part these large hares, with long hind legs and long ears, are native to open, arid country in the West and Southwest. The white-tailed jack rabbit, known, too, as the prairie hare and the plains hare, is the species seen in the Northwest. In addition to living in open prairie country, the white-tailed jack is found on open mountain slopes to a height of 12,000 feet.

This species, weighing from five to ten pounds, has an all-white tail that measures three to four inches in length, and black-tipped ears from five to six inches long. In summer the animal has a grayish-brown coat. In winter, however, the fur of those animals on the northern part of the range becomes entirely white except for the black-tipped ears, while the hares on the southern part of the range only acquire a lighter version of the summer coat.

Except for the pronghorn (see page 233) the white-tailed jack is the speediest animal in the Northwest. It bounds over the tall-grass country of its range in broad jumps of twenty feet, bouncing high into the air every so often. The distinguished naturalist Elliott Coues writing in the 1870's, well described the movement of the white-tailed jack:

The instant it touches the ground it is up again, with a peculiar springy jerk, more like the rebounding of an elastic ball than the result of muscular exertion. With a succession of these high jerky leaps the animal makes off generally in a straight course; there is nothing of the dodging or scuttling that marks the running of the smaller rabbits.

Like all hares the white-tailed jack is abroad generally at night or when the sun is low, feeding on almost any available green plants, including sagebrush, rabbitbrush, and snakeweed. One-quarter and perhaps one-half of the year-round food of this hare is grass. During the day the animal rests in one of several forms distributed over a circular range that is probably no more than two miles in diameter.

In winter the animal tunnels into the snow for warmth and protection from snowy and gray owls, and also seeks protection beside clods of earth in plowed fields.

Across the deserts of the Southwest, dotted with clumps of spiny mesquite, the black-tailed jack rabbit travels at speeds which sometimes attain a rate of forty-five miles an hour. A lean and lanky animal, this hare makes broad jumps of nearly fifteen feet, alternating these with "spy" leaps of four or more feet into the air, for the purpose of observation.

This species (*L. californicus*) is sometimes called the jackass hare because of its eight-inch ears which are tipped with black. The top side of the three- to four-inch tail is also black, and the sandy coat takes on a grayish cast in winter, but does not turn white. Like the females of the other species of jacks, the female with a black-topped tail is larger than the male. She may weigh as much as seven and one-half pounds, though the average weight is usually four to five pounds.

The black-tailed jack is more abundant and has a wider distribution than the white-tailed species. The western border of this hare's range extends from Oregon to Lower California and on the east from the southernmost part of South Dakota to Texas, and then south into Mexico.

During cyclical peaks in their populations the animals are agricultural pests, often destroying acres of field crops in a single night; they also compete with livestock for range. Frequently the black-tailed jack and less frequently the white-tailed species have to be controlled or eliminated by strychnine-treated baits, or hunted by organized drives.

In addition to feeding on grasses and crops, the black-tailed jack eats cacti. Sometimes the animal even tackles a spined variety such as the hedgehog or cholla. To eat one of these plants, the jack chews

all around a spiny area, then carefully pulls out the loosened section, and finally pokes its nose into the spine-free opening to bite out some of the pulp.

There is a long mating season for all jack rabbits, including the two species of antelope or white-sided jack rabbits (*L. alleni* and *L. gaillardi*). These two species live in small areas of Arizona and New Mexico. Of course the season varies within the combined ranges of these animals; it is shorter in the North than in the South. All four species indulge in strenuous antics before actually mating. There is a great deal of chasing back and forth and fights occur between buck rabbits.

A pair of battling jacks puts on a regular boxing match. Each rabbit rears up on tiptoe and rains blows at the other. Some battles are silent, others are accompanied by growling or grunting. From time to time one jack or the other delivers a blow with a hind foot. This is comparable to a human punch with brass knuckles, for the hind foot of a jack is heavy and equipped with sharp claws. If the kicking rabbit connects, its opponent is apt to be torn wide open. Blows are supplemented by biting and tearing chunks of skin out of the ears. As soon as one sparring rabbit weakens, he races off to be followed for a short distance by the victor, who quickly gives up the chase and claims a mate.

The number of young born to jack rabbits varies with the species: a female black-tailed jack usually has three to four young, though there may be one or as many as six; the female white-tailed jack has an average litter of four, though there may be only one or as many as eight.

Young jack rabbits are born in an oval-shaped nest, which is scooped out in the ground and protected by brush or thick grasses. This "delivery room" is lined with fur which the female pulls from her body. Shortly after birth, a young jack, weighing anywhere from two to six ounces, starts nursing. Although this young hare is so precocious that it can stand up and take a few steps right after birth, the little animal probably stays with its mother about four weeks. No one knows when a young jack rabbit strikes out for itself, and the animal is rarely seen until it is at least half-grown.

Both young and adults are preyed upon by bobcats, foxes, wolves, and coyotes. In some areas jack rabbits and cottontails make up more than fifty per cent of the coyote's year-round diet. Various snakes and other reptiles include baby jacks in their diets; both of our eagles, and some owls and hawks prey on them. And of course like all other hares and rabbits many jacks succumb to tularemia.

The other member of the hare family in America is the European common hare (*L. europaeus*), which was liberated at various places in the East in the early 1900's. This animal, often weighing as much as twelve pounds, is now abundant in New York in the Hudson River Valley, parts of Connecticut and Massachussets, and in Ontario. Introduced in the hope that it would be a desirable game animal, the European hare has turned out to be a serious crop and orchard pest—as unwelcome an addition to our wildlife as the introduced rabbit in Australia. Lacking natural controls in Australia the animal increased so rapidly that rabbits now occupy one-third of the continent. This plague of rabbits is the result of the introduction of twenty-four European animals released on December 29, 1859. Six years later, Thomas Austin, on whose estate the rabbits were freed, had killed 20,000 rabbits, and in later years Australia exported 700 million rabbit skins and 157 million frozen carcasses in a single decade.

In Australia and in England, where rabbits also reached plague proportions, the animals are being brought under control by releasing rabbits infected with the virus disease, myxomatosis. This control, spread from rabbit to rabbit by the bloodsucking anopheline mosquito, has been so successful in England that a Reuters dispatch in *The New York Times*, February 10, 1956, said that the scarcity of rabbits in England will result in a one hundred per cent increase in the price of men's hats. So many rabbits have been killed that furs used in making hats now have to be imported from as far away as Australia. Since the disease arrived in England, the price of imported rabbit fur has increased from 84 cents a dozen to as much as $3.08 a dozen. All of which seems to prove that man should not tamper with the ecological arrangement worked out by Nature in the first place.

EASTERN COTTONTAIL RABBIT

Sylvilagus floridanus

The left hind foot of a rabbit is supposed to prevent any kind of accident. A time-honored theatrical custom is to present a young actor with a rabbit's foot, which must be placed in his first makeup box and is used to apply rouge.

The superstition concerning the luck of the rabbit's foot originated in the belief that young rabbits are born with their eyes open, and thus have the power of the Evil Eye and can shoo away the Evil One. On these grounds the left hind foot of a North American rabbit is valueless, for all our rabbits are born with their eyes shut— one of the characteristics at birth that differentiates rabbits from hares, which are born with their eyes open.

In North America the rabbit is represented throughout the greater part of the United States, southernmost Canada, and Mexico by nearly seventy species and subspecies belonging to the genus *Sylvilagus*, with the eastern cottontail having the greatest distribution.

Usually the cottontail has a short, bushy tail, whose white underside looks like an exploded cotton boll as the animal hops along with its tail raised. A reddish-brown animal weighing two to three pounds, the cottontail has ears that measure two and one-half to three inches from the notch, and relatively short legs which cause the animal to run instead of leap like our various hares. And among cottontails the female is usually larger than the male.

On its range the eastern cottontail hops along on a zig-zag course over a territory that may be as much as twenty acres. In spring and summer the animal seeks such foods as clover, grasses, grains, and endless native green plants; in fall and winter it eats grains and twigs and gnaws the bark of shrubs and fruit trees.

When the snow is on the ground the course of this rabbit can be followed along the borders of woods and marshes. Although the cottontail's tracks are slightly smaller than those of the varying hare the pattern is similar, with their small, narrow prints—sets of paired hind feet—and the toe-width equal to that of the heel.

The animal feeds late in the afternoon, the early evening, or at any time during the night. Most cottontails spend the greater part of the day resting or sleeping in their forms—depressions in the earth—or in their dens or burrows. If the snow is deep and fluffy the cottontail moves about as little as possible, for the hind feet are not adapted to snowshoeing like those of the varying hare. The female cottontail is more apt to be inactive in winter than the male.

Although severe winter weather limits the movements of the rabbit, it does not altogether interfere with the mating season; in the northern half of the United States mating begins in January and lasts for nearly seven months. In the South and on the Pacific coast the cottontail breeds during the entire year. Frequently one or more males, or bucks, seek the same female, or doe. The spot at which contending males meet is often dotted by bits of fur—signs that a fight has taken place.

During a courtship two cottontails sometimes face one another and indulge in a *pas de deux* worthy of a ballet company. One of the rabbits leaps suddenly straight up into the air, and the second animal dashes beneath the leaper before he returns to earth. Such antics may be repeated a number of times—presumably until the animals tire or love triumphs.

The female stays with the male of her choice for two days, then turns on him and drives him away with a fury that occasionally includes biting fur from his flanks. About a month later the female delivers her young which are known as fawns. Frequently the female mates again within twenty-four hours of delivering her young. Thus there may be three, four, or even five litters a year.

Shortly before the young are born the female selects a nest site. Such a site, usually in an open field, is excavated by the female with her forepaws to make a saucerlike depression. Often cow or horse tracks or skunk scratchings are enlarged until the nest measures about seven by five inches and has a depth of three to four inches. This depression is lined by various grasses and bits of fur which the female yanks out of her breast and belly with her teeth.

Not infrequently the female is away from the nest, feeding, when she is ready to drop her young. The average litter of cottontails is five, though there may be only one or then again there may be eight.

Spring litters are generally the largest. Once the last of the litter is born and fed, the mother carries the young, if away from the nest, to the spot she prepared for them. When all the fawns are safely stowed away, the mother covers her naked, pink offspring with a blanket of grasses and fur.

At birth a young cottontail measures about four inches in length. The eyes and ears of the little animal are sealed. Only a line indicates where the eyes will open, and the half-inch ears lie flat on the head.

Twenty-four hours after birth a young rabbit is covered by a thin fuzz; four days later there is enough fur on the head to show how the animal will look as an adult; and at the end of the first week fur covers the entire body and the color pattern is easily discernible. At about this time, too, the eyes begin to open and the ears begin to stand upright. The eyes and ears of a rabbit are important adjuncts in the animal's fight for survival; the eyes bulge and permit the rabbit to see to the side and slightly to the rear as well as to the front, and the ears turn backward to catch sounds from the rear.

During the period in which a young rabbit is helpless the mother stays nearby. If an adult rabbit or a squirrel comes near the nest, she drives the intruder away. Several times each night the female comes to the nest and nurses her litter by squatting over the nest so that each fawn can reach a nipple. By the time a young cottontail is nearly two weeks old, the little animal is ready to make its first trip away from the nest.

A fawn and its litter mates start eating the greens within a few yards of their birthplace. Through the day each animal hides in a small individual form protected by grasses and shrubs. At night the young return to sleep in the nest, where they huddle together for warmth. About two weeks after birth the cottontail leaves the nest for good. Two or more of the animals in the same litter may stay together or near the mother for some little time, but eventually they go their separate ways to seek territories of their own.

From the moment it is born until its death from natural causes—perhaps three years at the most—the cottontail's life is a prolonged and constant fight for survival. Most of these rabbits live less than a year in the wild, though captives have lived to be five years old. Farm operations kill many rabbits in the nest; heavy rains may flood

Front   Hind   ⅙ *actual size*   Front   Hind

The distance between front and rear prints averages about 12 inches; and between pairs of footprints, about 26 inches

nests and drown the young; and dogs, cats, crows, snakes, and red squirrels prey on nestling rabbits.

Once the cottontail leaves the nest it becomes the staple food for many valuable fur animals, with the weasel the greatest predator. Red, gray, and kit foxes, minks, dogs, and cats kill numberless rabbits, and among the predatory birds that feed on the cottontail are the barn, barred, and great-horned owl, and the marsh and the red-tailed hawk. Man is probably the greatest predator; almost thirty percent of the shotgun shells discharged each year are fired at the cottontail. In 1938 it was estimated that two and one-half million rabbits were killed in Michigan; four and one-half million were killed in Missouri in the same year; and Ohio and Pennsylvania together accounted for seven million. And drivers of cars are responsible for the deaths of many rabbits, which become confused by the blinding headlights and are unable to get out of the way.

Hunters and those handling rabbits or cooking rabbit meat should wear gloves while dressing the carcass and thoroughly wash their hands afterward. The cottontail is prone to a number of parasites and a number of diseases, including tularemia or rabbit disease—highly infectious to man and fatal to rabbits, hares, ground squirrels, and many other rodents. A person may contract tularemia by handling an infected animal or eating one that has not been well cooked. One of the best ways to avoid contracting this painful, long-lasting, and sometimes fatal disease, is to avoid cottontails that look or act sick— a rabbit suffering from tularemia does not scamper off like a healthy one—and to cook all rabbit meat thoroughly. Such cooking renders the germ harmless.

As adults, rabbits are usually silent, but sometimes scream if injured. Young rabbits utter a faint squeak when hungry, but otherwise are as silent as their parents. Rabbits indicate danger by thumping with the hind feet, sometimes with the right and sometimes with the left, which is not the good luck charm it is supposed to be.

WOODCHUCK

Marmota monax

The woodchuck has achieved a special prominence in the animal kingdom through the old tongue-twister: "How much wood would a woodchuck chuck if a woodchuck could chuck wood? Why, a woodchuck would chuck as much wood as a woodchuck could chuck if a woodchuck could chuck wood."

The ability of a woodchuck, or groundhog, a fat, heavy-bodied rodent with a flattened head, to chuck wood is no better than the animal's ability to make long-range weather forecasts. Legend has it that if, on February 2 at eleven o'clock in the morning, the woodchuck sees its shadow upon emerging from its burrow after several months of hibernation, there will be another six weeks of winter. If, on the other hand, the animal does not see its shadow, then winter is over and an early spring is at hand.

The woodchuck's reputation as a wildlife weather prophet dates back to Colonial times. In European folklore, the badger is supposed to come out to look for its shadow on Candlemas Day, and early European settlers here transferred this myth to the woodchuck—an animal that is more interested in finding a mate than in looking for its shadow upon emerging from hibernation.

In the northernmost part of its range, the woodchuck begins hibernation earlier than animals in the South; in the Province of Quebec, for instance, it may start the big sleep in the middle of September. A woodchuck—also known as a whistlepig and popularly called a 'chuck—settles down for winter either in a grass bed at the end of its tunnel or in an unlined side chamber. A 'chuck buries itself alive, by sealing off the sleeping chamber with dirt scraped from the far end of the room. Once this operation has been accomplished, it rolls up in a ball, head between its hind legs. Breathing slows down until it almost stops, and the pulse becomes faint. The animal gets colder and colder until finally its temperature drops to somewhere between 40 and 57 degrees Fahrenheit. Now the woodchuck is in true hibernation, insensible to touch and sound.

When a woodchuck emerges in the spring, it has a lean and hungry look and its yellow-brown coat hangs loosely; the animal has lost from one-third to one-half its weight during a hibernation of five or more months. But no matter how hungry a male woodchuck may be upon emerging from its burrow in the spring, the animal at once starts to look for a mate. This quest to perpetuate the species is a determined one and frequently involves fights with other males seeking mates. Contending animals squeal and growl and snap at one another with white incisors; hides and ears and tails are chewed; sometimes as much as half of the six-inch, hairy, and flattened tail is bitten off. Eventually the weaker animal beats a retreat and the victor takes a mate.

From this union in March or April comes a litter of woodchucks that is born about a month or so later. A litter may consist of two to six, but four is average. At birth a young 'chuck is pink, naked, wrinkled, and blind. It is less than four inches in length and weighs about one to one and one-half ounces.

A female 'chuck sits on its haunches or stands on all fours to nurse its young. At the end of a four-week nursing period, a young 'chuck's eyes are open and the coat is well developed, and it is ready for its first trip above ground. Just before this eventful move, the mother 'chuck brings the month-old animal some vegetation to nibble on, and thus the youngster acquires a taste for clover, a favorite food, or other foods that grow near the burrow entrance.

By midsummer a young 'chuck is driven from the home burrow and takes up residence in one nearby. The youngster is still watched over by its mother; at the first sign of danger, the adult female gives a whistle similar to, but much less powerful than that of the hoary marmot (see page 51). At this period in its life, a 'chuck weighs about four pounds and measures about twenty inches in length. Not until the end of the second year does a woodchuck attain full growth; eighteen to twenty-six inches in length and five to ten pounds in weight. Extra-large 'chucks weigh as much as fourteen pounds. In captivity a woodchuck's life expectancy is four to five years; in the wild, somewhat less.

As soon as a woodchuck quits the area in which it was born, the animal establishes a home—a ground tunnel that it digs itself. A

Left Front
⅔ actual size

Track pattern, walking

tunnel may be on a hillside, in a gully, or in a forest (the original home of the woodchuck), but the preferred site is a bushy wood border at the edge of a clover-dotted meadow. A woodchuck digs two or three burrows, several hundred feet apart. Each burrow usually has two or more openings; the entrance hole has a large pile of freshly removed earth, but exit or plunge holes do not have the circular earth mound around them. Burrows vary in depth depending upon the soil. In soft earth, a tunnel may be as much as six and one-half feet below the surface of the earth; in hard soil, the tunnel may be three to four feet below the surface or even less.

Generally a woodchuck burrow has several tunnels leading to rooms measuring fifteen to eighteen inches in diameter and seven to ten inches in height at the ends of principal chambers. A sleeping chamber is usually high up in the tunnel system, to avoid flooding, whereas smaller chambers are lower and are used for hibernating or as toilets. A woodchuck cleans these toilet rooms regularly, carting wastes to the surface and burying them in the entrance mound, where the animal spends a good deal of time sunning itself.

Tracks around a mound are similar to those of a chipmunk, but three times larger; unpaired foreprints staggered behind paired hind prints. Fore toes with long claws scuff the snow after a winter's hibernation.

You can often see a woodchuck early in the morning or late in the afternoon or early in the evening—the times when the animal feeds, except on rainy days when it stays underground. A woodchuck eats so little animal food—occasionally snails and insects—that for all practical purposes it can be called a vegetarian. On a home range of less than one hundred yards in greatest length, a 'chuck eats leaves, flowers, and soft stem parts of buttercups, clovers, coltsfoots, white daisies, dandelions, Indian paintbrushes, and thistles. Bark of young wild cherries, hickories, maples, and sumacs is scratched or nibbled loose and eaten. The animal likes blackberries, cherries, and raspberries, and also windfallen apples.

Some woodchucks eat acorns and one tame 'chuck in Ohio even eats ice cream from a cone while sitting on its haunches, with the cone held between dark-brown forepaws as the animal licks away the ice cream. A 'chuck climbs trees and shrubs for fruits, and though it does not feed on aquatic life, it can swim, using a dog-paddle stroke.

A woodchuck eats all sorts of farm produce and can put away one and one-half pounds at a feeding of such growing crops as alfalfa, barley, corn, oats, soybeans, wheat; bean plants are relished and melon patches are often raided. In addition to being a glutton, a woodchuck spoils crops by trampling them down, makes mowing difficult by the earth it brings to the surface, and endangers livestock that might break a leg by stepping into a 'chuck hole.

If woodchucks become pests in agricultural areas, their destruction over *limited* areas is justifiable. In some states they are protected animals and game laws should be consulted before starting a control program.

According to the United States Fish and Wildlife Service, the surest and most practicable method for controlling woodchucks on the average farm is to gas the animals in their dens. Various types of gases may be used; gas cartridges especially prepared by the Fish and Wildlife Service; calcium cyanide dust, carbon disulphide, and gasoline engine exhaust. Only active burrows should be gassed and this should be done during April and May when there is less chance of damage to other wildlife. To receive specific instructions for woodchuck control, write the Fish and Wildlife Service, United States Department of the Interior, Washington 25, D. C., and ask for the leaflet "The Control of Woodchucks."

Nature has provided some controls for the woodchuck, whose mounds create dusting spots for birds and act as incubators for eggs of mud turtles. The 'chuck's burrows are sometimes taken over as temporary or permanent homes by foxes, opossums, skunks, rabbits, and weasels. When feeding, a woodchuck spends about half of its time watching out not only for foxes and weasels, but for bears, coyotes, eagles, hawks, wolves, and mountain lions as well as farm dogs—against which a 'chuck puts up a good fight. Tularemia is another 'chuck-killer, and man, of course, is one of the animal's greatest predators.

'Chuck-hunting is a rifleman's sport, and thousands of the animals are killed with a single-shot .22; but any caliber rifle, preferably with a telescopic sight, can be used. Late summer is best for 'chuck-hunting—then the animals are fat in anticipation of approaching hibernation. But no matter what season a hunter goes out for 'chucks, he has to be fast and have sharp vision as the animals are quick and wary and streak for a hole at the slightest hint of danger—even the reflection of sunlight on a rifle barrel sends them scurrying. An injured 'chuck, when wounded by a hunter or hurt by a predator, tries not to die underground—if possible such an animal drags itself out of its burrow.

Flesh of all woodchucks, except the very old, is good eating. In preparing a woodchuck for the table, you should remove the small, red musk glands under each foreleg and the one at the small of the back. Then wash the carcass well, remove excess fat, and soak overnight in a strong solution of vinegar and water to which onion and salt have been added. Next morning remove the carcass and scrub it clean. One of the easiest ways to cook a woodchuck is by stewing —parboil for twenty minutes, then drain, and cover with freshly boiling water. Add sliced onions, chopped parsley, one-half cup of diced celery, cloves, salt, and pepper. Cook until tender and thicken the liquor with flour to make gravy. (For other woodchuck recipes, refer to game cookbook listed in bibliography.)

You won't have a dish equal to roast pheasant, but you will find that this legendary weather prophet is good eating. And what is more the woodchuck is one of the few animals easily hunted or seen without traveling too far from home—if your home is anywhere within the animal's range extending from Labrador and Nova Scotia south to Virginia and Alabama, west to Kansas, and north through Minnesota and Central Canada to the northern Rocky Mountains.

HOARY MARMOT

Marmota caligata

A hoary marmot looks as if it had on blackish-brown boots or *caligae*, the name for the military boots of Roman warriors and the source of the animal's specific scientific name. Full-face, a marmot appears rather bulky, but actually it is a slim, almost skinny animal with a fine coat of gray-black fur interspersed with white-tipped guard hairs.

You will find hoary marmots along the timber line on the rocky and flowery slopes of mountains from northwestern Alaska and the Alaska Peninsula to central Washington and Idaho. Their clear, shrill whistles are among the few sounds that break the silence of the high altitudes and the reason French-Canadian fur traders in the Rockies named the animal *le siffleur*, the whistler.

The hoary marmot, about twice the size of a woodchuck, shares its French name with the woodchuck of eastern Canada, but whistler should be reserved solely for the hoary marmot, whose call can be heard a mile away on a windless day. The yellow-bellied marmot (*M. flaviventris*), which lives at lower altitudes than the hoary marmot, has a less powerful call, and the common woodchuck (*M. monax*, page 45) is more of a chirper than a whistler.

Sounded from a rocky lookout in a marmot village, a hoary marmot's whistle alerts every living thing within earshot, including the grizzly bear that preys on marmots. All the other mammals of the area pause in their respective activities to see what the danger is, while the marmots drop out of sight, like sailors being piped below decks, into their burrows among the rocks. When the danger is past, a marmot sentry gives a low whistle—apparently an all-clear. Soon after the safety signal is given, marmots pop out all over the community. To save themselves from golden eagles, marmots have a defense system of shallow shelter holes, dug along pathways from burrows to feeding grounds, and the mammals duck into these when an eagle starts a threatening swoop in their direction.

A hoary marmot is a vegetarian who enjoys wild-lettuce blossoms and those of other mountain plants in its regular diet. It munches the petals with the air of a gourmet savoring a favorite gastronomical delight. When eating flowers and ever on the alert for hawks and mammal predators including the bobcat and the cougar, the marmot stands up to grip the nodding white stalks of wild lettuce or the swaying blue spines of lupine. Stalks are pulled down by forepaws so that the marmot can nip off the blossoms with its large front teeth, which grow rapidly and continuously and are kept ground down by constant use. Mountain phlox and rosy douglasia are eaten, too, along with wild vegetables such as shining white onions. After unearthing onions, the marmot rears up and holds the bulbs between its paws and nibbles off the rootlets. Sometimes the bulbs themselves are eaten, but more often they are discarded.

Playful, noisy, and sociable, marmots often engage in antics resembling a dance. One animal extends an invitation to dance by tapping another on the shoulder. A chance to dance is seldom refused. The animals dance nose to nose and forepaws to forepaws in an arched upright position. Suddenly, as if on signal from an unseen caller, the dancers push away, curving backwards, only to swing into place again with such force that their buck teeth meet with a click that sounds like colliding billiard balls. The dance ends when one partner breaks away and races off to drop down exhausted on the grass or take a sunbath on a warm, flat rock.

Marmots also like tobogganing. In the spring, not long after hibernation, but before the deep snows have melted, the animal will deliberately run downhill, brake itself, and then skid ten feet or more. In the summer, when two or more marmots are frisking around a burrow, one will suddenly rear up and fling itself downhill, tail-over-teakettle, to be followed in a similar fashion by its companions.

⅔ actual size

Hind

Front

A marmot spends about seven and one-half months in hibernation, a period of suspended animation when biological fires are banked. It awakens from this long winter sleep early in the spring, the exact date depending upon altitude and latitude, and may have to tunnel up through as much as ten feet of snow to make this yearly debut above ground. There may be little food around when the animal emerges, but that does not seem to matter; at first the marmot acts as if drugged, taking little interest in the world around it. Then, as the snow melts and the greening of plants begins, it starts to eat, gorging until belly drags on the ground. The den is also refurbished; damp, winter-worn hay is hauled out and replaced with freshly cut grasses from nearby mountain meadows.

As a rule the animal does not mate until it is about two years old. The four or five resulting young are born in May, and by the time the female is preparing for hibernation, the young are shifting for themselves. All marmots in a community get ready for hibernation by fattening themselves to the bursting point, though for about two weeks before going underground for the last time of a current year, they eat nothing. Then, snug in winter-proof burrows, they curl up into tight little balls—safe for at least another seven and one-half months from enemies that like the flavor of the flower-eating whistler.

PRAIRIE DOG

Cynomys ludovicianus, C. leucurus

The Great Plains, generally level, treeless, and semiarid, extend in a continuous belt three to four hundred miles wide from western Canada to Mexico. The natural vegetation of buffalo and grama grass and other short, drought-resistant grasses make the Plains resemble a closely pastured meadow. Once the Plains were a wasteland occupied by scattered bands of nomadic Indians, roving herds of buffaloes, and innumerable prairie dogs, whose almost endless "towns" covered many square miles of this natural grazing land.

Today no such towns exist. Prairie dogs, plump, short-eared rodents with coarse buff fur, are far less numerous than they used to be. Except for a few scattered towns on public lands—those not reserved for special purposes—about the only places to see prairie dogs except for zoological parks are such federal installations as National Parks and National Wildlife Refuges. At places like Wichita Mountains National Wildlife Refuge in southwestern Oklahoma, Theodore Roosevelt National Memorial Park in western North Dakota, and Wind Cave National Park in southwestern South Dakota, the short-legged prairie dog still stands at the entrance of its chambered burrow like a guard posted to watch for marauders.

Once a prairie dog notices that danger is at hand the animal becomes ramrod stiff and sounds off with a shrill alarm—a piercing chirp or whistle. This signal is accompanied by a flip of the three-inch tail, an upthrust of the sleek body, and an extension of the small forepaws skyward. These movements are simultaneous and executed with lightning speed immediately before the animal ducks into its burrow.

From the tunnel's entrance the prairie dog watches every movement of an intruder with intent, beady, black eyes; if danger is imminent, the animals all over town retreat to the lower depths of their tunnels. On the other hand if the cause for alarm is not serious the animals stay in their listening rooms—chambers at one side and just below the tunnel's entrance. When the prairie dogs find that all is well, they pop out in relays like so many jack-in-the-boxes.

The burrow of the prairie dog is one of the most elaborate dug by any of the North American burrowing mammals. The "Yearbook of the Department of Agriculture" for 1901 described one such burrow excavated near Alma, Nebraska:

In this case the burrow went down nearly vertically to a depth of fourteen and one-half feet below the surface when it turned abruptly and became horizontal. The horizontal part was thirteen and one-half feet in length. One-third of the horizontal part and two old nests and passage ways were plugged with black earth brought in from the surface layer, which was very different from the light-colored clayey earth in which the greater part of the burrow lay.

Four or five feet below the entrance was a short side passage [the listening room] probably used as a place in which to turn around when the animals come back to take a look at the intruder before finally disappearing in the bottom of their burrows. It was also used, apparently, as a resting place where they bark and scold after retreating from the mouths of the burrow.

To make such a burrow the prairie dog uses its front feet, which are equipped with long, sharp claws. As the animal digs with its front feet, it passes the earth back under its belly and kicks it out behind with its rear feet. Some of the earth is used to build the crater-shaped mound that encircles the burrow entrance. A mound is built in flat country to prevent the tunnel system from being flooded in times of unusual rainfall. Generally the black-tailed prairie dog (*C. ludovicianus*) builds such mounds, whereas the shorter-tailed, more slender white-tailed species (*C. leucurus*) does not make a mound. Inhabitants of grassy uplands and mountainous areas, the white-tailed members of the family need not deflect water from their tunnels; natural drainage prevents flooding.

To build one of the crater-shaped mounds round the six- to eight-inch burrow entrance, the prairie dog carries double armfuls of moist earth to the desired spot. The earth is rammed and packed into a firm condition by repeated drives of the nose. As the animal works it holds its twelve- to sixteen-inch body in a curved position with the shoulders bent. In this position the body acts as a powerful machine to drive the hammerlike muzzle into the earth. A completed mound may measure four feet in diameter and as much as two feet high.

Deep in the burrow is a chamber that often measures nine by

eleven inches. This chamber is lined with grasses and is the delivery room in which young prairie dogs are born. The mother mates either in February, March, or April; some thirty-odd days later the young are born in litters that usually number five. At birth a prairie-dog pup is blind, hairless, and weighs about half an ounce. By the time the little animal is about four weeks old it is well furred, and about a week later the eyes open and it makes its first feeble bark.

Hind

Actual size

Front

In another week a pup and its litter mates make their initial trip aboveground, where they start eating green food. Although weaning begins then, the mother still nurses her offspring; she sits upright to do so. By the middle of September a pup has about doubled its weight and is completely weaned. Immediately after weaning her pups the mother leaves, and shortly thereafter the pups take off one by one to move into convenient nearby vacant burrows, which may be occupied by the same animal for as long as eight years.

Although the prairie dog is omnivorous, the animal eats far more vegetation than any other foods. Within their towns the animals strip the landscape of all plant life. The black-tailed species eats some grasshoppers, but its mainstay consists of such western plains grasses as wheat grass, brome grass, grama grass, and other short-grass growths. The white-tailed prairie dog eats some grubs and adult beetles, larvae of moths and butterflies, and grasshoppers, but shrubby plants, weeds, and grasses make up the bulk of this animal's diet, which includes Russian thistle, sagebrush, prickly pear, wheat, and saltbush. In captivity the prairie dog eats practically any food, but is particularly fond of cakes and fruits, with watermelon at the top of the preferred list.

Since the prairie dog lives in a semiarid climate, the animal seldom has the opportunity to drink water. After an infrequent rainstorm it drinks from puddles in the town, but ordinarily the animal relies on its ability to manufacture water in its body by the metabolic conversion of carbohydrates.

As the prairie dog scuttles around its town during the day on a home range of no more than forty acres in diameter, the animal has to be on the lookout for the badger, the bobcat, the coyote, the black-footed ferret, the raven, the eagle, and the rough-legged hawk. Although many stories have been written about the joint occupation of dens by prairie dogs, rattlesnakes, and burrowing owls, there is no truth in the statement that these plains creatures live together in any sort of harmony. Owls and snakes are often found in prairie-dog towns, but these animals are there as predators and destroy large numbers of young. If a prairie dog escapes a snake invading its burrow, the animal stays away from the burrow until the snake leaves.

By fall most prairie dogs are as fat as animals that are ready for hibernation. Although the prairie dog does go below ground for varying periods during the winter, the animal is not a true hibernator. During mild winter days even in the northern part of its range the prairie dog is frequently out. Vernon Bailey, chief field naturalist for the old Bureau of Biological Survey, once saw a white-tailed prairie dog eating sagebrush tips in the Green River Basin of Wyoming when the snow was a foot deep and following a night when the thermometer had registered 22 degrees below zero.

The prairie dog, whose generic name, *Cynomys*, means dog-like mouse, was given a number of names by early explorers in the West. Among these are barking squirrel, prairie squirrel, *petit chien*, and wishtonwish.

George Wilkins Kendall, the author of *Narrative of the Texan Santa Fe Expedition*, published in 1844, describes a visit to a prairie-dog town:

On several occasions I crept close to their village to watch their movements. Directly in the center of one village I particularly noticed a very large Dog, sitting in front of the door to his burrow. By his own actions and those of his neighbors it really seemed as though he was the president, mayor, or chief—the "big Dog" of the place. He received at least a dozen visits from his fellow Dogs during the hour that I watched. They would stop and chat with him a few moments, then run off to their domiciles. All this while he never left his post for a moment, and I thought I could discover a gravity in his deportment not discernible in those around him. Far be it for me to say that those visits he received were on business, or had anything to do with the local government of the village. But it certainly appeared so. If any animal has a system of laws regulating the body politic, it is the Prairie Dog.

Kendall's observations on the prairie dog were corroborated during the early 1950's. The animal's social behavior was studied by the staff of the Roscoe B. Jackson Memorial Laboratory, Bar Harbor, Maine. The staff concluded that the social behavior of the prairie dog resembles that of clannish human communities. Within a prairie-dog town, clans or cliques of as many as forty dogs are formed. The members keep out strangers regardless of sex or age. Young and old dogs of both sexes do the excluding. The dogs cannot talk, but they do vocalize or communicate in some sort of language and thus warn of danger and incite to combat.

Although the orange-colored lenses of the prairie dog's eyes act as filters permitting the animal to withstand the sun's intense glare, the animal generally goes below ground during the hottest part of the day, after an early morning feeding. Late in the afternoon the prairie dog emerges from its burrow and feeds until sundown, which is curfew. Then, as darkness closes down, quiet settles over the mound-dotted villages of the chunky little animals, once as much a part of the Great Plains as the ponderous buffaloes, but like them surviving only in sufficient numbers to give us a limited picture of the wildlife belonging to the Great Plains of another day.

Along with pocket gophers and ground squirrels, prairie dogs are frequently responsible for the destruction of many acres of range and great quantities of agricultural crops. In 1951 large amounts of natural resources, particularly range forage, were being lost through depredations of rodents on public and Indian lands. Officials of the Indian Service, the Forest Service, and the Bureau of Land Management together with those of the Fish and Wildlife Service made a survey of the extent of the damage by these rodents. The survey showed that some nineteen million acres of public and Indian lands required rodent control to conserve range and forest resources.

In rodent-control operations during the next three years more than 30,000,000 acres of land were treated for the elimination of prairie dogs, ground squirrels, pocket gophers, jack rabbits, field mice, rats, porcupines, woodchucks, and moles.

POCKET GOPHER

Geomyidae

Apparently the pocket gopher delights in living alone, for it pursues this way of life with a singleness of purpose that makes it a confirmed recluse among mammals. The pocket gopher, a busy, combative little rodent, is so fond of solitude that it does not even fraternize with its own kind, except when a short-lived urge to mate impels it to seek a female. If gopher tunnels intersect, openings are immediately plugged up, and when two gophers meet the animals usually fight until one is killed.

Pocket gophers, in one form or another, are native to Central and North America and occur from sea level to above timber line at 13,000 feet. Within the United States there are three main classifications of gophers: the eastern and western pocket gophers and the chestnut-faced pocket gopher. They occur in all states west of the lower Mississippi River, the Wabash River, and Lake Michigan, and in large areas of Alabama, Georgia, and Florida.

A pocket gopher has a sturdy body nine to ten inches long, including a three-inch tail. The tail, rather thick, almost hairless, and extremely sensitive, serves as a feeling organ as the animal shuffles back and forth in its labyrinthine tunnels. A gopher's head is broad, its neck is thick, and its shoulder muscles are powerful—a combination of physical characteristics that aids the animal in its endless digging. Forefeet, however, are the gopher's real digging equipment. Unusually strong, the feet have three toenails that make the loosening of dirt easy. Long, prominent teeth are practically outside the mouth cavity and they are also used in digging.

Tunnels of a pocket gopher vary in depth from six inches to a foot below the surface of the ground; they are from one and one-half to three inches in diameter, depending upon the size of the animal making the tunnel. A tunnel is dug dog-fashion; dirt is loosened by the front feet, then thrown back under the body. Once a pile of loose dirt is accumulated, a gopher does a quick about-face by somersaulting with a vigorous boost from its tail, then joins fore paws before its nose and bulldozes the dirt to the surface, where a fan-shaped pile is made. Before the gopher returns to further digging in search of food or to make chambers for storage or living quarters (including a chamber used solely for toilet purposes), the outlet is closed by a dirt plug.

The gopher, whose scientific family name means "earth mouse," gets its common name from two sources. "Gopher" is an Englished form of *gaufre*, a French word meaning "honeycomb." Early French settlers in this country used the term for various burrowing animals that make a network of tunnels. "Pocket" is of simpler derivation; a gopher has actual pockets or pouches that are entirely outside its mouth. These pockets give the gopher the name "pouched rat." They are lined with soft fur, or hair, lighter in color than that on the body. Fur of the body is soft to the touch, glossy, and varies in color—light buff, yellow, gray, many shades of brown, and sometimes almost black—depending upon species and locality.

Gopher pouches are expandable affairs in which food is transported to one of the smaller chambers excavated for storage. Most of the gopher's food is secured from underground, and consists of the fleshy roots of fruit trees, below-the-surface stems of various plants, including alfalfa, peanuts, and potatoes, and flowering bulbs like those of the tiger lily, and similar vegetation. It also likes the leaves of the dandelion and the cat's ear, nipped off on rare, hurried trips aboveground—usually taken early in the morning or late in the afternoon or on days when the sun is not shining. Out of its tunnel, a gopher is wary and seems apprehensive.

To secure root foods, a gopher tunnels directly to the source of supply from beneath, and will follow a row of potatoes across a field. If it is hungry, it nips off and eats the root at once. The plant withers and dies. If the food is to be stored, the plant is drawn down into the tunnel, nipped into convenient carrying lengths, and quickly stuffed into both cheek pouches with front paws. Then the gopher scurries off to one of its various chambers and deposits the load. This is accomplished by running the paws along the sides of the face to push the food out. As soon as the food is safely cached, the gopher scampers back for another load. One gopher is known to have stored as many as fifty tiger-lily bulbs in its burrow.

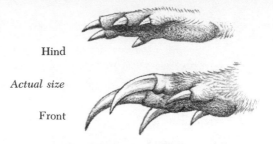

Hind

Actual size

Front

According to the United States Fish and Wildlife Service, which has conducted a gopher-control campaign since 1915, the greatest damage caused by pocket gophers is the destruction by root injury of trees and plants in fields, gardens, lawns, meadows, parks, and pastures, and the covering of much growing vegetation with excavated earth. Gopher mounds prevent close mowing of hay and damage farm machinery.

Irrigation systems are sometimes ruined by the work of pocket gophers. In Idaho gophers tunneled into the banks of an irrigation ditch, and prevented the watering of 18,000 acres of cultivated land because the water seeped away in the gopher burrows. And in southwestern Colorado, gophers undermined the roadbed of The Rio Grande Railroad, a small-gauge road, to such an extent that ties and rails settled and caused an engine to jump the track.

Natural enemies of the pocket gopher act as a population control but the gopher has less to fear from predators than do rodents that feed entirely above the ground. A gopher seldom leaves its burrow system; when it does, such trips are quickly conducted except in the case of a male looking for a mate. Long-eared, great-horned, and barn owls catch some gophers; a pair of barn owls may take from three to six gophers daily when feeding young. Hawks and house cats and coyotes, foxes, skunks, and wolves eat gophers, and the badger, a faster digger than the gopher, goes right into the ground after it. The king snake, known as the gopher snake in some areas, and the bull snake, eat gophers for their infrequent meals, and the weasel kills these rodents in their tunnels.

Digging of the tunnel systems is a perpetual task for the gopher. It repairs any break at once, and also digs short, steeply pitched sumps, similar to those in mine shafts, for drainage. Burrowing goes on day and night, four seasons a year, with layoffs for rest every two hours, though one gopher, under observation, dug for eight hours before stopping to rest. In winter tunnels are made under the snow and filled with earth brought up from burrows. Fall and spring are the periods of greatest activity; fall is the time of preparing for winter by laying in food, spring for perpetuating the species.

Because they are such solitary animals, gophers are not prolific. Only during mating season do the animals have any kind of family life, and apparently some males are misogynists, as many females go through the spring without breeding. Females that have mated average litters of five in some areas, and in warm climates, some bring off two litters a year.

Pocket gophers are born in nearly globular nests of fine, dry grasses, or shredded stubble. They are blind, hairless, and without cheek pouches at birth. After a nursing period of about ten days, they start to develop and are brought vegetable food by their mother, and in a month and a half they are weaned. Shortly after that they begin to shift for themselves, and almost at once start digging small tunnels, where they take up their solitary existence.

Along with the habit of digging and living alone soon after birth, a young gopher displays other traits similar to an older one, including the inclination to attack anything that moves. The attack is accompanied by angry wheezes and savage bites—bites that can cut deep into the toe of a heavy leather boot.

A gopher's personal and feeding habits are to its credit. It is clean and a strict eater of vegetable matter, from which it gets about the only liquid in its diet; most gophers seldom, if ever, drink free water. A gopher locates its food by a sense of smell, the means by which it also locates its mate. Its sight is extremely poor, and may account for its abrupt attacks on any moving thing, no matter what the size.

Gophers are too small to be of any value commercially, but they do make good eating—something to be remembered if you get lost in gopher country. The vegetable diet makes the flesh tender and well-flavored, unless the gopher has eaten wild onions, of which it is fond. The dark, fine-grained meat tastes somewhat like squirrel.

Over the centuries the gopher's constant burrowing has done much for the soil by aerating it. But today this type of soil conditioning is less valuable than it used to be, and about the only favorable thing you can now say of a gopher is what the old lady remarked of the devil, "Well, nobody can say he's idle!"

BEAVER

Castor canadensis

When a storage dam at Canada's Chalk River atomic-energy plant failed, two beavers were released in the water impounded by the leaking dam. As the animals like a constant water level, they set to work to repair the dam and soon had it watertight.

Impoundment of water is perhaps the most important contribution that the beaver makes to man's economy and to wildlife's requirements. In the Silver Creek area in eastern Oregon, two trappers removed six hundred beavers during one winter, with the result that in subsequent years ponds and grassy meadows disappeared. Only a few hundred tons of pasturage were left out of an estimated 15,000 tons (worth three to five dollars a ton); ranchers had to dig wells and pump water for their stock, and farmers on the lower reaches of the creek saw their lands revert to desert. The trappers realized about five thousand dollars from the beaver pelts, but farmers and ranchers lost hundreds of thousands of dollars; fishermen could no longer take trout from the creek and its tributaries, as natural trout-rearing ponds were a thing of the past. So for want of beaver, a productive agricultural, livestock, and wildlife area was lost.

The beaver, largest North American rodent and second largest in the world, is found in various forms in most of North America from northern Florida and extreme northern Mexico northward to tree limits. The animal's primary range coincides roughly with that of aspen and cottonwood growths—its preferred habitat.

In appearance a beaver looks much like a large, fat woodchuck, with a black, horizontally flattened tail that is scaly, oval in outline, and ten to twelve inches long. A beaver's tail serves several purposes: it is used primarily as a rudder to enable the beaver to paddle through the water at a speed of about four miles an hour; as a scull when the animal is swimming more leisurely; as a prop when the animal stands up on its hind legs to cut down a tree; and as a warning mechanism.

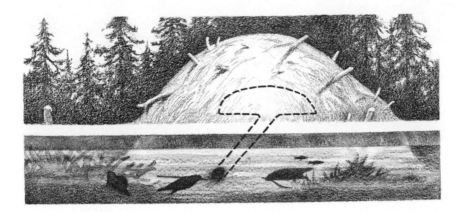

The beaver sounds an alarm by bringing the tail quickly up over the back, then down with such force on the surface of the water that the resulting crack can be heard for half a mile on a quiet night. Almost simultaneously with the crack—sounding like the wallop of a flat board on the water's surface—all beavers in an area dive.

A beaver can stay submerged about seventeen minutes before having to come up for air and the animal has been known to swim half a mile underwater. Nostrils and ears have valves that close automatically when the beaver goes under water and open again when it surfaces. Its lips are loose enough so that they can be drawn together tightly behind protruding teeth; thus, like the muskrat, the beaver can submerge and cut and chew without getting its mouth full of water. Small eyes, in tightly fitting lids, apparently see better under water than on land. The handlike front feet with long claws are not used in swimming but are curled tightly to the breast; large hind feet, webbed like the feet of a goose, are used as paddles.

Two coats of fur keep a beaver warm and waterproofed. A soft, thick undercoat of dull brown fur is for warmth, and a long, shining overcoat of chestnut brown fur acts as a water repellent. A beaver takes good care of its coat; as soon as it quits the water, the animal wipes and combs its fur with its claws. Second toenails on each hind foot are split lengthwise and appear to act as a fine-toothed comb for removing lice and parasitic beetles. This wiping and combing redistributes the natural oil in the fur and makes the animal waterproof again.

Beavers live in colonies, with the average colony containing about six animals, though there may be twelve if an area can support that many. During winter a beaver family usually consists of two parents, juveniles of about one and one-half years of age, and young of the current year. Young beavers are born in late April, May, or early June of monogamous parents that mated in January or February. During mating season males fight and occasionally you will find a beaver with a badly torn skin.

Glands in the groin, known as castors, are larger in males than in females, and give off a pleasant musky odor, stronger during mating season than through the rest of the year. Sometimes, though rarely, a beaver is called a "castor" and a hat made of beaver fur is known as a "castor"—a Latin word that means "the exceller."

A beaver litter usually consists of six kits, as the young are called. At birth a kit weighs about one pound and measures about fifteen inches long, including its three and one-half inch flat tail; eyes are open and the body is encased in fine soft fur. A kit soon starts swimming with no instruction from its parents.

If you canoe by a beaver lodge, whose roof is not chinked with mud to allow ventilation, you can sometimes hear the whimpering of kits. In addition to whimpering—a sound very much like the wail of a newly born human baby—beavers mumble like old men, hiss when angry, and cry like a hurt child when injured or frightened.

At the time a two-year-old beaver is driven from the lodge in the early spring, the animal weighs about thirty pounds. At maturity a beaver measures thirty-five to forty inches and weighs about forty to fifty pounds; old males often weigh in at sixty pounds and one behemoth caught in Wisconsin during the 1951 trapping season weighed eighty-two pounds. Beavers may live to be ten years old in the wild; as much as twenty in captivity.

If the area in which a beaver is born will not support additional animals, a two-year-old migrates to a suitable spot along a stream and starts a dam-building program. A beaver is well equipped to cut down aspens and cottonwoods and other trees of sapling size, with which to build a dam. Four large, orange-colored front teeth, with chisel-like tips, are mounted on a powerful set of jawbones and are backed by large grinding molars. With this combination a beaver gnaws through a three-inch aspen in about twelve minutes, and under normal circumstances fells from 200 to 300 trees a year. An acre of aspens ordinarily supports a beaver family of six for about one and one-half years. Gnawed tree stumps, chips, and V-shaped wedges on standing trees are sure signs that you are in beaver territory.

Felled trees are gnawed into lengths of two to six feet, and are then dragged to the water or floated down beaver-made canals if the tree-cutting is carried on some distance from a pond. Gripping the log in its teeth, a beaver tows it to the dam foundation—a mixture of mud, stones, and debris of all kinds. The log is anchored to this mass, butt-end upstream, and is followed by as many logs as necessary to complete a dam that will maintain a constant water level two to three feet in depth. At first water may pour through the dam, but eventually every hole is plugged with mud on the upstream side until the structure is watertight. Dams of varying dimensions are constructed, depending upon the animal's requirements. Most dams are 3 to 4 feet high and less than 300 feet in length; one in Routt National Forest, Colorado, however, was 4 feet high and 500 feet long; the longest ever recorded was on Jefferson River, near Three Forks, Montana, and measured 2,140 feet.

A beaver generally constructs a conical lodge near the center of its pond. A lodge, built of rocks, sods, and sticks plastered with mud, rises 6 to 8 feet above water level and measures 15 to 25 feet in diameter at water level. The one chamber in the lodge is 18 to 24 inches high and about 6 feet in diameter, and has an elevated floor through which a plunge hole penetrates to the depth of the pond. Adults sleep on the bare floor, but newly born kits sleep on a matting of grasses, leaves, roots, and twigs, which later are eaten by the inmates of the lodge.

In the days when men were searching for fur, principally beaver, in the Pacific Northwest, a beaver lodge saved the life of John Colter, discoverer of the Yellowstone area. The Blackfeet Indians captured and stripped Colter, and made him run over a course that was carpeted with the needle-sharp cacti of the Northwest.

Colter was a fast runner and had outdistanced all the pursuing Indians but one. Colter stopped dead, whirled around, and lunged at his pursuer. The Indian, completely taken off guard, dropped his spear, the shaft of which splintered as it hit the ground. Colter snatched up the broken shaft, plunged it into the Indian's breast, then ran on, dived into the Madison River, and came up inside a beaver lodge, where there was air space above the water level. And there Colter stayed, numbed and blue, until he escaped after dark. Seven days later he arrived at a fort on the Big Horn, after walking two hundred miles, naked and living off the land.

It was fortunate for John Colter that beavers along the Madison River were lodge-building animals, not bank beavers as those animals that dig bank burrows are known. In a bank burrow, a chamber, located well above average high-water mark if possible, is about two and one-half to three feet across and one and one-half to two feet from floor to domed ceiling. A tunnel, sometimes fifty feet long but usually less, connects the chamber to the water.

Although both types of home and a beaver's general way of life give it comparative safety, the animal has some enemies. Bears, bobcats, cougars, coyotes, lynxes, wolves, and wolverines all prey on it, and it is subject to various diseases, many of which have not been identified. Some beavers are killed while felling trees, though deaths from this cause are not numerous. Man, the beaver's greatest enemy, takes about 150,000 animals a year in the United States and Alaska. On the raw fur market, pelts of prime fur average better than $20.00 a pelt (before World War II, the price was about $35.00).

The beaver, a strict vegetarian, eats a variety of foods. Cattails, lily pads, grasses and sedge roots, and canes of raspberry and blackberry are part of the diet. All summer long the beaver cuts small amounts of aspen trees and eats the twigs. But compared to fall activity, summer is a period of leisure for the beaver. In the fall the animal patches its lodge and dam, sometimes with the aid of the family, sometimes alone, and starts laying in a winter food supply. Aspens and other trees, including alders, beeches, birches, cherries, maples, and willows, are felled, cut into convenient carrying lengths, and towed out in the pond near the lodge. Here the logs are sunk and anchored to the bottom by stones or rammed into the mud. This submerged pile of logs is the beaver's winter larder; when a pond is iced over, a beaver leaves its lodge by way of the plunge hole, swims under the ice to the anchored pile, and selects a log. The animal returns to the lodge with its meal, and there eats the bark from the log with a corn-on-the-cob technique. A beaver sits up, holds the piece of wood in its front paws, and revolves the log as bark is chewed off.

Unlike many rodents it is not subject to striking fluctuations in populations. Economically the beaver is more of an asset than a liability, though in some areas beavers may flood and kill acres of low-land trees that are good food and cover for deer. Drainage ditches and culverts are often dammed by the animals, which also burrow into and weaken dikes. And the damming of trout streams sometimes raises water temperatures above the point that trout can stand. Where beavers cause such trouble, the animals should be live-trapped and removed to other areas.

On the other hand, the benefits they yield are great—so great in fact that Idaho and Wyoming among other western states trap beaver where the animals are too numerous and release them where the animals' dam-building proclivities are needed. In remote areas the animals are dropped by parachute. They are placed in crates attached to parachutes. When the crate strikes the ground one end of the beaver's container drops open and the animal walks out. Usually two males and two females are dropped in an area.

The ponds created by parachuted beavers and by those that have reached an area by more usual methods provide firebreaks, help maintain water tables, act as settling basins where silt is deposited, and create havens for waterfowl. Mallard and wood ducks nest on beaver dams and migrant geese and ducks rest and feed at the ponds. Damming of cold, densely shaded mountain streams often causes an

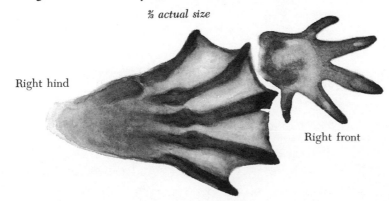

⅔ actual size

Right hind

Right front

accelerated growth of native brook trout; many such streams never produce trout of more than four to seven inches in length, but when streams are dammed trout of nine to twelve inches in length develop. This increased size of the fish is the result of warmer water and additional sunlight permitting growth of greater numbers of insects, crustaceans, and minnows for trout food. The beaver thus helps to establish a food chain that produces larger trout. A food chain, a whole series of creatures linked together by their food habits, is somewhat similar to the situation described in the popular verse by Augustus De Morgan:

> Great fleas have little fleas upon their
> backs to bite 'em,
> And little fleas have lesser fleas, and so
> *ad infinitum.*

If the beaver, once nearly extirpated over most of its range by relentless trapping, is given a chance, the animal, like the muskrat for which it provides habitat, will maintain itself *ad infinitum.*

EASTERN CHIPMUNK

Tamias striatus

The naturalist John Burroughs once provided a chipmunk with five quarts of hickory nuts, two quarts of chestnuts, and a quantity of shelled corn in a three-day feeding experiment. This animal carried it all away in its expandable cheek pouches. Each load was tucked into the pouches with the forepaws, first on one side, then on the other, until it was evenly balanced.

Some food of the chipmunk, an alert, tawny little animal with bright eyes enclosed by dark stripes, is cached in convenient spots on a territory that is no larger than two acres. The better part of the food, however, is carried to the burrow, where it is stored for winter use or to be eaten during periods of extremely warm weather when the animal also stays underground.

The burrow of the chipmunk is about two inches in diameter; for the first five inches it is vertical, then the shaft slopes off and continues to a depth of about five feet. If the animal lives its normal span of four or five years, it continues excavating until the tunnel may reach a length of twenty or thirty feet, and have several chambers. The room at the greatest depth is the toilet; two or three of the smaller rooms are for storage and often contain a bushel of food; and the largest, about a foot square, is used for sleeping quarters. This chamber contains a bed of shredded grasses and leaves. Food is stored under the bed. In the fall the chipmunk's resting place may be nearly as high as the ceiling, but by spring it may be almost down to the floor, if a great deal of the stored food has been eaten.

It is difficult to locate the entrance of the chipmunk's home, for the animal usually disposes of the excavated soil which has been pushed to the surface with the nose and tiny front paws. The chipmunk generally deposits the earth several yards away from the entrance. Sometimes, however, it leaves the earth nearby, then makes a second entrance. The smaller amount of dirt from the newer opening is pushed well away, so there is no indication that this is the chipmunk's home; the first entrance, marked by a quantity of dirt, is plugged up—a camouflage, apparently, to fool predators.

Although sociable, most chipmunks live alone except at mating time or when there are young in the burrow. Mating takes place from the first of February until the middle of March. During this period the male visits burrows of various females until he finds one that is ready to mate.

Some time in April the female gives birth to four or five young. The little animals weigh about one-ninth of an ounce, have their eyes closed, and are naked and red. They develop rapidly, and by the end of a month they look and behave like adults, whose slender bodies, measuring nine to eleven inches from the tip of the snout to the fleshy tip of the tail, are marked by five dark and four light stripes.

Throughout its range in deciduous forests and brushy areas of the greater part of the eastern United States and southeastern Canada, the chipmunk eats a variety of foods. It is abroad at all times during the day, gathering the fruits and seeds of the blackberry, wild cherry, elderberry, dogwood, partridgeberry, woodbine, and many others. Acorns, beechnuts, hazelnuts, and walnuts are in the diet, too, and though not an expert climber and leaper like the tree squirrels, the chipmunk goes aloft to get these nuts. Such crop plants as corn and wheat are occasionally eaten, but the animal does little damage.

Although primarily a vegetarian the chipmunk eats mice, some small birds and their eggs, snails, and occasionally small snakes. Its consumption of cutworms, beetles, June bugs, and wireworms helps the gardener to keep these pests under control. Sometimes the little animal, using the stalk-and-pounce technique of the cat, nabs a resting dragonfly; less often it catches a low-flying butterfly.

As the chipmunk scurries about seeking food, often calling to others of its kind with a soft "chuck, chuck," it has to be on the lookout for badgers, bobcats, foxes, small hawks, and barred and screech owls. Snakes and weasels prey on chipmunks, too, and frequently go right into a tunnel after their quarry. Cats kill many of these little creatures, and so do boys with .22 rifles and slingshots.

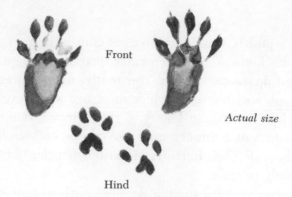

Front

Actual size

Hind

In late summer or early fall, you frequently see the chipmunk gathering its winter supplies. Look for it around hollow stumps, along stone fences, or in rocky pastures, and in large city parks. You may see the animal standing on its hind legs, with an acorn held in its tiny front paws. As the chipmunk revolves the nut or shifts it to chomp through the shell and get at the meat, it keeps one bright eye cocked in your direction. If you don't see the animal itself, you may find the caps and hulls of acorns or the hulls of other nuts on a flat rock. Sometimes a warm winter day brings the chipmunk aboveground; then you may spot its dainty, almost birdlike tracks in the snow (in summer look for them in dust, sand, or mud). The unpaired foreprints are usually staggered behind the paired hind tracks, and there is no tail drag.

Represented by eight species, the western chipmunks belong, like the chipmunks of eastern Asia, to the genus *Eutamias*. One race, the least chipmunk (*E. minimus neglectus*), lives in northern Michigan, Wisconsin, and northeastern Minnesota, also an area occupied in part by the eastern chipmunk.

It is easy to differentiate the western from the eastern one when you see them together. Except for the large and somewhat reddish Townsend's chipmunk (*E. townsendii*) of the Puget Sound area, the western species is smaller, has a longer tail, and is grayer than its eastern counterpart.

In one form or another the western chipmunk is found west of the Great Plains, from the southern parts of Mackenzie and Yukon Provinces to central Mexico. Within this range the animal lives in a variety of habitats—desert, forest, and mountain. In a timbered area you often see one on the end of a yellow-pine log. From this perch the animal may utter any one of its three calls, jerking its tail as it does so. At long but regular intervals it gives a somewhat low-pitched bark; at frequent but irregular intervals, it utters a high, chirping note; and when danger threatens, a guttural, scolding note is used.

The burrow of the western chipmunk is not so extensive as that of the eastern species. In a burrow or under the roots of a stump or a bush, the animal uses shredded grasses, leaves, and bark to make a nest that is about the size of a coconut. Here two litters are born each year, with the litters varying in size from two to eight. Young western chipmunks stay with the mother for about six weeks, then leave home to establish territories of their own.

The animal eats a wide variety of berries, fruits, nuts, and seeds, soft parts of plants, mushrooms, and many insects. Sometimes it does such a thorough job of collecting tree seeds that it hinders reforestation during the critical years following logging operations; at other times, however, the animal helps in reforestation of burned areas, where it buries food. Such caches are often forgotten, and sprout and grow. The numbers of insects harmful to forests eaten by the western chipmunk and the garden pests consumed by the eastern species are a credit to the animal about which a *New York Times* editorial once commented:

The little creatures are exquisitely graceful without being vain, well-dressed without being showy, friendly without being intrusive. Moreover, they are fun-loving without being silly, wise without being assertive, cautious without being afraid—and all over the scene without being bores. A human being might ask no more of his friends.

EASTERN GRAY SQUIRREL

Sciurus carolinensis

Legend has it that when the squirrel lived in the Garden of Eden it had a tail similar to that of the rat. Horror-stricken, it drew this appendage across its eyes at the moment Adam and Eve ate of the Forbidden Fruit to shut out the sight of their perfidy. As a reward the squirrel was given a great feathery tail of grayish black overlaid with white-tipped guard hairs.

The eastern gray squirrel, whose general color gives the impression of pepper-and-salt gray, must be a direct descendant of that Garden of Eden squirrel. It has the same type of tail, and often sits with it curved up like half a silver lyre, or as the first word of its scientific name expresses it, "he who sits in the shadow of his own tail." In addition to being decorative, and the reason for the common names "bannertail" and "silvertail," the squirrel's nine-inch plume is functional. It serves as a rudder during spectacular leaps, as a poncho or blanket in stormy or cold weather, and as an emotional outlet by which the animal expresses its feelings in a series of rippling jerks.

From the Atlantic seaboard to the western edge of the forest belt in Louisiana and Montana, a gray makes its home in woods composed of beeches, oaks, and hickories. The woods do not have to be pure stands and often are mixed with pines. In such habitat a gray lives either in a vacated woodpecker's hole or in spherical leafy nests, known as drays. All are usually forty to sixty feet above the ground. One type of leaf nest is built close to the trunk and is constructed of leaves, twigs, and bark. The nest measures about sixteen inches across on the inside and about twelve inches from top to bottom. Occasionally this nest is used to bring off a second brood of young or a summer brood of a female that has mated late. The other leaf nest, with a side entrance and looking somewhat like a crow's nest from underneath, is built well out on a branch and is used for resting or loafing—a prerogative of the male who, once the mating is completed, leads the existence of a bachelor.

The female is far too busy with her litter of five or six young to take time off to rest, though she sometimes moves herself and her young to a second nest if the first becomes unbearably flea-infested. In the North, gray squirrels are born from late February to the end of April; in the South, about a month earlier. Second and summer litters arrive from mid-July to mid-August. A gray squirrel is born with eyes closed and remains in that condition for five weeks or longer. It develops slowly; two months elapse before it can scamper around the home tree. It does not reach full size, seventeen to twenty-three inches, and full weight, one to one and one-half pounds, until it is two years old, but may mate when it is only a year old. Life expectancy of a wild gray squirrel is about eight years.

A gray squirrel is essentially a vegetarian, though individuals may sometimes eat birds or their eggs, or such exotic fare as the griddle cakes that my father used to bake for squirrels in Troy, N. Y. Regular diet changes with the seasons; in early spring, a squirrel eats buds of various trees, including the elm, and the flowers of others, including the sugar maple, whose sap it likes. Cuttings beneath elms and maples at this time of year may pile up to a depth of several inches and are one way by which you can tell that a gray squirrel is present.

Mulberries, huckleberries, and blackberries are all included in this animal's diet. And where a field of ripening corn is adjacent to a gray's home, you will discover its tracks—many sets of smaller paired fore prints which, in a bounding leap, are about half an inch in back of the larger hind prints—leading to and from the field.

As a rule corn-crop depredation by squirrels is not great unless there is a large concentration of the animals that can bite through the rough shells of hickory nuts in less time than it takes to say "*Rodentia*." This is the name of the order to which squirrels belong, for they are gnawing mammals with a double set of incisors. And as a rule squirrels in an area do not result in a conflict for use of land for grazing and other purposes, though squirrels compete to some extent with hogs for mast—a collective term for nuts. Mast is a wildlife food of great value; it contains a high percentage of car-bohydrates that produce heat and energy—two factors necessary if bobwhite quail and other game birds and mammals are to withstand

the storms and cold weather of winter. Mast also has a high content of protein, a tissue-builder. Oaks, particularly the white oaks, in addition to being valuable timber trees, are equally important as mast-producing trees for grouse and wild turkeys and deer, bears, raccoons, and squirrels. Crumbs dropped by squirrels when they eat acorns are picked up by quail and songbirds.

The gray's fondness for nuts of all kinds—acorns, pecans, and hickory nuts among others—causes it to be called the forest planter. A squirrel does not retrieve all the hundreds of nuts that it buries, though the percentage is high. Each nut is cached separately in a little cup-shaped hole. Many of the forgotten nuts sprout to produce seedlings. As a result the gray must be considered a good agent of conservation where the spread of nut trees is desirable.

A gray squirrel's worst enemy is man, who considers it an excellent small-game species because of its sporting qualities and edibility. Many people, of course, prefer to watch squirrels rather than to hunt them. Antics of squirrels are amusing as the animals scamper up and down tree trunks, using all four feet independently in the manner of red squirrels. If a park squirrel is tame enough to take a peanut from your hand, do not hold the nut too tightly. If you do, you may get nipped by teeth sharp enough to puncture the skin as the squirrel tries to get the nut away from you. If you happen to be bitten by a squirrel, use an antiseptic on the wound; many squirrels have scabies and some are apt to be rabid.

Gray squirrels are most active during the first three or four hours of the morning and during the last hours of full daylight. It is at these times that they are hunted. Grays are seldom, if ever, hunted for pelts, beautiful but of no economic value. (Fur coats are made from skins of Russian and Siberian squirrels.) At any season during bad weather, a squirrel holes up for short periods, but never actually hibernates or estivates. In winter several animals may occupy the same den, and sometimes when the nut supply fails, numbers of squirrels emigrate to another area.

A good hunter goes where squirrel food is abundant. The "splat, splat, splat" of hickory-nut cuttings, for instance, dribbling down through the trees in a grove of shag-barks is a sure indication that a gray is feasting somewhere overhead and that sooner or later in moving to a fresh feeding station will give the hunter an opportunity for a shot. At first hint of danger, a gray streaks for its hole, or if unable to do that, flattens out on a limb until it looks so similar to a gray lichen that even with 20/20 vision it is practically impossible to spot, let alone pick off with a .22 rifle by barking—stunning the squirrel by hitting the limb just below the frozen animal.

The eastern gray squirrel and three races of westerns (*S. griseus*, *S. nigripes*, and *S. anthonyi*), species of the Pacific slopes from northern Lower California to north-central Oregon, have many natural predators. Among them are the Cooper's hawk, the goshawk, and the red-shouldered hawk, the barred owl and the horned owl, and the fox, the bobcat, and the coyote. These predators catch their quarry on the ground, where the squirrels spend a great deal of time the year round, getting, burying, or retrieving food. Tree-climbing snakes, including the spotted chicken snake, go into dens for young squirrels, and in the West the pine marten gets some in trees.

A gray squirrel cries frantically when hawks and owls are around. The most common call is a loud, raspy note, that sounds something like a fast-repeated "Yak, yak, yak." There is also a bark, often harsh and impatient, then again rather soft and inquiring. And there are lesser calls uttered as the squirrels "talk" among themselves.

Frequently a gray-squirrel litter contains a black or melano and sometimes, though much more rarely, a white or albino. But whatever the color, they have bushy tails similar to the one bestowed upon their ancestor when Adam and Eve ate the apple, whose seeds, in fact, are liked by gray squirrels.

RED SQUIRREL

Tamiasciurus hudsonicus

The Chippewa Indians had an appropriate name for the eastern red squirrel, an exuberant little mammal and the smallest tree-climbing squirrel within its range. The Chippewas called the red squirrel *Adjidaumo*, meaning "Tail-in-the-air." This squirrel goes about its business in most evergreen forests of northern and western North America with a bushy, horizontally flattened tail held at an angle that gives its owner a devil-may-care appearance.

A red squirrel is easily recognized by its rufous color and whitish underparts and size—about six inches smaller than a gray squirrel. Ears are pointed and in winter have prominent reddish tufts, a characteristic that makes the red the only eastern squirrel so adorned. Each eye, sharp-sighted as a hawk's, is outlined by a ring of white.

A noisy little creature and usually heard before it is seen, the red squirrel barks, spits, and whickers all day long as it scampers through the trees of its home range—an area that is in the neighborhood of one-half to one acre. If you invade a red squirrel's domain, it scolds frantically, jerking its tail and stamping its tiny furred feet as it sounds off with "chickaree, chickaree, chickaree." Its defiant call has given in the name "chickaree" in the West, where there are two species of red squirrels: the Douglas chickaree (*T. douglasii*), which lives west of the Rocky Mountains, and the pine squirrel (*T. fremontii*), which is found from southern Wyoming to the Rocky Mountain region. These squirrels are sometimes called "bummers," a corruption of "boomer" which is the term for the red squirrel in the southern Appalachians.

At birth a red squirrel is blind and naked and weighs about one-fourth of an ounce. It is one of a litter of four or five, sometimes even seven, that are brought off in late May or June. The lying-in home for the female, born the previous spring, is usually a deserted woodpecker's hole, but sometimes it is an aerial nest of globular shape or an underground chamber of six to eight inches in diameter.

The aerial nest, close to the trunk and thirty to forty feet above the ground, is woven of bark, moss, and twigs, and of pine needles, dry grasses, and fallen leaves of nearby hardwoods. The underground chamber is one of several, used for resting or the storing of food and connected by numerous tunnels, whose entrances do not have dirt mounds.

A young red squirrel acquires a covering of fine, downy fur about ten days after birth, is nursed until it is five to seven weeks old, and leaves the home nest for good in late summer or early fall. From that time on, the squirrel leads a solitary life, living and working by itself until it dies at the age of five years, though it may live a little longer if its sharp incisors remain in good condition. There are fluctuations in the numbers of squirrels in a given area from year to year, with the greatest numbers occurring every fifth or sixth year.

Nuts and seeds of various pine trees are the principal foods of the red squirrel—an animal that eats almost constantly. Sometimes it stores as much as a bushel and a half of hickory nuts in a hole in a tree. In eating a hickory nut a squirrel gnaws through the shell so as to strike the kernel broadside and thus easily extract it. Pine cones, cut off and thrown to the ground by a red squirrel with an outward jerk of head or paw, are later picked up and lugged to a storage pile, known as a midden. A midden is usually at a central location in the squirrel's range, and is laid up around a log, stump, rock, or tree, always in a cool, moist spot. The moisture in the area acts as a preventive that keeps the cones from opening and losing their seeds. A midden contains from three to five bushels of cones, and some have contained as much as ten bushels.

Like the gray squirrel, which it may drive from its territory, the red has a sweet tooth. In the spring when sap is running up in maples and black birches, a red squirrel often laps the sap from a natural break in the bark. If nature does not provide such a source, the squirrel taps the tree by gouging out several small saucerlike depressions on the top sides of the limbs and laps from these as they fill.

This little animal eats berries of many shrubs, including the blueberry, the cranberry, and the partridgeberry among others, and the fruits of herbaceous plants, such as the bunchberry and the strawberry. Bark and roots, many insects, carrion, and eggs and young birds constitute part of a squirrel's diet. And when it comes to mushrooms, a red squirrel is so fond of them that it even digs for subterranean varieties. Gathered mushrooms are spread on the bark of trees to dry or tucked into crevices of old stumps. A mushroom-studded stump is a good indication that you are in red-squirrel territory. Varieties of mushrooms eaten include the fly and the destroying angel, both man-killers to which the red is immune.

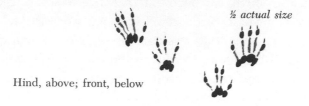

½ actual size

Hind, above; front, below

As it goes about its daily business, occasionally stopping to take a sunbath stretched flat out on a limb, a red squirrel has to be constantly on the alert for a host of enemies. Bobcat, lynx, mink, and weasel pursue it, and the marten, an animal that runs faster and leaps farther than the red, is a relentless hunter. The marten follows a red squirrel to the highest branch, where the pursuer shakes the pursued free and then races to the ground to kill it.

Among the hawks that a red squirrel has to watch out for are the broad-winged hawk, the goshawk, the marsh hawk, the red-shouldered and the red-winged hawks, and the sparrow hawk. And when the squirrel is abroad on a moonlight night, barred, horned, and spotted owls are the predators it must dodge.

A red squirrel is a good swimmer and sometimees escapes an enemy by taking to a pond or stream, often swimming a mile to make a getaway. But the safety of water is only comparative; a red is in danger of being pulled under and eaten by a good-sized pike or yanked out of the water by a hungry gull. In trees, a red is preyed upon by the black snake that goes into the nest and crushes the young.

The footwork of a red squirrel is nimble and varied to suit the occasion; on the ground it frisks about with short, springy leaps; in a tree it gallops along with fore and hind legs moving in pairs. It descends a tree trunk head first and at a trot in which the four feet are used independently, one foot being placed at a time and with back feet reversed to act as brakes. It makes jumps of as much as eight feet, with tail extended and legs spread wide. Most jumps are successful, but sometimes distance is miscalculated and the squirrel plummets to the ground. Apparently such a fall does not even knock the wind out of a squirrel, for it is up and away and into a tree with a speed you would hardly think possible.

Economically, a red squirrel is not important, though in some parts of Alaska and Canada skins are sold as fur. Like the gray squirrel's planting, that of the red in some localities is desirable and the pruning it does, by cutting off twigs, is useful. On the other hand, a red squirrel is a nuisance in camp; it gnaws window frames and other woodwork, and in some areas it is a host for ticks. Esthetically the red squirrel's value is immeasurable; the woods would not be the same if the Chippewas' "Tail-in-the-air" were not around to liven things up with its almost constant chatter and endless activity.

EASTERN FLYING SQUIRREL

Glaucomys volans

Flying fool, enormous eater, deep drinker, and apparently something of a mathematician, too, the little flying squirrel of most of the eastern United States and parts of Mexico is the sensational member of the squirrel family. This animal broke into print in 1624, when Captain John Smith wrote on it in his "History of Virginia": "A small beaste they haue, they call Assapanick, but we call them flying squirrels, because spreading their legs and so stretching the largenesse of their skins that they haue bin seene to fly 30 to 40 yards."

Smith's observations on the distance Assapanick could fly, or more properly glide, are quite accurate. Flights of flying squirrels have since been measured at 150 feet or more.

The animal whose scientific name can be freely translated as "silver-gray mouse that flies," has the gear necessary for gliding. Running from fore to hind leg, on either side of its 3½-ounce body, is a membrane, or fold of skin, stiffened by a cartilage extending from each foreleg. Thus equipped, it can soar with the greatest of ease.

A flying squirrel takes off from a limb high in a tree for a point near the ground. Before launching itself, the little mammal appears to make a visual measurement of the proposed leap. It will lean first one way and then another, apparently computing the distance to its chosen landing-spot by geometric triangulation. This range-finding is habitual with flying squirrels, according to E. P. Walker, assistant director of the National Zoological Park in Washington, D. C. That a flying squirrel gauges distance is evidenced by what happens when it does not measure its proposed leap. If you startle one by rapping on the base of its tree-trunk home, it will pop out and take off without pausing. Such a leap may land it on the ground or in the water. To land in water is disastrous, for a flying squirrel with its encumbering membranes is one of the few mammals that cannot swim.

Once a flying squirrel has measured the distance to its destination, it prepares to take off by gathering its tiny feet together. Then with a mighty spring, it leaps into the air, with legs spread out at right angles to the body. This action stretches wide the flying membranes so that the air rushing by underneath fills them as a parachute is filled. Immediately before landing, momentum is checked by an upward sweep, and the squirrel makes a treefall, spreadeagled and face upward on the spot of its choice. Shock of landing is absorbed by the hind feet; they strike the landing surface first.

In these glides the squirrel can change its course to one side or to the other with ease. This flight control makes it possible to avoid twigs and tree trunks and apparently comes from manipulation of the tail. Horizontally flat, the feathery tail is held straight out in the takeoff, but is flipped upward just before the landing. Another aid in controlling flight is varying the slack in one or both membranes. As soon as one glide is completed, the squirrel scrambles up the tree trunk on which it has landed, and prepares for another airborne descent, always at a 40- or 50-degree angle.

Undoubtedly it was this mastery of the air that intrigued England's first King James, and made him want a flying squirrel as a pet. The Earl of Southampton, a member of the Virginia Company's Council, mentioned the King's wish for a flying squirrel in a letter to the Earl of Salisbury, the King's Secretary of State, saying:

Talking with the King by chance I tould him of the Virginia squirrills which they say will fly . . . and hee presently and very earnestly asked me if none of them was provided for him and whether your Lordship had none for him, saying that hee was sure you would gett him one of them. I would not have troubled you with this but that you know so well how hee is affected to these toyes. . . .

In addition to being superb gliders, the King's toyes are excellent "second-story men." Tenants in a seven-story, stucco apartment house near Washington's wooded Rock Creek Park found that a pair of flying squirrels paid nightly calls at a sixth-floor window for a ration of pecans, after running straight up the side of the building.

The animal that can do all this, and also hang head down by a toe, is a little creature of mouselike appearance. It has moderately long fur—dense, fine, and of velvety texture. The upper part of the body is grayish fawn-brown with a blackish undercast. The body below is creamy white, while on the sides the blackish undercast prevails and makes a striking contrast to the white underparts. A nocturnal mammal, it has large eyes; they are circled by black and have a somewhat dreamy look.

A flying squirrel is an articulate little animal. For ordinary occasions, it utters a "chuck, chuck, chuck," much like the chatter of gray and red squirrels. When angry or alarmed, short, sharp squeals are in order. At other times, the vocalizing is similar to a bird song —a clear and musical chirping note. This note, sometimes harsh, is repeated for several minutes in succession.

In disposition no animal is more gentle or more curious than the eastern flying squirrel, which frequents almost any hardwood area within its range—even close to, or right in, an urban section, if there are beech and maple trees, its first choice, or oak and hickory trees, its second choice. A closely related, slightly larger species, the northern flying squirrel, *G. sabrinus*, of Canada and Alaska and parts of the Northwest, likes coniferous forests in which there are a few scattered hardwoods.

The flying squirrel's home is generally a deserted hole of a woodpecker—most often that of a downy but frequently those of hairy and pileated woodpeckers. The hole is lined with shreds of bark, dry leaves, moss, feathers, fur, or other soft material. Sometimes an outside nest is built. This structure is like the leaf nests of the gray squirrel, but has a warm inner lining and is snug enough for winter living. But whatever sort of nest a flying squirrel lives in—often with several of its kind, as it is gregarious—the nest is always near water. The little creature is a greater drinker than even the gray squirrel. It consumes nearly two jiggers of water a night or the equivalent of two gallons for a man.

If you rap on the tree-trunk home of an eastern flying squirrel with an axe handle, it will peek out to see what is up. Feed one and it will become tame in a week or two. After that, it may adopt you to a point where it will move in and take up residence in any pocket of your coat or shirt. It will stay curled up there all day, oblivious to the activity of the wearer of the garment.

Well after dark, a flying squirrel pops out of its hole to begin its night life—gliding, and eating and drinking. While feeding it has to be on the lookout for feral cats, owls, and raccoons, martens, weasels, and bobcats, and tree-climbing snakes. A flying squirrel is a huge feeder as it burns up energy fast. Primarily a vegetarian, its diet includes buds of trees in winter—as it does not hibernate—corn, berries of all kinds, mushroms, persimmons, wild grapes, blossoms of the sugar maple, and seeds and nuts. Nuts are necessary to keep teeth sharp. Hawk moths, May flies, and June bugs are eaten, and the larvae of many insects. Occasionally it eats eggs of wild birds and even devours birds, though not in sufficient numbers to make the animal a predator that needs to be controlled. In fact, as far as is known, a flying squirrel does not seem to exert a great influence on the plant and animal community in which it lives. It has some influence, of course, as all forms of life play a part in plant and animal communities.

Starting late in February, one or more litters are born each year. From three to six come into the world at a time. About the size of a quarter, they are naked, red, and wrinkled as raisins, with membranes fully spread and transparent. A young flying squirrel does not open its eyes until about the twentieth day after birth. At ten or twelve weeks, it can glide skilfully and takes to the air as readily as a duckling does to water. Apparently it is born with the innate know-how of gliding and needs no coaching from parents: tossed into the air, it automatically goes through the correct maneuvers to bring it to a safe landing.

In addition to being precocious about gliding, a young flying squirrel is smart about grooming at an early age. Before one is two months old, it makes it own toilet: baby fur is combed with the nails and washed with the tongue. At about three months, a young squirrel gets its adult coat of fur which, from then on, is changed annually, starting in September. Even though it acquires its adult coat at three months, the squirrel is not fully grown until it is about one and one-half years old. In the wild a flying squirrel's life expectancy is nearly five years; in captivity, it is about six to seven years, though one pair owned by a dealer in wildlife pets lived to be thirteen years old.

As pets flying squirrels are more readily available today than they were in King James's time. A Virginia dealer ships them to every state in the Union and exports them to Argentina, Scotland, France, and Switzerland. He has never shipped any to Asia, which has the largest flying squirrel in the world—a "monster" measuring four feet from tip of nose to tip of tail.

WHITE-FOOTED MOUSE (DEER MOUSE)

Peromyscus

In North America there are more than 250 forms of native mice. One of these is the white-footed mouse, whose distribution is about as widespread as that of any North American mammal. Hardly an acre south of the Arctic Circle is without some form of this big-eyed, big-eared mouse whose neat appearance and white undersides differentiate it from the slightly smaller, grayish-brown house mouse. In all there are more than fifteen species and at least seventy-five geographic races of the white-footed mouse, with the long-tailed member of the family occupying the most extensive range.

The white-footed mouse is also known as the deer mouse because the color and the pattern of its coat are somewhat like those of the white-tailed deer. In some areas this animal is known as the "vesper mouse" due to the buzzing or trilling it makes—a sound far different from the squeak most of us associate with a mouse. The long-tailed species of white-footed mouse bears the scientific name *Peromyscus maniculatus*, meaning "slender mouse with little gloves." And never was a name more fitting; the fore and hind feet of this sleek, long-whiskered little creature look as if they were encased in spotless white gloves.

This mouse is particular about its appearance and frequently spends fifteen to twenty minutes on its grooming. A white-footed mouse washes its face and long, sensitive whiskers much as a cat washes. After this part of the body is gone over with painstaking care, the animal licks and smooths its fur—a combination of buff to dark brown on the upper parts of the body and pure white on the belly, legs, and feet.

Neat about its person, the white-footed mouse is sloppy about its home. It does not bother to leave its nest to go to the toilet. In a short time the nest—perhaps in a ground burrow, an abandoned bird's nest, or a hollow log or tree—becomes so foul that the inhabitant has to move to another. Nests are located within the confines of a small, well-defined territory.

Each night the animal wanders over its territory in search of food; a male travels the farthest, perhaps as much as a hundred feet, but a female stays much closer to home, perhaps not going more than thirty feet. The white-footed mouse is generally abroad in search of food during the first two or three hours of the evening and again early in the morning. Only extreme hunger brings the animal out during the day or on moonlight nights. Although practically omnivorous, the white-footed mouse has a decided preference for dried seeds and berries; sometimes the animal stores as much as a quart of seeds for winter use in some convenient cranny.

When forest populations of white-footed mice become overabundant during cyclic peaks, the animals are a menace to reforestation. Feeding on tree seeds the mice destroy the crop which is needed for reforestation after logging. On the other hand if there are not so many mice in a given area that they hamper reforestation, the animals are valuable in keeping under control a white grub which attacks the roots of tree seedlings. The mice also bury more tree seeds than they actually need for food. Some of these "planted" seeds are forgotten and sprout, thus the white-footed mouse is responsible for some new forest growth. The forester's problem is to keep the white-footed mouse population at a level that is beneficial.

Although the white-footed mouse does some damage in agricultural regions, the animal is much less destructive to growing crops than the meadow mouse (*Microtus pennsylvanicus*). The meadow mouse and other members of the American vole family—the pine, the red-backed, the tree, and the lemming mouse—are so numerous and have such a wide distribution that they cause substantial damage in agricultural areas.

In addition to its cereal diet the white-footed mouse eats beetles, craneflies, caterpillars and cocoons, grasshoppers, moths, and many other insects. The animal also devours centipedes, slugs, snails, and spiders, and the carcasses of small birds and mammals, including other mice.

As it hunts the white-footed mouse gallops in a zigzag manner from place to place over its many types of home range. To catch live prey the animal stalks and then pounces in the manner of a hunting cat. The victim is bitten or beaten to death. The prints left by the mouse as it hunts are dainty, paired sets of prints seemingly in one hole; the width between prints is anywhere from 1½ inches to 1¾ inches. The prints of the front feet show only four toes, while those of the hind feet show five. The drag of the long, furry tail is often evident across heavy snow, through which the animal may also tunnel while seeking food.

Whenever the white-footed mouse is abroad it has to be on the lookout for a host of predators. All the flesh-eating animals hunt the creature, which is much less fleet than the weasel, the coyote, and the fox. Predatory birds, particularly the owls, which are night-hunters, feed on this mouse. Snakes and some of the larger shrews devour it too. But in spite of all these predators the animal is able to maintain its great numbers due to its fecundity.

Depending upon the species a female white-footed mouse may have from one to nine litters a year. In the North the breeding season starts in March and lasts until October. During the winter most of these mice live alone, but at the approach of spring a male starts looking for a mate. During the first part of the courtship the female fights off the advances of the male. Shortly, however, she stops resisting. But with this change in her attitude the male drops the initiative and makes no further advances. Then the female becomes the pursuer and finally entices her prospective mate into her nest, which may be in a variety of locations. The male stays with the female a few days, then leaves or is driven out.

At the end of a gestation period of twenty-one to twenty-eight days an average litter of four is born. Sometimes there is only one mouse in a litter for some species or as many as nine for others. The mice are born in a nest of carefully shredded materials, with a plug of this material acting as a stopper for the entrance hole so that it is warm in the nest wherever it may be: in a roofed-over bird's nest; in a tree hung with Spanish moss; in a beach burrow similar to the one made by a sand crab; in a spherical nest, sometimes a foot in diameter, woven around several branches in a bush; or in a house.

Except for its whiskers a young white-footed mouse is naked when it is born. The little animal is as crinkled as crepe and its eyes and ears are sealed. Weight at birth varies with the species. One of the smaller species weighs from one twenty-fifth of an ounce to one-twelfth of an ounce at birth, while those of the larger species may average one-fifth of an ounce.

Shortly after birth the young mice attach themselves to the mother's nipples for hours at a time and so firm is their grip that she can move around without having any of them drop off. When danger threatens the nest the female moves her litter wherever necessary, even carrying it up into a tree.

Hind, above; front, below

Actual size

Generally the time of weaning is the time for breaking up the family of white-footed mice. The young animals may be abandoned in the nest, or driven from the nest by the mother, or may leave of their own accord. For the first few months of its life a white-footed mouse is dull gray on the upper parts and white underneath. The gray hairs are gradually shed and replaced by dull, pale-brown hair, which in turn gives way to the deer-brown of the adult coat by the time a mouse is a year old. Once a year this mouse has a complete change of fur, which becomes sparser in summer and denser in winter.

This composite life history of the long-tailed species of white-footed mouse is in general typical of the life histories of all white-footed mice, whose family contains more than half the rodent species of North America.

Apparently the role nature designed for our native mice, primarily vegetarians, is to supply food for a host of birds and mammals, primarily flesh-eaters. For a complete listing of our native mice, or other animals with innumerable species and subspecies, consult the *Field*

Books of North American Mammals, by H. E. Anthony (G. P. Putnam's Sons, New York, N. Y.).

In addition to our native mice, there are two introduced forms of house mouse, a commensal animal—that is, one that lives in, with, or on another. The house mouse of the northern United States (*Mus musculus domesticus*) was transported from northern Europe to America by early Colonists, and the other form (*M. m. brevirostris*) was apparently carried by early Spanish explorers to Latin American countries and the southern United States.

The house mouse is referred to in the Bible, and historical records, including the writings of Aristotle and Pliny, mention mice as pests to mankind long before rats were mentioned in the same category. The generic name of the house mouse, *Mus*, means to steal, and is a fitting one for these tiny robber rodents. The tremendous potential destructiveness of these numerous little animals may be realized from reports concerning the California mouse plague at Buena Vista Basin in 1926. Part of one of these reports says:

A stack of barley hay literally alive with house mice had been completely riddled and all the grain consumed. Of ninety-one stacks of wheat sown on January 20, only fragments of the outer hulls remained on January 23. Shortage of crops due to the mice in 1926 is thus estimated at 10,000 stacks of barley, more than this amount of milo maize, besides greater amounts of wind-lodged maize that would have otherwise served as feed.

In addition to being an agent of destruction for crops, the house mouse transmits certain diseases of mankind, particularly several forms of food poisoning. From 1938 to 1945, the Public Health Service records indicated more than 12,000 cases of food-borne diseases in milk, more than 100,000 in water, and nearly 60,000 in food as a result of contamination by house mice.

On the credit side, the house mouse in its albino form is used for laboratory research. More than a million albino mice are raised each year for research purposes, particularly in the field of medicine. But even though the house mouse contributes to man's welfare through its use for laboratory research, the country would be better off if the animal had never been introduced in the United States.

WOODRAT

Neotoma

The woodrat—also known as the pack, trade, or cave rat—is a small creature with large, well-furred ears, large, bright eyes, soft, buffy fur, and white feet. Most species of woodrats have a rounded tail, covered by close-lying fur. One, however, is an exception: the bushy-tailed form (*N. cinerea*) of rocky areas in the far West has a fluffy tail that is similar in appearance to the tail of the flying squirrel.

Save for the eastern species (*N. floridana*), the majority of woodrats occupy territories in western North America from the southern part of Yukon Territory down to Mexico. Throughout their range these busy, inquisitive animals follow the practice which earned them the name "trade rat."

They might well be called the kleptomaniacs of the animal kingdom. Seemingly the woodrat cannot resist picking up an object—particularly a bright or shiny one—and lugging it home. If the animal spies a fragment of mirror, it usually drops the length of stick or bit of cactus it may be carrying, and picks up the mirror. As a rule the woodrat comes out ahead in trades, particularly when it purloins articles from camps and cabins during the night. Writing in *Arizona Wildlife Sportsman*, March, 1951, Ernest Douglas says: ". . . If the route [of the woodrat] chances to run through the cabin of a homesteader or tent of a camper, the trade may be for a bright can lid, a spoon, a bar of soap, a dollar watch, a biscuit, even a set of false teeth."

The articles gained by trade are lugged to the animal's home, which has some resemblance to a carelessly built beaver house. A bulky structure, it sometimes covers a ground area of four or five square feet. Homes are also built in trees, in clumps of mesquite or cacti, the crevices of cliffs, or in caves. Within any of these rubbishlike, stick structures is a globular nest, whose diameter is anywhere from six to ten inches. The nest is lined with soft, shredded materials of all kinds. Except at mating time or when there are young, each woodrat home is occupied by a single animal, which constantly adds to its domicile.

In early January a male woodrat becomes restless. This uneasiness takes the form of long night trips beyond its home range, which usually extends not more than fifty feet in any one direction from the nest. When the male finds a female who is in a mating mood, a stormy courtship ensues. The two animals fight and continue fighting even after the male moves into the home of the female. Some woodrats rear up on their haunches and tails and exchange blows like sparring partners. Eventually the animals come to tolerate one another, apparently deciding to bear and forbear, and mate. Shortly after the mating is consummated the male leaves.

Some four to five weeks later one to four young are born, with two an average litter. Northern species may have only one litter a year, while those in the South usually have several. A newborn woodrat is blind, deaf, and practically naked, and measures about four inches long including the tail.

At the end of three weeks' nursing period the little animal can see, and by the time it is three months old, it weighs about five ounces and has acquired a buff-colored coat similar to that of an adult. On leaving home the young woodrat either takes up residence in a nearby abandoned home erected by another woodrat or starts building one of its own.

Although primarily a night animal, it is frequently abroad during the day. The woodrat sometimes lies along a limb of a tree, with the tail hanging down, or sits on the ground on its haunches with the forepaws drawn up against the chest. If danger threatens, the animal thumps on the ground with one or both hind feet or vibrates the end third of its tail rapidly on the ground. Vocally the animal utters a variety of sounds: at mating time it gives a low chirp; during a fight, a short, shrill squeal is in order; and when danger threatens a woodrat makes a sound similar to a scolding red squirrel.

In addition to the mammals, such as badger, bobcat, coyote, fox, skunk, and ringtail, which prey on the woodrat, various reptiles include the animal in their diets, often slithering right into an intended victim's home. Barn and horned owls catch woodrats when the animals are out in the open—usually during the first hours after sunset or again early in the morning, the times when they are feeding or "trading."

The woodrat is a vegetarian. The eastern species, most numerous in the lower Mississippi Valley region, eats the rootstocks of goldenrod, leaves and twigs of the oak, and lengths of sumac, mesquite, and pricklypear. The white-throated woodrat (*N. albigula*) of the Southwest eats the pods and leaves of mesquite, the fruit of the pricklypear, carpetweed, and various other types of vegetation, and a few beetles and ants, which constitute less than one per cent of its diet.

The animal gnaws off the leaves and twigs with a slanting cut of its teeth. After it has cut for a while, the woodrat descends to the ground, picks up the twigs, and carries them to one of the storage rooms in its home. Some woodrats drink water, but others, particularly the desert forms, depend upon succulent foods for the necessary liquids in their diets.

Usually the woodrat does not in any way conflict with man's interests except at times of shortages in the regular foods. Then the animal sometimes eats the bark off trees. Such damage is slight. As a source of food for carnivores the woodrat is valuable, and some people say that it is better eating than quail. Indians, particularly the Apaches, have always eaten woodrats; in northern Mexico the flesh is sold in country markets. And with a life expectancy of three to four years in captivity, the animal makes a delightful pet, for it is intelligent and spotlessly clean.

EASTERN MUSKRAT

Ondatra zibethicus

A muskrat seldom strays far from water. Occasionally one of these small, densely furred rodents wanders along a highway or in a field, but such an animal is usually on the move as a result of drought, flood, or scarcity of food, or because it is looking for a mate.

Essentially an overgrown meadow mouse, with feet, fur, and tail adapted to an aquatic life, the muskrat occurs throughout the greater part of the continent from Bering Sea and the northern tree limits southward to Mexico. Within this range the eastern muskrat and fourteen subspecies and the Newfoundland muskrat (*O. obscurus*) live in rivers, lakes, ponds, swamps, and marshes.

Of these environments, the marsh is the most important, particularly coastal marshes like those around Delaware and Chesapeake Bays, where land is valued at ten to thirty dollars an acre a year for trapping purposes. A muskrat prefers a marsh that has an abundance of suitable aquatic vegetation for food and protective cover, fresh or slightly saline water for swimming and sanitation, and bottoms of peaty humus in which the animal can dig canals, underground tunnels, and runways.

In such a marsh the muskrat thrives and though you may not see any animals, their presence can be detected by signs of their activities and movements—dome-shaped houses, waste food particles floating in the water, air bubbles under ice, or little handlike tracks that show imprints of five fingers, and a quarter-inch-wide tail drag that is continuous when the animal hops or walks.

A marsh-dwelling muskrat builds several types of structures, including the dome-shaped nesting or dwelling house, also known as a bed or a lodge. This one, largest of all muskrat structures, is raised in water about two feet deep. Fibrous roots and stems of aquatic plants are used in construction. Freshly cut material is built up to a height that varies from sixteen inches to four feet; the walls are from four inches to one foot thick and are chinked with mud. Chinking acts as insulation to keep the lodge cool in summer and warm in winter. A lodge has several exits, known as plunge holes, so that the two or more occupants have free access to the water.

A lodge contains a dry, well-lined chamber which is a foot or more in diameter and some distance above the water line. In this chamber the first of three or more litters a year are born in late April or early May. Litters of the common eastern muskrat average six young. At birth a muskrat is about the size of a man's thumb, weighs less than an ounce, and is blind, red, almost naked, and helpless. After a nursing period of fifteen to eighteen days, a young muskrat's eyes open and it is covered with coarse gray-brown fur.

Young muskrats, known as mice, often nibble green vegetation before they are weaned at the age of four weeks, when incisors are sufficiently developed to give anyone handling the animal a real wound. At the time of weaning the young are driven from the lodge by the again pregnant female. Once a young muskrat is on its own, growth is remarkably rapid, and by the end of the trapping season in late February, a common eastern muskrat may weigh better than three pounds. By the following spring the animal is mature and ready to breed—a stage when the male battles savagely with other males for a mate. A female is attracted by the pungent scent secreted from glands under the skin near the groins. This musky odor is particularly strong at mating time and is the reason for the animal's name, given the Cree spelling of "Musquash" in Canada. The animal is sometimes known locally as "marsh rat" or " 'rat"; in Louisiana its official name is "marsh hare." The musk is often used in the manufacture of perfumes.

Near the dome-shaped house in which a young muskrat is born are several feeding shelters; these are easily differentiated from dwelling houses by the smaller size, more rounded, uniform shape, and low height—twelve to sixteen inches above water level. Feeding shelters contain a small central feeding platform above the water line, where a muskrat brings food to eat while protected from enemies and the weather.

A third type of structure built by a muskrat is the push-up or breather; this is generally found in frozen marshes of northern states and Canada along deep channels, river edges, and lakes. As soon as ice forms in the fall, a muskrat starts building push-ups by cutting holes of four to five inches in diameter in the thin ice. Fibrous roots, waterweeds, and other vegetation are pushed into the openings; sometimes air holes are stuffed with this material. A mass about the size of a man's hat is formed on the ice above the opening, and inside the mass a cavity is hollowed out which a muskrat uses as a shelter and a breather.

Cross-section view of a muskrat burrow: (a) den with tunnel to water under surface sheet of ice, (b) pile of vegetation hiding ground entrance, and (c) feeding station.

Bank burrows are dug by muskrats living along edges of waterways. Where a watercourse drains good farmland, muskrats often average six to eight breeding females a mile and have better pelts in size and quality than those of animals on streams that drain poor land. Entrances to bank burrows vary in depth and are usually under water. Tunnels lead back into a main burrow and then upward into one or more large nesting chambers high above the water level. Larger burrows have well-hidden surface entrances, with loosely plugged holes that serve as vents.

The muskrat's habit of burrowing into dams, levees, canal banks, and other earthen structures for retaining water often causes serious damage to the structures themselves and to adjacent agricultural lands by flooding or draining waters from irrigated crops. Dikes and levees in rice fields in the South, in Western irrigation projects, and in fish hatcheries have been ruined frequently by burrowing muskrats. For their control, carried on in accordance with state regulations, muskrats are trapped, shot, or dug out of their homes.

In Holland, to which the muskrat has spread from stock released in Bohemia in 1905 and in the British Isles in 1927, the animal is a serious problem. In fact the Dutch rank the muskrat as a public enemy. Since 1941, the Dutch government has been trying to exterminate the muskrat, which they fear may burrow into dikes. Muskrateers are employed to kill the animals and a bounty of five guilders ($1.50) is paid to private persons for every pelt turned in.

Although the muskrat is a pest animal in Holland, it is currently the most valuable wild fur animal in the United States. In the past decade the take of muskrat pelts has averaged 18,000,000 to 20,-000,000 a year, whereas average yearly take of opossum is about 3,000,000, skunk 2,500,000, raccoon 1,500,000, fox 900,000, and mink 700,000. Average price for a prime muskrat pelt is $2.50, though in some years top Northern pelts, like those from New York, have brought $4.00 to $4.55 on the raw fur market. Mutations, like the "Maryland white," bred in the swampy lands of Maryland, probably bring considerably more.

Track pattern, showing tail-drag

Fur of the muskrat varies from dark rich brown to a fulvous or reddish brown. Long, stiff, shiny brown guard hairs are closely interspersed among the short, soft, and exceedingly dense underfur. This gives the muskrat a coat that repels water like the feathers of a duck—a necessity, as the animal spends the better part of its life in or under water. The muskrat is further equipped for aquatic life by a ten-inch tail that distinguishes it from all other animals. The tail, thick, vertically flattened, and covered with small scaly areas, is held rigid as a rudder while swimming or let waver like a propeller. The tail is also used to slap the water when trouble is at hand. Large hind feet can be turned sidewise to reduce resistance to the water and though not webbed, they have fringes of short, stiff hairs that also aid in swimming.

A muskrat has four protruding, chisel-like incisors to cut its food,

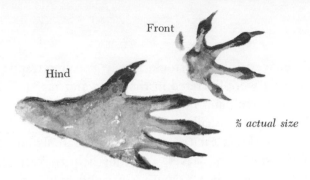

Front

Hind

⅔ *actual size*

which varies with the seasons and plants available. Though a vegetable eater for the most part, a muskrat feeds to a limited extent on
crayfish, crabs, minnows, mussels, snails, and sluggish fish like carp.
In summer a muskrat's food consists of leaves and roots of plants
such as arrowhead or duck potato, cattail, wild rice, water lily,
marsh aster, pond weeds, water weeds, and occasionally smartweed.

Foods of inland fresh-water areas, like those of the six North
Central States that produce the largest and the best pelts, are blue-
flag, cattail, broad-leaved cattail, and burreed; in the great muskrat-
producing marshes of the Atlantic and Gulf coasts, three-squares and
saltmarsh bulrush are staple foods.

In winter a muskrat lives mainly on underground parts of plants.
Unlike many other rodents the animal does not store great quantities
of food for this time of year and depends entirely on its ability to
dive and while submerged dig and gnaw loose pieces of roots and
lower stems of aquatic plants. Short, bristlelike hairs cover the lips
and protect them from sharp grasses and other rough plants. A deep
cleft between upper and lower lips permits the animal to open its
mouth wide enough to carry large mouthfuls of nest-building material or food. In summer some of this food includes such cultivated
plants as alfalfa, carrots, clover, raw peanuts, soybeans, and apples.

Muskrats like stalks of growing corn and may cut extensively from
cornfields near streams and ponds. But it takes a great deal of cutting
for the animal to pilfer more than a bushel or two of corn by harvest
time, and the loss can be compensated for by the sale of two or three
pelts of the animal which, on most farms, represents the greatest cash
value of any wildlife species.

In addition to a cash value, muskrats have wide value as a marsh-
management tool. At Stillwater Wildlife Management Area in western Nevada, disease had nearly exterminated the muskrat by 1948.

To speed recovery of local stock, nearly 800 live-trapped muskrats from California were liberated in the Stillwater marsh. These plantings were successful, and in the following years the muskrats made a fourfold increase annually.

Stillwater muskrats eat the rootstalks of cattails and build their houses of the stalks and leaves, and thus help to keep the plant in check and create open water where sago pondweed and other aquatic plants useful to waterfowl may grow.

In addition to its value as a fur animal and as a marsh-management tool, the muskrat is a source of food. There is a growing demand for the fine, dark-grained flesh that has a decidedly gamy flavor; it is sold under such names as "marsh hare" and "Chesapeake terrapin" in retail markets in the East and in the Middle West. Muskrat meat is served in many leading restaurants and hotels and for thousands of trapper families muskrat flesh is the best meat available in their daily diet.

A muskrat is generally most active from dusk until about eleven o'clock at night and again in the early morning, though the eastern species is frequently active during the day. In the open a muskrat has to be on the lookout for numerous predators that include the marsh hawk, the red-tailed hawk, and the great-horned owl. Bald eagles rob muskrat traps and one bald eagle in Maryland carried off forty traps and ate their contents at the nest. Mammal predators include the coyote, the red fox, and the marsh-dwelling raccoon. Minks, particularly buck minks, are one of the muskrat's deadliest foes. The black snake, the water moccasin, the alligator, the garfish, and the snapping turtle take many young ones, and on more northern marshes the pike and the muskellunge are occasional predators.

Diseases, too, kill great numbers of muskrats whose abundance follows a cyclic pattern. In Canada peak muskrat populations occur about every ten years; in the United States peak populations occur at somewhat longer intervals.

The muskrat survives due to its adaptability and the fact that it multiplies much more readily than other fur animals. In a suitable habitat it is a self-perpetuating resource that can be harvested without seeding, cultivating, or care of any kind—a boon not only to the country's 2,000,000 trappers but to all of us.

BROWN RAT

Rattus norvegicus

The rat that ate the malt that lay in
the house that Jack built.
       The Domicile Erected by John
                    GEORGE SHEPARD BURLEIGH, 1857

Long before Burleigh wrote about the rat, this omnivorous rodent was a pest to man. An ancient Greek treatise on farming advises that to rid your land and buildings of rats and mice, you should take a piece of paper and write on it as follows: "I adjure you, ye mice or rats here present, that ye neither injure me nor suffer another mouse or rat to do so. I give you yonder field (a particular field is indicated), but if I ever catch you here again, by the mother of the Gods I will rend you in seven pieces." After a paper had been properly inscribed, it was to be placed on an unhewn stone, "taking great care," the treatise admonished, "to keep the written side up."

The Greeks were not the only people to use the inscribed paper method for getting rid of rats. Centuries later the Welsh wrote out a letter-changing formula to rid a house or property of rats:

                    r.a.t.s.
                    a.r.s.t.
                    t.s.r.a.
                    s.t.a.r.

A paper so inscribed was then to be placed in the mouth of King Rat; but there were no directions on how to catch the King Rat or how to recognize such an animal.

Although present-day methods of getting rid of rats are much more effective, there are probably more rats than people in densely populated areas. Each year house rats cause losses amounting to millions of dollars and also transmit bubonic and typhus fever by means of rat fleas.

The two species responsible for these losses and the spread of these diseases are the brown (*Rattus norvegicus*) and the black rat (*R. rattus*). Originally these mammals were confined to Asia. The tree-climbing black rat, a slender grayish-black animal, probably migrated to Europe in the twelfth century, then by ships reached America at the end of the seventeenth century. By 1700 the black rat, also known as the ship, roof, or house rat, was common along the Atlantic seaboard.

About 1727 the second of these species, the coarse-furred brown rat, made its appearance in Europe, and reached America around 1775. This animal, whose sparsely haired, scaly tail is shorter than its head and body, drove the smaller black rat from much of the coastal range it had occupied. Today the range of the brown rat is practically the entire United States, a great part of Canada, and all along the coast of Alaska.

An adaptable, intelligent animal (as shown by maze tests with albino rats at the American Museum of Natural History's Animal Behavior Laboratory), the brown rat makes itself at home anywhere, utilizing the materials at hand for its burrows and nests. On Rat Island in the Aleutians these animals dig burrows in the bases of the cliff nests of bald eagles. Generally the brown rat lives in burrows under or near buildings or between the lower walls of structures. The tunnels of this species are dug by the cooperative efforts of many animals. The greatest length of a tunnel is probably no more than a foot and one-half. Rats also live in open fields, ditch banks, and trash or garbage dumps. Other outdoor homes are often found near grain or cane fields, and in salt marshes.

Rat dens, globular in shape, are about a foot in diameter; they are lined with any available soft material. In such a den the young are born during the warm months in the North, and all year round in the South, though in winter births of southern rats are not so frequent.

The number of rats in a litter may be anywhere from one to fifteen—or even as many as twenty-two. At birth a young rat is blind, hairless, and weighs about one-fifth of an ounce. About halfway through its nursing period of some three weeks, the young animal's eye open, and by the time it is fully weaned the animal is ready to leave the nest.

A brown rat is ready to breed by the time it is three months old, and continues to breed until it is two years of age. Litters of the black rat, restricted to coastal areas of the southeastern States, are

Black Rat

smaller. The black form, which makes its nest well up in buildings, was exterminated in interior areas by the larger brown rat.

Both species, good swimmers, are active all year. They eat a wide variety of foods, including refuse of all kinds, stored and growing grains and fruits, meats, packaged foods, soaps, and the dead of their own kind. They also eat book bindings, gnaw the insulation off electrical wiring, and gnaw through lead water pipes to get at water—of which they drink quantities.

Although not classed as carnivores these animals kill domestic poultry and wild birds, and frequently take both eggs and young chicks from beneath a setting hen without disturbing her. Rats kill adult birds by slitting the throat. Frequently rats fight over food among themselves, with the brown species squeaking or squealing as it does so. The sound made by the black rat is a twittering noise.

In addition to man, who destroys large numbers of rats, the animals have a number of natural predators. Hawks and owls, foxes, minks, skunks, and weasels kill numbers of them; dogs and cats also are rat-killers.

The yearly losses caused by rats in the United States through damage to property and the destruction and spoilage of foods has been estimated at two hundred million dollars. This amount is nothing in comparison to the animals' effect on health. Rat-borne diseases have resulted in the deaths of more people during the last five thousand years than the combined casualties of the wars taking place during those years.

Of the various plagues caused by rats, the one known as the Black Death was the most widespread and catastrophic. This plague (the bubonic type) began in Constantinople in 1347. By the time it had died out, the greater part of the European population had succumbed.

Although the last widespread European outbreak of plague was on the Volga in 1878–79, the Far East has had epidemics of plague in recent years. In Occidental countries constant warfare on rats by means of control campaigns, the rat-proofing of dwellings, granaries, and other buildings, insecticides to destroy disease-carrying fleas, and the treatment and control of disease by sulfa drugs and streptomycin have prevented such epidemics.

The brown rat is used by bacteriologists, biochemists, and geneticists in studies relating to human medicine. However since the house rat is adaptable, intelligent, and prolific it is necessary to kill these public enemies, excepting the laboratory strain, of course, whenever and wherever possible. For a leaflet on their control, write the Superintendent of Documents, Government Printing Office, Washington 25, D. C., for Circular 22, *Rats—Let's Get Rid of Them,* a publication of the Fish and Wildlife Service, Department of the Interior. This circular costs ten cents, and is a much more practical paper than those used either by the Greeks or the Welsh for getting rid of these pests.

CANADA PORCUPINE

Erethizon dorsatum

The rolling gait of the porcupine is usually deliberate and un-hurried, as if the humpbacked-looking animal had complete confidence in the impregnability of its quill defense. Some 30,000 hollow quills cover an adult porcupine from just above its black, beady eyes almost to the tip of its short, clublike tail. The quills are long and slender across the shoulders, short and thick on rump and tail.

The yellow or white quills have black or brown sharply pointed tips that bear hundreds of microscopic, diamond-shaped scales; these serve much the same purpose as barbs on a fishhook. Quills can be raised or lowered but cannot be thrown; there are no quills on the almost hairless belly, the snub-nosed face, or on the tough, scaly underside of the tail. As quills are lost in defense actions or moulted they are replaced by new ones.

When attacked a porcupine puts its nose between front legs and lowers its belly to the ground to protect those parts of the body not covered by quills. Then before going into action, the animal clicks its teeth or utters a kind of grumbling noise—apparently a warning to beware. If the attacker moves in, the porcupine spins around so that its rear is to the enemy, arches its back, and thrashes out with body and tail until hundreds of quills are embedded in the attacker. Quills work forward in the flesh, swelling as they do so, and burning like red-hot skewers. Quills in head, throat, or chest may eventually pierce a vital spot or cause infection; and as it is impossible for a wild animal to paw them out, a creature that has been struck in the mouth ordinarily becomes unable to eat and dies of starvation. On the other hand, great-horned owls and bears, mountain lions, and wolves have been found full of quills and proved otherwise to be in reason-ably good condition.

The porcupine's generic name, *Erethizon*, means "the one who rises in anger"; its common name comes from two sources: "porcus," a Latin word meaning pig, and "épine," a French word derived from the Latin "spina," meaning spike or thorn. One of the porcupine's colloquial names is "quill pig" and another is "porky." In some areas the animal is called a "hedgehog," a misnomer, as the porcupine is a rodent (second largest in North America) and the hedgehog of Europe is an insectivore.

The Canada porcupine of the East and the yellow-haired porcupine (*E. epixanthum*) of the West are found in woodlands of most of northern North America. The Canada porcupine lives as far south as West Virginia and west to Minnesota; the yellow-haired porcupine lives in Rocky Mountain regions south to Mexico.

For its home a porcupine uses the crevice of a ledge, rock debris below a cliff, a hollow tree or log, the exposed parts of a stump, or a brush pile. In such a spot the female repairs to bear the single young which results from a fall or early winter mating—a mating preceded by a strenuous courtship which includes a great deal of nose-rubbing along with falsetto cries by the male and squalls by the female.

A young porcupine is born during April, May, or June, after a gestation period of more than two hundred days. At birth a Canada porcupine is larger than a newborn black bear, weighs from twelve to twenty ounces, and is ten inches long. Its eyes are open and a dense coat of long black fur (the yellow-haired porcupine develops the yellowish cast at a later date) covers the body. In the fur are hundreds of soft quills which harden within one-half hour after birth. If the little animal is frightened, it performs a defensive action similar to the one executed by an adult; sometimes a young porcupine plays in the same way. If captured young, a porcupine makes a delightful and affectionate pet and may live to be seven years old. Wild porcupines probably have a life span that is considerably shorter.

During the first ten days of its life a young porcupine nurses frequently as the female sits on her haunches and tail. At the end of this period the young animal starts to eat green herbs and is weaned soon thereafter. From birth a young porcupine is able to walk, albeit in a somewhat wobbly manner, and from the second day of its life the young animal is able to climb, though first ascents are cautious and only into the lower branches of a tree.

Hind   Front

⅔ actual size

By the time a porcupine is six months old and weighs several pounds, it climbs as well as the mother from which it has now parted. And when mature, about a year later, the animal weighs eight to fifteen pounds, sometimes as much as thirty-five pounds. Full-grown it measures about twenty-five to thirty-five inches in length, and is ready to mate.

The mating interval is about the only time a porcupine seeks one of its own kind. Occasionally the animals den together in winter or come from miles around to feed on garden stuffs, truck crops, or orchard fruits. In Maine porcupine raids on sweet corn at the time the ear is in milk have drawn as many as thirty animals to a one-acre field, leaving the area ravaged as though cattle had broken in to feed.

The porcupine, an excellent climber and an efficient swimmer—the air-filled quills give the animal buoyancy—is active all year. The animal generally goes about its business at night, grunting as it does so, on a home range of approximately five acres. Sometimes after a stormy spell, the animal feeds during the day or suns sprawled out on a leafless limb.

Common signs of porcupine activity are bean-shaped droppings at den entrances, and barked trees. Patches gnawed by a porcupine low on a tree can be differentiated from the barking of elk or moose by the irregular outline, neatly gnawed edges, and small tooth marks. Additional signs that indicate a porcupine's presence are toed-in tracks resembling the imprint of a human foot and a zigzag tail drag in dust or snow that looks as if someone had gone along lightly brushing the dust or snow with a whisk broom. Porcupine tracks and those of any other wild animal serve as clues to relative abundance and supply needed information for wildlife management—particularly in regulation of trapping.

In the spring a porcupine, a strict vegetarian, eats the flowers and catkins of the maple, poplar, and willow. As soon as these are "out of season," the animal shifts to the new and tender leaves of such trees as aspen and larch. During the summer herbaceous meadow and field plants are eaten and in winter the foliage of such evergreens as hemlock and white, ponderosa, and piñon pine are part of the diet.

Principal winter food is the inner bark—cambium and phloem layers—of a number of trees. With its large, yellow, chisel-like teeth the animal chips off the outer, corky layers of bark and discards these to eat the succulent layers of bark just beneath, containing stored quantities of sugar and starch.

In the Northeast trees often selected for a porcupine's winter feeding are such valuable timber trees as the beech and the sugar maple, the white and yellow birch, and the white pine and the white spruce. The animal usually selects the dominant and thriftiest trees, leaving the suppressed and poorer ones to perpetuate the stand. Sometimes a porcupine stays in and feeds on one tree for days at a time.

Complete girdling causes a tree to die; even spot damage may seriously affect growth and timber value. On a pole-sized tree, porcupine feeding usually occurs in the upper fourth of the main stem, and although the tree may not die, it becomes spike-topped and quite useless for lumber and for shade.

Though the most serious economic losses from porcupines are caused by their winter feeding habits, the animals endanger domestic livestock. A porcupine in a pasture arouses the curiosity of most farm animals, which in trying to get a closer look usually get slapped across the muzzle. Scores of quills are thereby driven deep into tongue and muzzle and range cattle often die following such an encounter. Dogs never seem to learn to leave porcupines alone. A Vermont veterinarian earns a good part of his income from treating dogs that have been worsted by porcupines.

A porcupine's craving for salt makes the animal a nuisance, too. Anything touched by human hands leaves a trace of salt. Farm-tool handles, saddles, and canoe paddles are often damaged overnight as a porcupine gnaws away. A Forest Service employee once parked his car at the foot of a trail leading to his fire lookout station, forgetting to roll up the windows. When he returned a week later, he discovered that a porcupine had worked on the steering wheel until little more than the spokes remained. Porcupines also gnaw on old deer antlers and bones to get at the minerals contained in them.

Porcupines are controlled by hunting, trapping and poisoning, and fencing. No large-scale program of control, particularly one of poisoning, should be conducted without the advice and guidance of someone thoroughly familiar with the animal's habits.

Nature provides some controls for the porcupine. The bobcat, the red fox, the lynx, and the mountain lion attack it. The fisher is probably the porcupine's deadliest foe, as this predator has learned to flip over a porcupine and rip open the defenseless soft belly and eat out the carcass. Where there are fishers there are not so many porcupines, though not all fishers escape injury by quills; some die from quills and pelts have been taken in which there were numerous, flattened quills. Sometimes the coyote, the black and grizzly bear, the wolf, and the wolverine use the fisher's tactic on porcupines. Among the many diseases to which a porcupine is susceptible, tularemia is perhaps the greatest control.

The porcupine contributes little to man's economy and wildlife's requirements. Quills are used by Indians in fancywork, and twigs cut down by feeding porcupines are eaten by deer and elk. The animal eats quantities of mistletoe, but frequently after ridding a tree of this parasitic growth a porcupine starts on the tree itself.

If you are ever lost in the woods and need a meal, remember that a porcupine is the only animal an unarmed person can kill by hitting over the head with a club, and is therefore protected in some areas. No preparation is needed to cook a porcupine. Place the carcass on a bed of coals, heap more coals over it, and roast for thirty or forty minutes. Upon removal from the fire, skin and quills can easily be pulled off. The white meat is said to be tender, but it is apt to have a pine-bark flavor. In a pinch, however, porcupine meat would keep you from starving to death. Also remember that a porcupine never attacks, so if you leave the animal alone there is no danger of getting some of those 30,000-odd quills embedded in your flesh.

NUTRIA

Myocastor coypus

An adult nutria, or coypu, looks something like a stunted beaver. Long whiskers make the short-eared head appear broad, heavy, and coarse. The whiskers might be useful as a grip for picking up the animal, but four, powerful orange-colored incisors, which can inflict a severe wound, make it advisable to stay away from the front end of a nutria. The only safe way to handle this marsh dweller is to pick it up by its long, round, and scantily haired tail. The nutria's tail differentiates it from the beaver and the muskrat, whose tails are flattened and naked.

The nutria's tail serves as a rudder as the animal pushes through the water with webbed hind feet which, with its clawed front feet, make a combination unlike that of any native animal in the United States. Like the beaver, the nutria slaps its tail against the water as a warning signal, though it has few predators. Owls and hawks and minks and raccoons probably get some young and may occasionally kill an adult in the open.

A few nutrias were introduced from South America in 1899, but not until the 1930's were many brought in for fur farming. The experiment was unsuccessful; the animals did not do well in captivity and upkeep soon exceeded sales value. In 1940 about thirty pairs of animals were set free in the Louisiana marshes by discouraged breeders of fur animals. Later the freed nutrias were joined by others that escaped.

If ever an immigrant took kindly to a new country, it is the nutria. The animal flourished and now thrives in the vast coastal marshes of Louisiana, where conservationists believe that in time receipts from sales of nutria pelts will be greater than receipts from muskrat pelts —a crop that has brought as much as $15,000,000 a year. Nutrias are doing well in Washington, where they were freed by discouraged breeders, and in Texas, to which the animal migrated from Louisiana or was introduced. In Texas the nutria is used as a marsh management tool to create open water. Ten or twelve nutrias released in a small, weed-choked lake clear it of such pest plants as waterlily, cattail, cutgrass, and arrowhead in about six months. Nutrias are in Alabama, Mississippi, and New Mexico, and have been planted in several states, including Maryland. A few pioneering animals have migrated to Iowa, Michigan, and Ohio, and even western Canada—quite an outpost for the South American animals, which, where they are numerous, maintain about six active burrows to a mile of levee.

A young nutria is rat-sized at the time of birth—following a gestation period of 127 to 132 days—and is one in a litter of three to twelve. It is born with a dense coat of fur, is extremely precocious, and often starts swimming in few hours after birth. It nurses, half-immersed beside its mother, whose mammary glands are along the sides of her back. A young nutria is weaned when it is seven or eight weeks old. In keeping with this precocity, a female breeds by the time it is six or eight months old, and continues to produce a litter every four months or so after the initial one. Young are born either in a grass-lined bank burrow, whose diameter is seven or eight inches and whose entrance is just above the water line, or in a floating nest constructed of aquatic plants, that is similar in appearance to a muskrat house. During cold weather the floating nest is used by a family group that snuggles close together to conserve body heat.

At maturity a male weighs about twenty to twenty-five pounds, a female about five pounds less. A male, known as a boar, lives to be six years old, but a female only lives to be three due to the frequency with which she bears young.

In color the fur of the nutria is dark amber, and though a pelt is five times larger than that of a muskrat, only the fine, dense belly fur is used in making a coat. A coat of prime skins commands a price of around fifteen hundred dollars. The coat might be mistaken for beaver, as the fur is not well known in the United States in spite of the fact that the nutria has been "at home" here for more than fifty years—a period during which the animal's long guard hairs were used primarily to make hatter's plush.

Like the muskrat the nutria digs into banks of irrigation canals and small dams and levees. Corn and other vegetables and alfalfa and rice are eaten when regular foods—the soft portions of shoots and tubers of bull's tongue, pickerel weed, and water hyacinth among others—are in short supply. However, the price of $3.50 to $6.00 paid on the market for pelts should keep the nutria population well under control and should compensate for any damage done by this addition to our wildlife.

In South America the nutria was thought to be a species of otter by early Spanish explorers. They named it nutria, Spanish for otter. As nutria—a misnomer, as the animal is a rodent not a weasel—it was hunted in Argentina until nearly exterminated. As a result the value of pelts rose until the price quoted on Canada's raw fur market for extra large pelts in 1929 was $13.50.

South Americans started raising nutria in captivity in 1922. The animals used for breeding purposes were wild ones and were bought for as much as one hundred dollars a pair. These breeding animals were the ancestors of those in the United States, and France, Germany, Russia, and Switzerland, and the Scandinavian countries.

A nutria occupies a habitat niche in this country not used by other marsh animals and eats the coarser vegetation that does not appeal to the others. It prefers deeper and fresher water than the muskrat, and even in waters that have been stocked with fish, the nutria has never been known to eat the fish. It has never shown any inclination to eat eggs of waterfowl nesting in the same area. So it seems that as a naturalized citizen the nutria has much in its favor. What effect the animal will eventually have on our native wildlife populations, our plants, and the balance of nature will only be known in the future. But whatever the effects of this exotic, the animal seems to be here to stay.

England, however, has already learned that the nutria, or coypu as the animal is known there, is a pest. It destroys sugar-beet crops by nibbling off the tops of growing plants, and also causes flooding. The animal burrows deep in the banks of rivers and drainage canals at water level.

The nutrias in England are the descendants of those which escaped from about fifty nutria farms established in Britain during the 1920's. As the animal has no natural enemy in Great Britain, it is feared that well-established colonies may build up rapidly in the wet, low-lying regions of East Anglia, where shotgun patrols have been organized to kill the animals on sight.

COYOTE

Canis latrans

One of the first American naturalists to hear the yelping cry of the coyote was Thomas Say. In the early 1800's Say was a member of expeditions to the Rocky Mountains and up the Mississippi and Minnesota Rivers under the direction of Stephen H. Long, who was to determine the source of the Minnesota. On these trips Say heard the call of the coyote and named the animal *Canis latrans*, the "barking dog." Anyone who hearts the coyote's serenade at twilight or the animal's early morning reveille realizes with what precision Say made his choice.

The coyote, whose name is a modification of the Aztec word *coyotl*, is a dog-like animal weighing from twenty to fifty pounds. The fur is tawny, the tail is bushy and black-tipped, and the ears and nose are sharply pointed. All nineteen races of the widely distributed coyote have similar coats except the pale-gray desert form; and all coyotes have longer, lighter-colored fur in winter than in summer, when the coat takes on tones that blend with summer vegetation.

Originally the coyote, known as the brush wolf in forested regions and the prairie wolf in plains country, was confined to western North America, where it lived from plains country to timberline. Today the coyote has extended its range eastward and northward until the animal is found in several eastern states and Canadian provinces and in Alaska, where it first appeared about 1900.

Some of the local populations of coyotes in eastern states include a cross between coyotes and feral dogs. Known as coydogs or doyotes, these hybrids look more like coyotes than dogs, but run faster than dogs and are said to be more cunning than coyotes, whose intelligence is so highly regarded by Mexicans that they use the expression *"muy coyote"* to denote someone who is shrewd in a crafty way. These hybrids cannot be tamed like the coyote, which if caught as a young pup makes an interesting pet that may live in captivity as long as fifteen years.

By the time a female is two years old she is ready to mate. Sometimes she is fought over by two males seeking her favors. Surprisingly the female often mates with the vanquished male which, like all males of the species, is monogamous for at least a year and possibly for the lifetime of the female. Matings take place in January and February; about sixty days later the female delivers her young in the hollow base of a tree, a hollow log, among rocks, in a cavern, or in a burrow.

A burrow is dug in loose soil. Sometimes mated coyotes dig a new tunnel, but more frequently they enlarge one that has been vacated by a badger, fox, or skunk. The tunnel of the coyote is anywhere from one to two feet in diameter and from five to thirty feet in length. During the excavation of the main tunnel and its several branches, the dirt is pushed back to the entrance and deposited outside in a low, fan-shaped heap. At the burrow's end is a chamber, whose ceiling varies from a foot below the surface of the ground to as much as six feet below. Sometimes the chamber is ventilated by a hole in the ceiling and like the entire burrow it is scrupulously clean, for the animals deposit wastes outside.

The annual litter of coyotes is born during April, May, or June. A litter may contain as few as three pups or there may be as many as nineteen. Usually there are five to seven little coyotes which come into the world well furred, but with their eyes closed. Although the male leaves the female at about the time she is ready to whelp, he stays in the immediate vicinity of the den, bringing the female food all during her confinement and while she is nursing her young.

Food is dropped at the entrance of the den by the male for his mate who, after eating it, regurgitates the food in a partially digested form. This "baby food" is given the pups to start the process of weaning. By the time the pups are five or six weeks old, they go outside the den; under the watchful eyes of the mother, they frolic and tumble about like young dogs. In another month the male returns to the den, and both parents take their offspring on field trips. On such expeditions a young coyote and its litter mates are shown how to hunt for small mammals. By fall the half-grown animals are well drilled in the ways of a coyote; they then leave the parents' territory which will not support the entire family. At this time a great many young coyotes die—victims of mammal predators, accidents, and the traps, poisons, and guns of man.

On a home range of several hundred acres the coyote—sometimes alone and sometimes with a mate—jog-trots or lopes along in quest of its prey, occasionally "playing dead" to lure such birds as ravens and magpies close enough to be caught. When walking or trotting the twelve- to fifteen-inch tail of the coyote hangs down, but when the animal increases its speed to as much as thirty miles an hour, the tail is raised.

Although the coyote eats a little of everything, about three-fourths of its food is rabbits and rodents. Carrion makes up the greater part of the remainder of the diet, which also includes domestic and wild birds, grasshoppers and beetles, fish and crayfish, some big game, and some vegetation. The animal is particularly fond of watermelons and in the words of John E. Hearn, Chief of Predator Control for the Texas Game and Fish Commission, "the coyote is able to pick out the best melons in a patch without even having to thump them."

As the coyote hunts daily throughout the year, it has to be on the lookout for various predators. Wolves, cougars, and golden eagles regularly kill coyotes. Occasionally deer and elk trample the animal to death and sometimes the quills of the porcupine cause the death of a coyote.

The diseases of the dog family, to which the coyote belongs, cause the deaths of many animals, with rabies and distemper the greatest killers. Internal parasites, such as tapeworms and roundworms, and external parasites, such as mange mites, bother the animal. And of course man has been trapping, poisoning, and shooting it in planned campaigns since 1875. Then the first large-scale operation was undertaken to rid coyote country of the animal where it conflicted with man's interests. In 1906 a campaign was undertaken for the removal of predators from the Kaibab portion of the Grand Canyon Forest. During the twenty-five years of this particular predator-control operation, 4,889 coyotes were killed.

Belatedly it has been learned that the complete removal of coyotes from an area is not always the wisest method of predator control. A number of years ago a western state put on a campaign to rid the state of coyotes. The campaign was so effective that the coyote became a vanishing species there. In a few years ground squirrels had increased to such a degree and caused so much crop damage that a large-scale federal and state poisoning program was put into effect. Coyotes would have done the job at much less expense, and while keeping the ground-squirrel population in check, these natural predators would have acted as garbage men, sanitary engineers, and health officers in the removal of carrion, garbage, and other refuse that the omnivorous coyote considers edible. In areas where the wolf has been extirpated, the coyote is taking over the larger animal's ecological role.

But in spite of being shot, trapped, and poisoned at an estimated rate of 125,000 animals a year, the coyote survives. The animal's fecundity, adaptability, and cunning in outwitting man are the reasons for its survival.

Probably the somewhat angular, doglike tracks of the coyote will never vanish from its range nor will its weird, wild voice ever be stilled in North America as we know it. An old Indian legend has it that the coyote will be the last animal on earth.

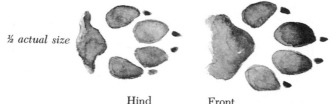

½ actual size

Hind   Front

GRAY WOLF

Canis lupus

Today the gray wolf is found in northern Wisconsin, upper Michigan, northern Minnesota, and possibly parts of some Prairie States. Outside the United States this rough-coated animal with erect ears and bushy tail trots through wilderness areas of Canada, and in Alaska roams from the islands of the southeast to the Arctic coast and as far west on the Alaska Peninsula as Unimak Island. In such areas the gray wolf—known also as the timber wolf and the lobo wolf—still raises its long muzzle skyward to give its deep-throated cry or to utter the high, plaintive note which the animal uses at or near its den.

For its den site the wolf may choose a rocky cavern, the base of a hollow tree, an abandoned badger or coyote den, which the wolf enlarges to suit its self, or a tunnel dug out by the female in a sandy, brush-covered bank. The female prepares such a den early in her pregnancy, which is the result of a January or February mating; she presumably stays with the same male for life. About three months later the female gives birth to her young, in April or May. The usual number of wolf pups in a litter is six or seven, but there may be anywhere from five to ten.

At birth a wolf pup has a fuzzy coat of black, brown, or gray fur. For the first week or ten days of its life the animal is blind and for the first three weeks it subsists solely on its mother's milk. To start weaning her offspring the mother feeds them bits of partly digested food which she regurgitates. The food that she predigests is brought to her by the male, who is most solicitous of his mate and young.

As soon as the young are strong enough the family leaves the den and the training of the pups is undertaken by both parents. By example the older animals show their offspring how to hunt, how to protect themselves, and all other phases of the wolf's existence. The little animals follow the parents' tactics until they become proficient in the ways of the wolf, which include the ability to swim.

During the winter following the birth of the young the family stays together. The family group may be joined by other wolves and these animals all travel and hunt together over a roughly circuitous route that covers many miles. As they move about at a rangy trot with tails held high, the wolves leave tracks somewhat hexagonal in outline. The front tracks, four to five inches in length and three and three-quarters inches to more than five inches in width, are larger than the hind tracks; in the prints the front toes show a wider spread than those of the hind feet. Sometimes a wolf hunts alone and its tracks are found along a solitary route that is a hundred or more miles long.

Although wolves prey regularly on caribou and other big game, the bulk of their food consists of mice, pocket gophers, rabbits, and ground squirrels. Sometimes the wolf stalks its prey but usually several animals working together run down such big game as antelope, bighorn sheep, caribou, deer, elk, moose, and muskoxen.

Not speed but endurance is the power by which the wolf catches its prey. The animal, less fleet than most of the big game it hunts, lopes along at about twenty miles an hour—and can maintain this rate hour after hour. Eventually the distance between the wolf and its quarry narrows until the predator reaches its prey—usually young, old, sick, or crippled animals. Then with a final burst of speed the wolf closes in with a sidewise lunge which causes the quarry to stumble. This gives the wolf an opportunity to jump and make its kill, snarling as it tears open its victim's throat.

The wolf is an enormous feeder; at a single meal it often eats one-fifth of its body weight. The weight of wolves varies with individuals. It may be anywhere from sixty to one hundred pounds or even one hundred and sixty pounds for animals in the far north, where there is a white species (*C. tundrarum*).

If natural foods are not available the wolf kills and gorges on any livestock and domestic poultry to be found within its range. Because of such predation the animal has been hunted and extirpated from most of its former range, which included the greater part of North America except for arid regions in the West and Southwest. Although some wolves become cattle and poultry killers the animal should not be killed off in areas where it does not conflict with man's activities. Like any other carnivore the wolf does not eliminate its own food supply, but serves to cull the weaklings and prevent over-abundance—a law of nature that has gone almost unrecognized since Colonial times.

In 1630 Massachusetts established the first American wolf bounty law. In the intervening three hundred years, it has been estimated that more than $100,000,000 has been paid out in such bounties. But in spite of the bounty system (in effect since Roman times) and other methods of eliminating wolves, the animal has survived, due, some biologists believe, to its unusual cunning. Only the encroachment of civilization on the wolf's habitat has been effective in reducing the numbers of animals in the United States.

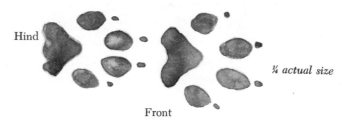

Hind

¼ actual size

Front

In addition to the gray wolf, there is another species in North America, the red wolf (*C. niger*). This smaller animal is apparently unrelated to the European forms and has lines something like those of a greyhound. The red wolf inhabits parts of Texas and Oklahoma, the Mississippi valley, and parts of Florida.

The present-day wolves of North America are not so large as those which roamed the continent during the late Pleistocene age. Fossil remains in lime and sandstone deposits and skeletons from the La Brea tar pits in southern California show that only the gray wolves of the Arctic approach the size of their prehistoric ancestors.

The North American species seem to be less ferocious than those in Europe. In fact our wolves are retiring animals, which seldom, if ever, attack man, and were respected by the Indians for their cunning and sagacity. But in Europe the attitude is different. Although Romulus, the legendary founder of Rome, and his twin brother, Remus, were suckled by a she-wolf, the animal has the reputation of a man-killer, particularly in France, Germany, Rumania, and Russia. During the unusually severe winter of 1955–56 in Europe, starving wolves were reported to have left their woodland haunts in Germany and Italy to search for food in nearby towns, and in Italy wolves were said to have lunged at passing cars along a highway nine miles from metropolitan Naples.

Stories of werewolves, or turnskins as they are sometimes known, have been the basis of horror tales since the time of Petronius, when the Roman satirist wrote about a werewolf in his "Satyricon." In the Middle Ages there were many trials of people accused of lycanthropy, the assumption of the form and traits of a wolf by witchcraft. One of the most celebrated of these trials was that of Giles Garnier in 1573; he was accused of having devoured several children while in the form of a werewolf, and was condemned to be burned to death.

Despite the horror induced by wolves and werewolves through the ages the animal has been considered a symbol of power, cunning, and strength. Since the days of Beowulf, the legendary Teutonic heroic figure, men have incorporated "wolf" into their names. Anglo-Saxon kings and nobles used such names as Berthwolf, Cynewolf, and Wulfred to suggest that they were endowed with wolfish characteristics.

In America the wolf is not associated with the supernatural, but the Indians had such a high regard for the animal's cunning and prowess that they used the name in various combinations for their warriors. Hugh Monroe, an employee of the Hudson's Bay Company, and later a famous free trapper, was named "Rising Wolf" by the Blackfeet. Today one of the mountains in Glacier National Park is known as "Rising Wolf Mountain" in memory of Monroe, whom the Blackfeet considered wise as a wolf.

RED FOX

Vulpes fulva

'Twas the sound of his horn brought me from my bed,
And the cry of his hounds, which he oft-times led,
For Peel's view-hallo would waken the dead,
Or the fox from his lair in the morning.
                    JOHN PEEL. Old Hunting Song Refrain. 1832.

Probably of all the foxes in North America the red fox is the one most frequently routed by the deep-mouthed cry of the fox-hound. The red fox is the most numerous and most widely distributed of our foxes and in some one of its twenty-odd forms the animal is found throughout the greater part of the continent. Only coastal areas of the Southeast and southern California, some areas in the South-Central states, and parts of the Southwest are excepted from this range. There is also an area in the Northwest Territories in which there are no red foxes.

Within this range the red fox lives in widely differing habitats: you may find the animal with its triangular ears and white-tipped tail in open woodlands, along bushy borders which edge marshes and swamps, in treeless mountain areas, or even in suburban communities. The fox is so adaptable that it has been little affected by the changes in terrain resulting from the widespread cultivation of the land. In fact the creation of farmlands seems to have been a boon to the fox, as it has flourished in contrast to less hardy or adaptable species that have dwindled in numbers or become nonexistent.

On an individual range of not much more than a mile in radius, the sharp-faced fox, ears alerted for the slightest sound, trots gracefully along on a quest for a meal. The diet of the fox is varied and depends on the availability of different foods at different times and places. The animal eats mice and rabbits and other crop and orchard pests; small, ground-nesting birds, their eggs, and fledglings; snakes, and such insects as beetles, crickets, and grasshoppers. A great fruit eater, the fox devours quantities of fresh and dried apples, blackberries, grapes, raspberries, and strawberries among other fruits. It also eats grasses, and clay and gravel to supply some of the necessary minerals.

In winter the fox is more carnivorous and sometimes the animal even attacks the porcupine if food is scarce. When natural foods are in short supply the fox kills domestic poultry and young lambs and pigs. Not all the odds and ends of domestic animals found in the vicinity of a fox's den or lair are those of animals killed by the fox. Much of this discarded foodstuff is apt to be carrion lugged home from farm fields or dumps. If a fox finds or kills more than enough to satisfy immediate hunger the excess is cached—a peculiarity of the wild dog family to which the red fox belongs, but from which it is set apart by a peculiarity of its own. When the eye of the fox contracts the pupil becomes elliptical, but when the eyes of other wild dogs contract the pupils remain round.

To catch live prey the red fox either approaches a meadow mouse or other animals in a high-stepping but stealthy manner or steals up with the wriggling, belly-to-earth technique of a stalking cat. Once the prey is actually spotted, the fox pauses for a split second, then closes in with a rush or a pounce, and kills its victim with a quick snap of the jaws.

As it hunts or is hunted the red fox uses its tail, whose white tip differentiates it from other species of foxes, as a means of maintaining its balance. While hunting it has to be on the lookout for bobcats, coyotes, lynxes, and wolves, and the golden eagle. Most of the foxes caught by these predators are the young or the old, sick, and crippled. Foxes are adept in escaping predators, including dogs; the animals use such tactics as doubling back on the trail, taking to the water to destroy scent, or walking along stone walls, a trick that leaves a gap in the trail.

Although primarily an evening hunter the red fox is often abroad during the day. As the animal travels over its routes, it leaves dainty tracks in which four claws and small pads show. The hind tracks fit those of the front tracks perfectly. In winter pads seldom show as the feet are covered by a thick growth of fur. And in winter the red fox does not use a den but curls up wherever it happens to be and uses its tail as a blanket. The tail is arranged so that it covers the animal's little black nose and the little black feet to protect them from the cold.

Once the backbone of winter is broken, the male of the species

Kit Fox

Gray Fox

Arctic Fox

known as the dog fox, is ready to seek a mate with which it stays for the better part of the year. Matings usually occur during January and February and are preceded by fights among the males. The female or vixen prepares the den, which is frequently used year after year. A den may be one made by the fox in loose soil or it may be an enlarged woodchuck or porcupine burrow. Den entrances vary in size; those of old, often-used dens measure as much as twenty inches in width, while new entrances are about half that breadth.

Some dens have tunnels as long as seventy-five feet, off which there are numerous side chambers. Most entrances lack the earthen mound of many tunneling mammals and have numerous, well-defined trails leading to them. Usually the den of a fox can be identified by an odor that is somewhat akin to that around a skunk's home, but not so powerful. The entrances are also marked by fox hairs embedded in the earthen sides.

After a gestation period of about fifty days — during which the female becomes increasingly irritable—four or five and sometimes as many as ten kits or pups are born. During her confinement and for the first few days after delivering her young, the male brings the female food.

At birth a kit weighs about four ounces and is well furred. The kits of any litter may be of the same color phase or all three color phases may be present. One kit may be the typical reddish-brown-yellow, another may be black or silver, and a third may be a cross, an intermixture of red and black hairs. When the kits are about ten days old their eyes open and by the end of four or five weeks the fuzzy little animals come out of the den and play around the entrance under the watchful eyes of the mother and the father.

Weaning takes place at the end of eight or ten weeks. Then the kits are taken on trips during which they are taught to hunt, to swim, and all the other aspects of fox life. The family stays together until fall; then each animal goes its separate way. Although the male, weighing anywhere from five to fifteen pounds, is a great wanderer, the less-heavy female stays within a mile or two of the den; she may live in the same area for several years—perhaps her entire life span, which is undoubtedly less than that of captive foxes which have lived ten or twelve years.

The red fox is subject to rabies, which causes the animal to lose its fear of man. A rabid fox may wander around aimlessly, biting both wild and domestic animals. The bite of a rabid fox often causes the death of an animal, but is seldom fatal to a human being. Rabies, as well as encephalitis and distemper, seems to be nature's way of controlling fox populations when the animals become overabundant about every nine to ten years. In recent years outbreaks of rabies have become more frequent and have been controlled by shooting the rabid animals within a given area. Cattle losses resulting from the bites of rabid foxes are often extremely heavy. Dogs should be vaccinated to prevent rabies and people bitten by the rabid animals should receive the Pasteur treatment.

The red fox, trapped for its dense, soft, and reasonably durable fur, has been a source of revenue for trappers since the first quarter of the nineteenth century. Through the years the price of a prime pelt has varied, with the value running between ten and fifteen dollars in an average year. The red fox has been hunted in America since Colonial times for sport by varying methods, depending upon the locale and the prevailing customs. And the bugling of the American foxhound, considered one of the finest trail dogs in the world, rouses not only the red fox from its lair but two other forms of American foxes as well.

Sometimes a hound's bugling puts to flight the gray fox (*Urocyon cinereoargenteus*), a grizzled gray animal with a long, slender tail that is marked by a black line on the upper side. Also known as the "tree fox" due to its ability to climb trees, the gray is more of a night animal than the red fox and often lives undetected in the brushy country it prefers. On the islands off southern California there lives another species of gray fox (*U. littoralis*). Smaller than the mainland gray fox, this short-eared animal hunts for food cast up by the sea on the beaches of the islands, whose cactus beds afford it shelter.

Other North American species are the two kit foxes (*V. velox* and *V. macrotis*). These desert-dwelling animals, also known as the "swift fox" and the "long-eared fox," are the smallest of our foxes and spend more time underground than any other species.

The last of our foxes and probably the only one not put to flight by foxhounds is the Arctic fox (*Alopex lagopus*), an animal of the Arctic regions which comes as far south as the Aleutian Islands in Alaska. In summer this fox, with short, rounded ears, has brown or dark-gray fur; in winter the fur is pure white except the tip of the tail, which is black. In the Aleutian Islands and on the Pribilof Islands there is a blue phase of the Arctic fox, whose summer coat is brownish and a maltese shade in winter.

All these foxes are vocal: the bark of the male red fox is a short yelp, while that of the female is a shrill yap. The gray fox has a coarser bark than that of the red fox and at times the gray sounds something like a coyote. The bark of the kit fox does not have the volume of the red and often has a quality similar to the racket made by a scolding gray squirrel. The call of the Arctic fox is like the yapping of a dog.

These then are the voices of the foxes of North America which, to paraphrase a comment of Suetonius, "Change their fur but never change their habits."

BLACK BEAR

Euarctos americanus

The smallest and most widely distributed of our bears is the black bear, which was once abundant in most wooded and mountainous sections of the continent from Alaska and Canada south as far as Mexico City. Except for a few eastern and midwestern states it still occupies much of its ancestral range, though the animal is not so numerous as it used to be. The spread of civilization has reduced the population of the black bear—an animal that has a number of color phases.

Surprisingly enough the bluish glacier bear of Alaska, the brown or cinnamon bear of the West, and the white Kermode's bear of coastal British Columbia are all black bears. They may be identified as such by their straight profiles and short, rounded claws from which they get the name "short-clawed American bears."

The black bear with which most of us are familiar has a glossy black coat of long, soft fur, a brown snout, a white chest patch, and black claws. A full-grown male weighs anywhere from 200 to 300 pounds—occasionally as much as 500 pounds—and has a total length of 4½ to 6½ feet. It stands 2 to 3 feet at the shoulders, which are lower than the rump.

For the better part of the year the male is solitary, living by himself on a well-defined home range of about fifteen square miles. But in the late spring or early summer a male seeks one or more females. Mating bears often stand upright and hug one another. About seven months after a mating is consummated the young are born in January or February while the female is bedded down for her winter sleep.

During this winter sleep the animal's body temperature stays high enough to melt any snow drifting into the cave, windfall, or swampy thicket in which a northern bear has secreted itself. Since the body temperature is unchanged and the animal's breathing continues at the normal rate of four or five times a minute, the winter sleep of a bear is not considered true hibernation (a state in which breathing slows down until it almost ceases and the pulse becomes faint).

A bear is easily roused from its winter sleep and often wakes of its own accord to come out and prowl around for a few hours, days, or even longer. Generally a bear that interrupts its winter sleep is a slim one; fat bears den early and usually sleep the winter through. During the long sleep or dormant stage cubs are born while the mother is in a subconscious state that might be likened to the partial anesthesia induced by "twilight sleep."

Usually there are two cubs in a litter, though there may be one or three; four are rare, and five in a litter are exceptional. At birth a cub weighs nine to twelve ounces and measures about eight inches in length. The little animal is blind and toothless and so scantily covered by fine dark fur that it is practically naked. The mother rouses sufficiently from her dormant state to cut the umbilical cord and lick life into her young—a step described in the "Natural History" of Pliny the Elder when he wrote: "Bears when first born are shapeless masses of white flesh little larger than mice, their claws alone being prominent. The mother licks them gradually into shape."

After delivery of her young the mother continues to sleep for another two months—a period during which the cubs alternately suckle and sleep. By spring a cub and its twin are active roly-poly little creatures weighing about five pounds each; they spend hours lying on their backs playing with their feet and toes. Such baby antics are interrupted when they finally leave the winter quarters in the company of their mother.

Although far from steady on its feet, a young bear can climb well and scurries up a tree at the first sign of danger—usually announced by a warning grunt from the mother. If a cub does not move fast enough the mother cuffs it. Keen senses of hearing and smell help the mother to escape danger for her cubs and herself.

For more than half a year after birth the cubs and their mother roam over a home territory of about a ten-mile radius. The animals have no regular den and sleep wherever they happen to be. As the family travels about, the mother teaches her cubs to dig out chipmunks, mice, marmots, pocket gophers, ground squirrels, and woodchucks, and to dig up wild onions, wild parsnips, and other wild bulbous plants.

Occasionally bears eat porcupines, flipping the quilled animals over on their backs and eating out the soft bellies. This maneuver is not always accomplished without harm to the predator; bears have been found dead with quills embedded in their mouths. At fawning time bears seek the young of the antelope, the deer, and the elk. Bears probably do not kill many fawns; even a few days after birth a fawn can outdistance a full-grown bear, whose lumbering gait may attain a speed of twenty-five miles an hour for a short distance.

Black bears eat dead mammals and fishes, a great variety of wild berries and fruits, eggs and young of ground-nesting birds, ants, and the nectar and honey of wild bees and wasps. The animal also eats the larvae and the insects themselves, seemingly little troubled by the stings of the insects. Sometimes a bear becomes a cattle-killer, and such an animal has to be destroyed.

As a family ambles over its territory on well-established trails, the animals leave tracks with ball and toe-marks resembling those in a human footprint. Sometimes bears pause in their travels to rip off the outer bark of coniferous trees and eat the inner bark. Such trees frequently show the vertical marks of the bear's incisor teeth. Claw marks on trees up which a bear has scrambled are another sign to look for in bear country and so are the hairs caught on trees or bushes on which the animals have rubbed themselves.

At the end of the first summer a cub and its twin are ready to settle down for the winter sleep, after gorging on all manner of foods. When they awake the next spring the young bears are about sixteen months old, and by the middle of June the mother is no longer interested in her offspring. Ready to mate again, she either deserts them or drives them away. For another year or so twins may travel together, but when they are about three years old they separate to seek mates and from then on, except at mating time, they are solitary.

During the twelve to fifteen years of a wild black bear's life, the animal has few predators to worry it. Cougars probably kill some old or crippled bears and wolves sometimes attack a bear which is in a poorly protected wintering hideaway. Occasionally bears fight among themselves over a mate or food and one may kill another and eat the carcass of its victim.

Man is undoubtedly the black bear's greatest predator. The animal is hunted for sport, for the oil produced from its fat, and for its skins which have various uses. In the spring of 1953, seven hundred black bears were killed in the Lillooet district of British Columbia; their skins were needed to make 3,000 shakos for the Royal Guards to wear at the June coronation of Queen Elizabeth. Fortunately for the black bear Great Britain's coronations are infrequent and the life of a shako is forty years.

The model for the first essentially American toy is the black bear. Back in 1902 when President Theodore Roosevelt was on a hunting trip some members of his party captured a small black bear cub and urged that he shoot it. The President refused and instead adopted the little animal as a pet. Morris Michtom, a Brooklyn doll manufacturer and a great admirer of Teddy Roosevelt, used this bear as the model for a toy. Michtom got White House approval to call the toy "Teddy," and his teddy bear was the first of an estimated 30,000,000 to have been sold in this country.

Although most black bears run the other way upon meeting a man, the animals are unpredictable, particularly where they have had contact with people as do the bears in our National Parks. During the first half of the summer of 1955 fourteen people were bitten by bears in Great Smoky National Park in North Carolina and Tennessee. The black bear is crafty, persistent, and adaptable, and the animal is not always gentle in an attempt to get at food.

The National Parks warning states that "The feeding, touching, teasing, or molesting of bears is prohibited." In bear country it is wise to keep this admonition in mind in dealing with our smallest, most widely distributed bear.

GRIZZLY BEAR
Ursus horribilis

The grizzly bear appears on the recent list of endangered species issued by the National Wildlife Federation of Washington, D. C. Only a few hundred of these great, humpbacked bears with dished-in faces and grizzled coats are left in the United States. In

Grizzly   Alaska Brown   Black

Relative head sizes of the three species

the wilderness areas of Colorado, Idaho, Montana, and Wyoming, and in Yellowstone and Glacier National Parks, the long-clawed grizzly bear wanders over an individual territory that is about twenty miles in diameter and marked by well-defined routes which lead above timber line.

Outside the United States there are large areas that may still be designated as grizzly bear territory. In Alaska, the Yukon, and British Columbia, grizzly bears in considerable numbers roam over ranges in the mountains and across vast expanses of tundra. Alaska is reported to have more than 10,000 of these bears and though no figures are available, western Canada is supposed to have a good-sized population of this bear, whose scientific description was given by Lewis and Clark after their exploration of the headwaters of the Missouri and Columbia Rivers in 1805–06.

Like the black bear the grizzly has several color variations. A grizzly's fur may have a dark-brown cast, the usual color, or it may have a yellowish, grayish, or blackish tinge. The fur of all races is generally darker along the spine and on the legs and ears. Light-tipped hairs on the underparts of the body give the animal the grizzled appearance from which it gets its common name.

The life history of the grizzly is similar to that of the more common black bear. Grizzly cubs, however, grow more slowly than those of the black bear, and do not reach full size until they are eight to ten years old, about one-half of their life span in the wild.

A mature male weighs anywhere from 500 to 800 pounds, measures 6 to 7½ feet in length, and stands 3 to 3½ feet at the shoulder. Grizzlies have been recorded that weighed as much as a thousand pounds. A full-grown female weighs about 400 pounds and her other physical characteristics are scaled to this smaller weight.

Like the black bear the grizzly is a vegetarian for the better part of the year, but the animal is also a great meat eater. It preys on deer, elk, and moose, particularly those that are old, sick, or crippled, and carries off the entire carcass to cache at some convenient spot, where it is covered with dirt, rocks, or leaf litter. The grizzly returns to such a cache until the food is entirely consumed.

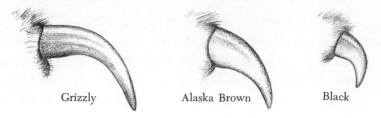

Grizzly   Alaska Brown   Black

Relative sizes of the claws

This bear is of prime interest to the big-game hunter, and during the 1950's about two hundred were killed each year. To preserve the animal in Alaska, the Territorial Game Commission has reduced the limit to a single grizzly or brown bear (a closely related species) except in southeastern Alaska. Such a measure should help to maintain a breeding stock so that this species in its various forms will be perpetuated, provided, of course, that wilderness habitat is always available.

ALASKA BROWN BEAR

Ursus middendorffi
(Kodiak Island Bear)

Among Alaska's many species and subspecies of bears is the Alaska brown bear, the largest carnivore on earth. This animal ranges up the mainland coastal mountains to the subarctic regions and among the mountains of the interior. Brown bears in one form or another are numerous on Admiralty, Baranof, and Chichagof Islands, the Kodiak-Afognak group, and the Alaska Peninsula, and are also found along the coast of western Canada.

The brown bear might be a coastal or island subspecies of the grizzly. At any rate they are closely related and there is a noticeable resemblance between the two types. Scientifically these two races have been separated into nine groups, made up of about thirty species and subspecies. In this assortment there is a wide range in color and size.

The Shiras brown bear of Admiralty Island is almost coal-black, while the Toklat grizzly is cream-colored. The grizzly of Norton Sound is comparatively small, but the Kodiak brown bear is the largest of them all.

At maturity a Kodiak bear about seven years old has an average weight of half a ton and an occasional one weighs as much as 1½ tons. Some brown bears measure 8 feet from nose to tail and stand 4 to 4½ feet at the shoulder. As a rule the brown bear has fewer light-tipped hairs than the grizzly and its dark claws are short, stout, and curved.

As the animal moves over the trails, crisscrossing its home range, it leaves staggered tracks, measuring 6 to 8 or more inches wide by 12 to 14 inches long for the hind feet, and 7 to 8 inches wide for the front feet.

Like all our bears the brown bear is solitary, but is inclined to be out during the day more than some species. Except at mating time— every other year for the female, sometimes every third year—the animal usually seeks its prey by itself.

When salmon are migrating several brown bears may be found fishing at one spot. To catch salmon the animal pounces on the fish in shallow water and pins the squirming fish down or flails one out of the water with a sweep of the great paw. Then grasping the fish between its jaws, the bear carries it ashore to eat. The brown bear also consumes quantities of vegetation, various rodents, and carrion of all kinds.

Late in the fall when the animal is fat, it stops eating and dens up on a mountainside for the winter sleep, from which it does not emerge until May. During the winter sleep of the female, twin cubs are born in January or February, and the pattern of the lives is similar to that of the black bear cubs. The nature of the brown bear is unpredictable; it is wise therefore to bypass this animal at some distance, particularly if it makes a coughing sound or growls—sure indications that the animal is in no mood to brook interference.

POLAR BEAR

Thalarctos maritimus

The polar bear is a strong and graceful swimmer. A huge, white animal, weighing from 700 to 1,600 pounds, this bear lives principally along the southern border of the ice pack in Arctic waters —a wet, cold, and bleak habitat, where the thermometer frequently registers 60 degrees below zero.

In winter the polar bear moves south to follow the food supply as the ice shifts; in summer the animal heads back to the frozen ice pack. A sudden advance of ice sometimes brings a polar bear as far south as Bering Strait in the Pacific or to Newfoundland in the Atlantic.

This species differs from our other bears in that it has a long neck, a smaller head, and a narrower skull. The animal has a seasonal change in its coat which matches the changing color of the ice floes. In winter the fur is the pure white of the dazzling floes; in summer the fur takes on a yellowish tinge matching the yellowed ice of the summer pack.

A polar bear spends most of its life roaming over a wide area in search of food. On land the animal's pace is rapid; its feet, well covered with hair except for small naked pads, act as snowshoes; in the water the animal swims along, using only its forefeet, to cover great distances at a rate of three to six miles an hour.

More carnivorous than other members of the family, the polar bear's diet consists of seals, walruses, porpoises, fishes, sea ducks such as eiders and scoters, other birds, and kelp and other marine and land vegetation.

Only pregnant females of this species den for the winter sleep. Dens are either in a pile of shore ice or in a drift of hard-packed snow. In such a spot one or two hairless and blind cubs are born in late December or early January. By the end of March the mother and the cubs—looking like toys with their fluffy white baby fur, their black shoe-button eyes, and black-tipped noses—leave the den and head for the sea. When the cubs are about ten months old, they quit the mother and, except for a mating period, lead a solitary existence. Sometimes two or more polar bears gather to eat the carcass of a stranded whale.

To hunt the polar bear is a dangerous undertaking, due not only to the bear's unpredictable nature but also because the hunt is conducted from a small boat among the ice floes. Man is the animal's only predator and hunts it as a trophy or to use the skin for a sleeping bag. The fat of this animal is widely used by the Eskimos, who also make garments of the pelts and ornaments of the teeth and claws.

Polar-bear meat should be well cooked, to avoid trichinosis. The liver should never be eaten; it contains so much vitamin A that it causes a sickness—hypervitaminosis—similar to the shock caused by an overdose of protein.

About one hundred polar bear pelts, worth six to eight dollars, as measured from tip of nose to tip of tail, are exported from Alaska each year. To see the animal, however, most of us have to go to the zoo.

Animals were not regularly exhibited in zoos in America until 1874. Then the Philadelphia Zoological Garden was opened in Philadelphia July 1, 1874; one of the attractions was a bear pit. Since then bears have been displayed in all zoological gardens, including the National Zoological Park, Washington, D. C. Among the various species of bears in the capital's zoo is Smokey, the black bear rescued from a New Mexican forest fire in 1950. Smokey is a reminder that each year forest fires cost the Nation nearly $70,000,000 for fighting this destroyer of wildlife, timber, and other resources of America.

RACCOON

Procyon lotor

The police of Greeley, Colorado, were once called by an irate husband to arrest a masked stranger who peered at his wife while she undressed. This peeping Tom turned out to be a raccoon perched on the crossbar of the door, watching the lady with a curiosity that is typical of most raccoons. The Greeley raccoon was hauled off to the pound, where, no doubt, it made itself completely at home, as raccoons are adaptable—so adaptable, in fact, that they have survived environmental changes that have wiped out less resilient species.

Wildlife, like vegetation, is modified as its habitat changes, and as our population jumped from nearly 25,000,000 in 1850 to almost 150,000,000 in 1950, competition for use of the land increased enormously. Many species, unable to adapt to changes resulting from large-scale use of the land by agriculture and industry, became extinct or nearly so. But the raccoon, a hardy creature, survived, though much habitat within its transcontinental range was modified or altered completely—as in areas where lands were stripped of all forest cover.

A raccoon, with its pointed nose, bushy, ringed tail, and bandit-like mask across piercing eyes, is one of our most familiar wild animals and in one of its more than thirty forms or races is native to every state. It likes partly cleared agricultural lands with stands of old oaks, beeches, and maples. In such areas the number of raccoons is related directly to soil fertility; good soil means numerous, robust raccoons; where cultivation is intense there are not so many. In most areas, perhaps one raccoon for every ten acres is a good average; sometimes there are large local populations as in Mississippi, where eight to ten animals an acre have been reported. Poor soil produces fewer, less healthy specimens that have little resistance to mange and a pneumonia-like disease that has not yet been isolated.

For its home, a 'coon likes a hollow tree, where a limb has been broken off or water has rotted out a cavity large enough to accommodate the animal's bulk of fifteen to twenty pounds at maturity. If you see such a cavity with an opening of about five to six inches in diameter, look for scratches made by five strong toes on fore and hind feet and grayish-black hairs around the edges of the opening—signs that usually indicate a raccoon's home. If a tree den is not available, the animal sometimes lives in a drain tile, a deep fissure in a rocky ledge along a lake shore or river bank, or in the kind of nest box set out for a wood duck.

Raccoon is probably the phonetic equivalent of *arakun*, from the Algonquin Indian word, *arakunem*, meaning "he who scratches with his hands." The scratcher sleeps the day away in its chosen home in one of two characteristic positions. In one the animal lies on its back with its forepaws placed over the eyes; in the other it rolls itself almost into a ball with the top of the head placed flat on the floor between the forelegs.

After the sun has set, a 'coon makes a sleepy descent. Although the animal usually descends tail first, it can scramble up or down a tree trunk almost as adroitly as a gray squirrel. When it reaches the ground, a raccoon commonly utters a sort of querulous, harsh call, similar to the cry of a screech owl, then starts off on a search for food to satisfy an appetite that is as insatiable as its curiosity.

The raccoon eats more fruits and vegetables than meat. As fruits ripen throughout the season, the animal gorges on cherries, grapes, hackberries, haws, persimmons, plums, raspberries, and dogwood, manzanita, and pokeweed berries.

In addition to berries and fruits, a 'coon eats nuts, grains, insects, and other invertebrates, and in summer sometimes raids cornfields adjacent to woodlands when corn is in milk. Stalks are pulled down or ears ripped off, and partly eaten ears are left scattered all over the field. Often corn depredations attributed to raccoons are caused by squirrels.

A favorite food of the animal is crayfish. If you see five-toed tracks, suggesting imprints of human baby hands and feet, in mud along a stream bank, you can be reasonably sure that a raccoon has been "fishing" there for the little lobster-like crustaceans. It catches a crayfish by dabbling a finger in the water. As soon as a crayfish clamps onto the finger, the raccoon flips the catch into its mouth and greedily devours it. To eat a clam, a 'coon inserts a fingernail between the shells and with a deft, semicircular motion rips apart the shells, tears out the flesh, which is popped into the mouth and speedily gobbled down.

½ actual size

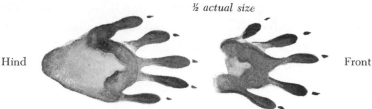

Hind   Front

Although its specific scientific name, *Lotor*, meaning "the washer," and the German name, *Waschbär*, meaning "washing bear," are appropriate, the animal eats quantities of food without washing it. Near water food is often washed time after time. An explanation for this habit, particularly in the case of live food, is that a 'coon does it for fun—as a cat worries a mouse.

A raccoon also eats eggs and young of ground-nesting birds and those of birds that nest in trees, and eggs of domestic poultry. Around waterfowl concentrations in a marsh, 'coon predation on nests of black and mallard ducks is a problem. Biologists in New York discovered that out of fifteen black-duck nests under observation, raccoons destroyed twelve and crows two. Of thirty-five mallard nests watched, raccoons broke eggs in twenty-six, and crows broke eggs in five. As a rule it is the individual, not an entire population, that has to be controlled as a predator, either by shooting or trapping.

In late January or February the polygamous male, larger than the female, seeks a mate, and in April or May from two to six young are born of the union. At birth young raccoons weigh 2 ½ ounces, have the ancestral black mask well defined, and are covered by warm, fuzzy coats. In about eighteen days, a young 'coon's eyes are open, and in about two months it is ready to start making nightly trips with the mother as guide and teacher.

First trips away from the home den, base of operations in a territory of about a mile, are rather short. Gradually they lengthen, until by the end of summer, when a young 'coon starts getting its heavy winter fur, it travels as much as five miles. Trips cease during really cold weather when food is scarce, and though a raccoon does not actually hibernate, it dens up, sometimes with several others, in a hollow tree, and sleeps out a cold snap. During mild weather, it pops out of its den at night to satisfy its enormous appetite by feeding on mice and rabbits or anything else that is available. And though mainly nocturnal, a raccoon likes to sun itself, and sprawls out in a variety of positions on the large upper limbs of trees during the day.

The animal is beneficial in spite of its depredations on crops and waterfowl nests, and its economic use is part of our country's history. In pioneer days raccoon skins were used as a medium of exchange. When residents of a mountain section in Tennessee organized the local "State of Franklin," salaries of public officials were paid in animal skins at the following rates:

> . . . secretary to his excellency, the governor, ...500 raccoon
> . . . clerk of the house of commons, ...200 raccoon
> . . . member of the assembly, per diem, ... 3 raccoon

Powhatan, the Indian chief and father of Pocahontas, gave John Smith a coat of raccoon skins, which, no doubt, the explorer was glad to wear during the winter of 1607, his first in America. Colonial frontiersmen wore raccoon caps with the tail hanging down one side. So great was the demand for the pelts here and abroad that late in the seventeenth century, Colonists passed laws prohibiting taxing or exporting pelts so that there would be sufficient skins for home consumption.

The fur of the northern raccoon is dense and durable; recently the annual take has been from one to one and one-half million pelts. As a fur animal the 'coon is outnumbered only by the muskrat, the opossum, and the skunk. Prime raccoon pelts bring an average of three dollars each, and as much as fifteen dollars in peak years.

The raccoon probably has more hunters on its trail than any other wild animal. In California during the middle 1800's, the carcasses were frequently shipped to market, where they sold for one to three dollars. 'Coon flesh is like dark meat of chicken, and if you make a sandwich with a slice of chicken and a slice of lamb, you will get some idea of the flavor of the meat.

In the fall when a red hunter's moon rides high in the sky and frost is on the pumpkin, the raccoon is at the mercy of its greatest predators—a hunter and his hound. A 'coon is no easy prey and only an inexperienced animal lets itself get treed. A seasoned raccoon runs for four or five miles after it is started, circles trees, runs along tops of log and rail fences, and swims streams. Sometimes a raccoon turns on a hound in the water and in the ensuing struggle drowns the dog by holding the dog's head under water with black forepaws. Not until a hunted 'coon is dead is a dog safe, and many a hound bears scars inflicted by the sharp teeth of a raccoon.

This mammal has few natural enemies because of its ferocity when cornered; and, barring accidents, the animal lives to about seven years in the wild.

Captive 'coons may possibly live to be fourteen years old. A raccoon makes a good though mischievous pet, if taken young, but in a year or two is apt to develop a cranky disposition. So in dealing with a raccoon treat it with respect. Remember you are dealing with an animal hardy enough and apparently intelligent enough to survive in a world greatly altered by our civilization.

RINGTAIL

Bassariscus astutus

Although the ringtail, a slim night-prowling mammal of parts of the West and Southwest, is related to the raccoon, it is not nearly so well known. The two animals are somewhat similar in appearance, but the splendid bushy tail of the ringtail puts to shame the stubbier one of the raccoon, an animal found in all forty-eight states.

A ringtail, whose scientific name means "clever little fox," is sleek and slender and has a slightly foxlike face. Big, bright eyes, spectacled by whitish rings, suggest a look of mild astonishment; big, round ears, cocked forward, seem perpetually alerted for the slightest sound that indicates danger. Its fur is fluffy, and is light brown on most of the body, but darkens along the back and is white on the undersides.

The tail is the eye-catching feature of a ringtail, and accounts for at least half of the animal's slender, total length of twenty-five to thirty inches. Brownish and flattened and ringed by alternating bands of black and white, the tail is not only resplendent but functional. As a ringtail scampers through the trees, it lets the tail swing out squirrel-fashion to balance itself. When frightened, the animal holds its tail over the back much as an angry squirrel does under similar circumstances, scolding or barking as it does so. And when a ringtail hunts in the open on moonlight nights, it arches the tail over the back, a habit that might fool some predators, including the great-horned owl, into thinking the little mammal too large to handle.

The animal has many aliases. Prospectors in the West gave it the name "miner's cat" because it is a regular mobile mousetrap, keeping a cabin free of rats and mice better than any domestic cat. Miners learned that a young ringtail makes an excellent pet. Older ones, especially males, are apt to be ill-tempered and far less adaptable.

Other names for the ringtail are coon cat, band-tailed cat, and raccoon fox. It is cat-squirrel in Texas, but mountain cat and ring-

tailed cat in California. In Mexico it is cacomixtle or tepe-maxtle—
Aztec-Mexican words meaning rush-cat and bush-cat. Cacomixtle is
spelled "cacomistle" north of the Border. Sometimes the animal is
known as civet cat, a misnomer, for the ringtail is not related to the
civet of the Old World.

Track pattern

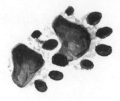

⅔ actual size

For its home, the animal with all these aliases likes a hole on the
lower side of a leaning tree that is near water. Such a den gives as
much protection from the rain as possible. An entrance so tight that
the ringtail has to worm its way in is the desired size; such an
opening keeps out many would-be intruders.

Summer cottages, ancient Indian ruins, and rocky ledges also house
the ringtail, which can leap ten feet from point to point on rocky
ledges with no trouble at all. A pair of ringtails once moved into the
top story of the Grand Canyon's El Tovar Hotel. They "paid" for
the space they occupied by keeping the premises free of rodents, and
a grateful management saw to it that each evening pretty waitresses
served the ringtails tidbits, while the dinner guests looked on in
delight.

When not hand-fed, a ringtail hunts packrats, lizards, ground
squirrels, chipmunks, pocket gophers, and occasionally birds, including sparrows, towhees, and thrushes. Figs, fruits of low-growing
cacti, madrone, yew, cascara, and manzanita are eaten. When dates
are ripening in the orchards of Lower California, where the ringtail
has still another alias, *babisuri,* it prowls around under the palms at
night with gray foxes and spotted skunks, picking up fruit that has
fallen to the ground.

A captive ringtail likes oranges. It eats this fruit with great care,
deftly scooping out the fleshy parts without spilling a drop of juice
on its white front. Green corn, the nuts of the oak, the pinyon, and
the ponderosa pine, and numerous insects complete the diet. A ring-

tail likes any form of sugar, and loves to lick honey from the end of a stick.

Like most animals with large eyes, this one is active mainly at night, though, as if sensing the benefits of ultraviolet rays, it does come out at noonday to sleep in the top of a tall tree. It is then that you might see a ringtail, as it often sleeps with its tail hanging down. In its nightly search for food, it covers a wide area and sometimes goes right into town. Early risers in villages on the Mexican tableland often see the dainty tracks of a ringtail in the dust of the streets. These tracks are rounded and toe-tipped like those of a cat, but show five toes in each track like those of a raccoon. Toes are semiretractable and between the pads there is dense fur.

The young are born in May or June. The average litter is three, with males in the majority. Sometimes only one is born and sometimes there are five. About the size of a kitten, a young ringtail is blind, toothless, and deaf because ears are temporarily sealed. A fine white fuzz barely covers the pink skin, and faint black rings show on the stubby tail, which gives no hint of the size to which it will grow.

When the animal is hungry it squeaks like an unoiled oarlock. Adults usually bark, though when frightened they snarl. At about three weeks, a juvenile ringtail switches from a liquid diet to one that is solid, principally meat, brought to it by either parent. In another month, it is taken on hunting trips that include excursions into trees. At four months it is turned out of the moss-lined nest, and is on its own.

COATI

Nasua narica

Coatis are "on the staff" of University Hospital at Ann Arbor, Michigan. Doctors at the hospital were concerned over the tears, melancholy faces, and sometimes a refusal to talk on the part of patients in the children's division. Animals were suggested as a form of therapy which might overcome ailments that did not respond to medical treatment. Among the animals brought into the hospital in response to this suggestion were coatis—slim raccoon-like mammals with long, rubbery snouts, long, slender tails, and a pale-brown mask across the dark eyes.

The coati is native to South and Central America, but has extended its range north in Arizona, where the animal is fairly numerous in the Huachuca Mountains, in southwestern New Mexico, and in Texas just above the Border. Not a great deal is known about the life history of the coati, whose scientific name, *Nasua narica*, means "the nosey one." The coati's long, upturned snout is ideal for grubbing out insects and roots, part of a diet that consists of birds' eggs—regularly those of wild birds, occasionally those of domestic poultry—nuts and fruits, and lizards, including the iguana.

Apparently the coati is always hungry; the animal hunts day and night, though it is inclined to be less active around noonday and at midnight. Sometimes a coati hunts on the ground, where the animal walks with all four feet flat on the ground, leaving tracks similar to those of the hind tracks of a raccoon and showing five toes; sometimes it hunts in the trees, where it leaps around, using its tapering, dark-ringed tail of twenty or more inches as a tightrope walker uses a pole, to maintain balance. When ready to return to the ground, it comes down out of a tree headfirst. When it is resting, either on the branch of a tree, such as a *palo verde*, or on the dry ground in some *arroyo*, the coati curls itself into a ball.

Generally rocky areas, not too heavily wooded, are the places to look for the coati, which has a number of names. Naturalists call the animal "coatimundi"; Mexicans use *choluga* or *cholla*; and Central and South Americans call it *pisote*. A vernacular term, *pisote*, is used when speaking of any coati, but *pisote solo* is used when talking about the male, which, except during a brief mating season, is solitary; and *pisote de manada* is used for the females which, with their young, travel in bands of fifteen or more.

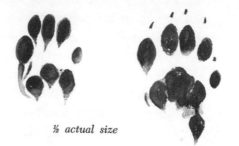

½ *actual size*

A company of coatis bounds along at a sort of rollicking gallop, with their constantly waving tails carried horizontally or at any angle up to ninety degrees; when feeding, the animals hold their tails straight up. As they travel, swimming if necessary to cross a pond or stream, they keep up a constant chittering, and their snouts are always twitching as if possessed by tics. When a coati wants to change or reverse its course, the animal does not turn around but pivots on its hind legs.

In Arizona young coatis are born in the spring or early summer— the result of a mating which took place about eleven weeks earlier. Their first home is apt to be a cavity among rocks. In such a place there are thought to be four to six animals born to a litter. Young coatis are darker than adults, and have tails on which the rings are considerably more distinct than those on the tails of older animals. By the time a male coati is fully grown, the animal weighs ten to twenty-five pounds, measures three to four or more feet, and stands about nine to twelve inches at the shoulder. Females are considerably smaller.

A coati is a nice animal to have around the house; it is affectionate, odorless, washes after each meal, and is easily housebroken, using newspapers or a sand box like a cat. A coati is so curious that it explores every inch of a house; bric-a-brac doesn't stand a chance when this animal is on the loose. Therefore if you plan to have a coati for a pet, it is wise to put away all breakable ornaments or else lay in a large supply of transparent, flexible, and waterproof household cement to mend the broken china or glass an exploring coati leaves in its wake.

A coati likes attention and if you leave one by itself the animal whimpers like an abandoned child. Other coati sounds are grunts, high-pitched screams, snorts, and hisses. If you keep a coati as a pet, you will not be able to have a dog or a cat, for the coati has no love for either animal. In the wild, coatis can get the better of most dogs which attack, and the animal is reported to be able to drive off ocelots and margays with which the coatis share a range.

In addition to being hard on ornaments, a coati is rough on draperies, up which it scampers with the agility of a monkey, shredding the fabric with its long, sharp claws. The animals quickly learn to walk a slack wire, and Olaus Murie, the naturalist, tells of seeing coatis on Barro Colorado Island, a wildlife preserve in the Canal Zone, walk such a wire to get pieces of bread suspended from the middle of the wire.

At the University Hospital in Ann Arbor wires were strung the length of the ward, well above the patients' heads and the wire-walking of the coatis brought smiles to the faces of the sober little patients. It would seem then that the coati, whose short, coarse brown or gray fur has no commercial value, does have a therapeutic value.

MARTEN

Martes americana

During the eighteenth century the American marten was so plentiful that the Hudson's Bay Company sold 15,000 skins in one year and Canada exported 30,000 skins to France in the same year. Today the animal—also known as the pine marten and American sable—is no longer abundant on many parts of its range through mature coniferous forests of the northern states from the Adirondacks to the Rocky Mountains, and north to tree limits. In some places the population often drops so low that closed seasons are necessary in specific areas—even in Alaska, once a great source of marten pelts—and the animal cannot be trapped on such federal areas as National Parks except with a permit for scientific purposes. In the Adirondack region, where martens are rigidly protected, they are reported on the increase.

One of our most beautiful and graceful forest animals, it has, according to Audubon, "the cunning, sneaking character of the Fox, the wide-awake, cautious habits of the Weasel, the voracity of the Mink, and the climbing propensities of the Raccoon." You might think that so endowed the marten would have had no trouble to survive on all parts of its range. But over-trapping and the lumbering and burning of vast areas were responsible for the drastic reduction in the numbers of this little animal—big-eyed, round-eared, and as restless as a gypsy.

After sleeping the better part of the day, it wakes late in the afternoon, and with what seems like an abnormal amount of energy, sets off by tree and by ground to hunt for chipmunks and squirrels, mice and woodrats, conies and rabbits, small birds, nestlings, eggs, and, if it can get them without wetting its feet, fish and frogs. Some berries, nuts, and occasionally honey are included in the diet. Unlike the weasel and the mink, the marten does not kill more than it needs; if the kill is greater than necessary to satisfy immediate hunger the animal buries the excess in the ground and returns to it later.

The marten often travels as much as ten to fifteen miles in one night and it is so fleet and so fierce that only the fisher is able to catch and kill it regularly, though the lynx occasionally preys on the marten and in the West the golden eagle is reported to take some.

On the ground or in the snow the animal leaves indistinct, elongated prints due to its partly furred feet, which become completely furred in winter. Prints vary in size from 1½ inches to 4½ inches, depending upon the condition of the earth or snow over which the animal travels. In a walking gait, such prints are 2½ inches to 9 inches apart, again depending on conditions underfoot—whether the snow is soft or well-packed, the earth soft or hard. On hard snow toe and heel pads show and in summer the long claws often leave prints. In a bounding gait, hind prints are placed in those of the front prints or slightly ahead of them and distances between prints may be as much as 3 feet.

⅔ actual size

The marten is a solitary animal, except for a mating period of about fifteen days in July, when the female makes a sort of clucking sound—at other times martens scream and snarl. The young are born the following March or April in a den lined with grasses or mosses in the hollow of a tree, in a hollow log, or occasionally in a burrow in the ground. Usually there are two or three in a litter, though there may be only one or as many as five. At birth a young marten weighs about an ounce, is blind, and has only a thin coat of fine, yellowish hair. The little animal nurses for six or seven weeks. At the end of this nursing period the mother brings it solid food. At three months a marten reaches adult weight; by that time it is ready to leave the family group. Captive martens may possibly live to be twenty years old; wild ones probably have much shorter lives.

An adult male weighs from 5 to 6 pounds, measures 2 or more feet, including its bushy 7½- to 10-inch tail. Females are somewhat

Track pattern, walking

smaller than males. Both sexes have soft, dense underfur covered by an outer fur that ranges from light red or gray to rich brown or black, depending upon environment (martens from Labrador are almost black, those from Alaska are light brown). Some animals have a yellowish or whitish patch and the ears are fringed with white hairs. Good pelts usually sell for twenty-five to fifty dollars.

To date fur-farming experiments with martens have not been commercially successful, although the animal has been raised in pens at the Department of Agriculture Experimental Fur Farm at Petersburg, Alaska; and before it closed the United States Fur Animal Experiment Station at Saratoga, New York, had made progress in breeding and rearing martens. At Saratoga the long gestation period —the result of delayed implantation—was shortened by subjecting pregnant females to increased amounts of electric light to simulate the lengthening days of late winter and early spring. One female there whelped four months ahead of schedule.

If the marten is to continue as a fur animal of economic value— until recently each year's catch amounted to half a million dollars— experimental fur farming will have to be carried on until martens can be raised in captivity like minks. Biologists of the Cooperative Wildlife Research Unit program are studying these animals in Montana.

Although so shy and secretive that few people see them, martens are so curious that they are easily trapped—one reason for their scarcity. A few feathers, a bright object, or an enticing scent will lure the animals into a trap. One biologist, studying Montana martens, trapped them with kippered herring. The same animals were trapped time and again. After being in a trap for several hours, one was so hungry that upon release it came right up to the biologist and ate out of his hand the kippered herring intended for rebaiting the trap.

FISHER OR PEKAN

Martes pennanti

Among the nation's rarer carnivores is the fisher or pekan—now more an animal of the Canadian forests than those of the United States. But there are still a few stateside areas left in which the fisher lives out its solitary life in swampy woodlands or heavily forested terrain near water.

Like a weasel in form, the fisher in size more nearly approaches an emaciated gray fox, but has shorter legs and rounded ears. In ever-diminishing numbers the animal lives in several northeastern states along the Canadian border, throughout the Rockies south to Yellowstone Park in Montana, in parts of the Sierra Nevadas, and perhaps in the Coast Range of Washington.

If you are fortunate enough to catch sight of it in any of these places, you will probably see the dark-brown to black animal bounding over the ground, swimming across a stream, or running over windfallen timber with the agility of a gray squirrel. If you spot a fisher coming down out of a tree, the animal will be descending head first. And if it spots you, the animal may pause and, hanging by its hind feet, pound the trunk of the tree with first one forefoot and then the other. Upon reaching the ground it may arch its back, snarl and hiss, and whip its bushy, thirteen-inch tail back and forth, to show its displeasure at your intrusion. For the fisher likes to wander by itself over its territory, stopping from time to time to hole up in one of several resting dens. Though not a hibernator, the animal often stays in a den during severe weather for several days. Its den has a noticeable odor, which is not so strong nor so unpleasant as that of other members of the weasel family.

Except for a mating period of two or three days in April, fishers keep to themselves. Matings occur when they are about two years old. Almost a year later, one to five young are born, with the average litter more likely to be three. Soon after delivering her young, the mother leaves them to mate again, as she is in heat for only two or three days once a year, at this season. According to some breeders of fur animals who have attempted to raise fishers, the female courts the male, coaxing him to her with a series of purrs and chuckles.

Once a female has mated it returns to the young—small, hairless, and blind—which may be secreted in a hollow high in a tree, a hollow log, or a cavity among rocks. All such hideaways are lined with grasses. After a seven weeks' nursing period, a young fisher's eyes open; at three months the little animal goes hunting with its mother; and by late fall the family disbands.

½ actual size

About a year after birth a fisher is fully grown: an adult male weighs about 12 pounds, though the weight of males varies greatly—sometimes it is as little as 5 pounds or as much as 20. Length of an adult male is 30 to 40 inches, including its bushy, tapering tail. An adult female is about one-third the size of a male and weighs about one-half as much. Both have dense and silky underfur protected by long, glossy guard hairs. On head, neck, and shoulders, guard hairs are tipped with white; over the rump the fur is denser and on the undersides it is somewhat lighter in color. Neither animal has a seasonal change in its coat. Because of its fine fur—that of the female is considered better than that of the male—the fisher is trapped. A pelt in prime condition commands a price of at least fifty dollars and may bring as much as seventy-five or one hundred dollars.

Though nocturnal, the fisher hunts during the day if hungry. Whether out by day or by night the animal has few predators other than man to worry it. For it can outrun any animals that might try to attack and can worst any that actually attack, including dogs trained to hold bears at bay.

Among the many mammals on which the fisher preys are beavers, chipmunks, marmots, martens, mice, rabbits, squirrels, woodrats, and sewellels or mountain beavers (*Aplodontia rufa*), burrowing rodents of the Pacific slope. The animal kills so many porcupines, by flipping them over on their backs and eating out the carcasses, that it keeps these rodents under control. Occasionally a fisher dies as the result of a porcupine encounter. If it kills more than it eats, excess food is buried and eaten later. Small birds, fishes, and some frogs, insects, and nuts and fruits make up the balance of the animal's diet.

As the fisher goes about its business, the animal leaves sets of tracks that vary in size and stride. When walking, a large male makes somewhat rounded prints in which the five toepads and the heelmarks show. Measuring about 1½ inches by 2 inches, the prints are about thirteen inches apart. In a bounding gait the distance between sets of prints is generally two feet; occasionally as much as four. All prints are similar to those made by martens, whose generic name, *Martes*, is the same as that of the fisher.

The name "fisher" is misleading as the animal does not fish, though it eats spawned-out salmon and robs traps baited with fish. Some early explorer, coming upon the animal eating fish by a streamside, probably thought it had caught the fish and so named it. "Pekan," a French word of American Indian origin, may derive from *un mauvais pekin*, which in vernacular French means "a nasty fellow" —perhaps a reference to the fisher's propensity for robbing traps. It has also been called "black cat," though not related to the cat family; "black fox," though it is not related to the foxes either; "Pennant's cat," after Thomas Pennant, an early authority on North American fur animals; and *tha-cho*. This last is a Chipewyan Indian term meaning "big marten," an exact description of the rapidly vanishing fisher.

LONG-TAILED WEASEL

Mustela frenata

Although American weasels include a total of thirty-six forms, there are three basic species: the least weasel, the short-tailed weasel, and the long-tailed weasel. The least weasel, North America's smallest carnivore, has a one-inch tail which is never black-tipped, while those of the short-tailed and long-tailed weasels are always black-tipped.

Of these three species the long-tailed weasel in its various forms has the widest distribution within the United States. Only western Arizona and a small area in southeastern California are excepted from the animal's United States range, which extends north into southern Canada and south into parts of Mexico.

Like all members of the weasel family, the long-tailed species may be identified by an elongated body, short legs, small head, with rounded ears set close to the skull. Males and females vary in size, with the male larger than the female, but both sexes are similar in appearance; under fur is short and dense and protected by long, glistening guard hairs. In summer the fur is light brown on the upper part of the body, yellowish white on the undersides. In winter the fur of most species, particularly in the northern parts of the range, turns white—hence the name "American ermine," though only one species of American weasel, the short-tailed (*M. arctica*), is closely related to the ermine of Europe.

The habitat of the long-tailed weasel is varied: farmland, prairie, swamp, or woodland, where there is a plentiful supply of water, are areas in which to look for the animal. In such an environment it makes its home in a log, stump, rabbit hole, rockpile, or in the burrow of a mole or pocket gopher; occasionally the weasel makes its den in a bale of hay, and sometimes in the winter nest of a field mouse that it has killed. Dens are lined with feathers, bones, and the fur of the weasel's prey. In such a den the young are born about eight months after a mating that usually occurs in July or August.

At birth each of those in a litter of four to twelve weighs about one-ninth of an ounce, is blind, and has some fine white hair on its wrinkled, pink skin. When the little animal is three weeks old, the mother brings it some solid food; when it is five weeks old, its eyes open and it is weaned; and by the time it is seven or eight weeks old, it is able to hunt.

By fall the animal attains adult weight. Weight varies among individual species and subspecies, depending upon their range. The least weasel (*M. rixosa*), for instance, has a slender, 6-inch body, a 1-inch tail, and paws the size of a mouse, while the long-tailed weasel of the West is larger than one of the East. A western male weighs 7 to 14 ounces, measures 14 to 23 inches, and has a tail 4½ inches to 7 inches.

The long-tailed weasel in winter coat

Although it is abroad at times during the day, the animal is most active at night when it hunts over part of a territory that may be as much as three hundred acres. The prey of the weasel depends on the character of the country, but small mammals, mainly meadow and white-footed mice, make up the greater part of the diet; in some areas nearly 70 percent of its prey is mice. Rats of various species, moles and shrews, cottontails, snowshoe hares, and pikas, squirrels, young birds, frogs, snakes, and lizards, and earthworms are eaten, too, together with domestic poultry. Sometimes a weasel cleans out a henhouse; then control measures are necessary. Occasionally it climbs or swims to get its prey, which, in the last part of the chase, is rushed and killed by a bite at the base of the skull.

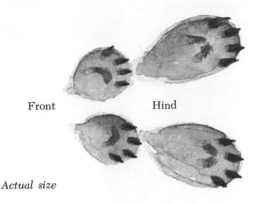

Front   Hind

Actual size

The fox, the lynx, the mink, the marten, and the fisher and some of the larger owls prey on the weasel, but the animal's agility and small size make it difficult to catch, and its musk secreted from an anal gland, is so nauseating that usually none but the hardy or the hungry attack.

As a weasel hunts, with tail held rigidly parallel to the ground or slightly raised, it leaves sets of twin prints, for the hind feet are generally placed in the prints made by the front feet. Four of the five toes show in the tracks which, in the case of the long-tailed weasel, may be spaced twenty to fifty inches apart. Sometimes in winter you can see the drag mark left in the snow by the tail, and sometimes distances between sets of prints follow a short-long, short-long pattern as the animal alternates its bounding or loping gaits.

Weasels, like other members of the family, are curious, and therefore easy to trap. The pelts are soft and durable and a good skin sometimes brings as much as a dollar. The best North American pelts come from Alaska. Today the fur is worn by anyone who can afford it, but during medieval times only royalty was privileged to wear the fur of this animal. Ermine spotted with pieces of black lamb is worn by the British on ceremonial occasions; fifty thousand pelts are supposed to have been used in the coronation of King George VI in 1937.

Savage though they are, weasels can be tamed and make reasonably good but vociferous pets. Young ones squeak and purr; adults bark, hiss, and scream. Captive animals have lived as long as five years, and have proved such good mousers and ratters that they live up to their generic name *Mustela* meaning "those who carry off mice."

MINK

Mustela vison

The mink has the land habits of the weasel and that animal's habit of killing more than enough to satisfy immediate needs; but it also reflects the water habits of the otter and to some extent, that animal's apparent fondness for play. With this combination of traits and its prolific nature the mink maintains itself in spite of man's encroachment on wilderness areas. In fact it has been so little affected by the urbanization of the country that the animal lives within the limits of large cities—even New York—if there is suitable habitat.

Never plentiful in any area, the mink lives along wooded streams, lakes, and marshes, including tidal marshes, throughout the greater part of North America from Mexico to the Arctic Circle. Only the southern half of Florida, parts of the Southwest, northern and western Alaska, and some areas of the northern Canadian Provinces are excepted from this range. The animals establish overlapping territories; an adult male has a home range of something more than thirty acres, while that of a female is considerably smaller.

A slender, light to dark brown animal, with short, close-set ears, short legs, bushy tail, and a constantly arched back, the mink occasionally hunts and travels by day, but is chiefly nocturnal. Hunting routes are neither definite nor well defined, but usually border streams or circle lakes. As the animal hunts, sometimes bounding along, sometimes moving stealthily, it leaves tracks similar to those of a gray squirrel. The somewhat squarish prints show four of the five toes on each foot, and in a bounding gait the imprints of the slightly webbed hind feet are a little ahead of those of the front feet or in them.

Small birds, eggs, fish and shellfish, frogs, turtle eggs, rats and mice, rabbits and squirrels, earthworms, waterfowl, and domestic poultry are all included in the mink's diet. It is particularly fond of young muskrats and tears apart a muskrat house to get at the young. It preys on older muskrats, too, killing them in the open or following them right into tunnels or houses.

The mink frequently establishes itself in the house of a muskrat which it has killed. Other types of mink dens are deserted woodchuck holes near water, cavities among rocks, hollow stumps of trees, and bank burrows. A burrow dug by a mink is about four inches in diameter and varies in length and depth depending upon the nature of the soil. In soft soil the animal may tunnel to a depth of three or four feet and to a length of ten or twelve feet. Sometimes a den contains a month's supply of food—one mink den by actual count held a store of thirteen muskrats, two mallard ducks, and one coot.

Left front

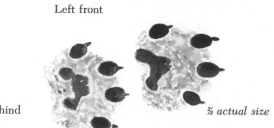

Left hind

⅔ *actual size*

Such dens are often lined with fur, feathers, or bones, and amid the remains of the parents' victims the young are born, about forty days after a strenuous courting and mating in February or March. The litter may number anywhere from three to ten, though it is usually five to eight. At birth a young mink is about the size of a pea pod and is covered by fine, light hair. The little animal is born with its eyes closed.

A kit nurses for about five weeks. During the latter part of this period its thirty-four teeth begin to pierce the gum lines. It is then that the mother brings the kit bits of solid food. At the end of five weeks the animal's eyes open and it is weaned.

Young minks are playful. Sometimes they slide down stream banks like land otters and occasionally float downstream, curled up and looking as if they were asleep. In their rough-and-tumble play they pounce upon one another, snarling and hissing. As they grow older and as adults, minks scream, bark, and utter a deep-throated purr.

A litter is schooled in mink ways by the mother sometimes assisted by the father who, though he may mate with several females, generally stays with the last one he encounters during the mating season. The family travels and hunts together over a range that often measures several square miles until fall, when the unit breaks up. Each member then establishes a home territory on which it lives alone—even the female is solitary until the next mating period. During cold weather minks often sleep away several days, curled up, using their tails as blankets to cover their heads. Wild ones lead such strenuous lives that they probably do not live as long as ranch-bred minks, which are old at ten years of age.

The bobcat, the fox, and the lynx, and the great-horned and snowy owls prey on it, but the mink is so fast and so ferocious that it usually worsts or escapes most animals that attempt an attack.

An adult male mink measures about twenty-four inches, has a tail six to eight inches in length, and weighs one to three pounds. Females are about one-fourth smaller. Both animals have dense, soft underfur protected by long, lustrous guard hairs; on the back the fur is generally darker than on the rest of the body and the tail is almost black. There is generally a white spot on the chest. Neither animal undergoes a marked seasonal change in fur.

Of all the weasel family, to which the mink belongs, none has a stench like the mink. The musk which it discharges at the slightest provocation is contained in anal glands similar to those of a skunk, but cannot be sprayed as a skunk sprays its musk.

Throughout the range minks vary in size and color. Away from the coast in Alaska, which produces the largest minks, the fur of the animals is of high quality, color, and durability, though not so dark as the fur of Labrador minks, which are almost black. In Louisiana, which produces more mink fur than any of the states, the fur is lighter in color and not so durable as that of northern animals.

Among North American fur animals the mink is one of the most valuable and was the first of our fur animals to be raised commercially. In 1866, H. Ressegue of Oneida, New York, operated a mink ranch and was soon selling breeding stock at thirty dollars a pair. Mink farming has had a steady growth since then, and during the last decade has increased enormously. In 1940 about 300,000 animals were raised on backyard "ranches" for auxiliary income and on regular mink ranches. By 1951 more than 2,000,000 ranch-reared mink pelts were sold on the raw fur market with a gross value of about $40,000,000.00.

Of this little animal which makes such a contribution to the nation's economy, Audubon wrote: "Next to the Ermine, the Mink is the most active and destructive little depredator that prowls around the farmyard, or the farmer's duck pond. The vigilant farmer may see a fine fowl in the clutches of a Mink moving towards a fissure in a rock or a hole in some pile of stones, in the gray of the morning."

Audubon further comments on the mink by saying of a pet one, "It waged war on the Norway rats in the dam, and caught frogs on the banks of the pond. It never attacked the poultry, and was on good terms with the dogs and cats."

Two other members of the weasel family (*Mustelidae*) now extremely rare in the United States are:

The black-footed ferret (*M. nigripes*), an animal of the Great Plains, where it lives in prairie-dog towns and is thought to feed on these as well as other rodents. Though similar in appearance to the long-tailed weasel, this animal is larger, has a black band across the eyes and black paws and forelegs.

The wolverine (*Gulo luscus*), an animal of the forests and Arctic regions of North America, seldom found south of Canada, though there may be a few in the mountainous regions of the West. The animal looks something like a cross between a skunk and a bear, has a shaggy dark brown or black coat, and a white stripe on each side of the body. This largest member of the weasel family is a gluttonous killer that robs traplines, and the number of wolverines in Alaska remains constant because trapping the animal is difficult.

STRIPED SKUNK

Mephitis mephitis

"There is no quadruped on the continent of North America," wrote John James Audubon, "the approach of which is more generally detested than that of the skunk. Even the bravest of our boasting race is, by this little animal, compelled to break off his train of thought, *hold his nose*, and run—as if a lion were at his heels."

The skunk, a glossy black animal with white stripes, is quite capable of making anyone hold his nose and run. Two glands near the base of the tail contain a thick, yellowish fluid known as n-butyl mercaptan. To discharge this fluid the animal everts these glands, which then look rather like diminutive nozzles. But before laying down a barrage the skunk gives warning: it turns backsides to an assailant, lowers its narrow head, stamps on the ground with first one small forefoot and then the other, growling as it does so. Finally the long plumy tail is arched over the white-striped back.

The arching of a skunk's tail is as significant as the hoisting of a red-and-white hurricane flag. If the maneuver fails to rout an enemy, a skunk whips its twenty-eight-inch body into a U-shape, so that the target is in the line of vision. The animal then discharges the musk from either gland or both in a fine spray, which carries ten to twelve feet or even farther if there is a favorable wind. Only a quick move in the animal's direction or actual injury causes a skunk to spray its musk—of such pungency that it can be detected half a mile away from the point of discharge. One discharge does not exhaust the supply—said to be luminous at night and produced at the rate of nearly one-third liquid ounce a week; there is sufficient musk for at least five consecutive discharges. However, a skunk never uses more musk than necessary and never discharges it if the tail is lowered.

The musk burns like acid on the skin and causes temporary blindness if it gets in the eyes. The copious tears induced by a direct hit bring relief in fifteen or twenty minutes; and bathing the eyes with water speeds recovery from the blindness. To rid clothes of the odor of skunk musk, some woodsmen suggest washing them in vinegar, a treatment which may fade them; others recommend hanging "skunked" clothes over a smoky fire of cedar or juniper chips to rid them of the smell; while a third group contends such clothing should be buried in the ground for several days, then sent to the dry cleaner's. A dog that runs afoul of a skunk can be washed in vinegar water. Skunked automobiles are sometimes an extra expense for owners. One motorist who hit a skunk received the following bill from a garage:

Washing car	$2.00
Allowing it in place...............	1.00

It is often impossible to avoid hitting skunks on the road, particularly at dusk when the animals are moving about, for they cross highways with a fine disregard for cars and trucks. But skunks are not troublesome if you stay beyond the "critical distance," the point at which any animal defends itself when surprised or cornered.

The striped skunk, a member of the weasel family, ranges over most of North America, from Nova Scotia, the Hudson Bay area, and the northern limits of British Columbia south into Mexico. Unlike many American mammals of economic value, this skunk has not decreased in numbers as the country has developed. In fact the animal is probably one of our commonest wild carnivores because its environmental requirements are elastic.

Open fields with plenty of dense cover and adjacent to water are good skunk habitat. Although the home range of the animal seldom exceeds half a mile in any one direction from the den, a skunk often covers six to eight miles in a night's erratic prowling. A den is any sort of natural cavity, open spaces beneath buildings, or abandoned burrows of badgers, foxes, woodchucks, or other tunneling animals within the extensive range. A burrow dug by a skunk is shallow and short and ends in a rounded chamber about two feet below the surface of the ground. The chamber is above the level of the tunnel to secure proper drainage and is lined with dried grasses and leaves— often pushed in head first by a female to ready the chamber for the birth of young.

Older females mate in February, while younger ones mate as late as May. The mating of skunks is a strenuous affair for the males; some males are monogamous, others polygamous, but all fight among themselves, hiss and growl, and in the general boisterousness of the occasion frequently spray one another. Eight or nine weeks after a mating the young are born. The usual skunk litter is six, but there may be as few as two or as many as ten.

At birth a young skunk or kit weighs about one ounce. Front claws are well developed and the black-and-white pattern is well defined, as if tattooed, on the crinkled pink skin, but the little animal is blind, hairless, toothless, and almost earless. A kit nurses for six or seven weeks with the mother sprawling over it or lying sidewise so that her six pairs of nipples are easily accessible.

Growth of a kit is rapid and a good coat of fur soon develops. Midway in the nursing period the eyes open and during the latter part of this period a young skunk follows the mother on nightly foraging trips. Occasionally a mother and young are out during the day. On expeditions either by day or by night the mother leads the kits around in single-file formation, with each little skunk about twenty inches behind the other and with each kit emulating every movement of the leader, who teaches the young to swim or shows them how to bat unwary minnows out of the water.

By fall the family disbands, with each half-grown animal going its own way. Skunks, with about one animal to every thirty acres, establish home territories that often overlap. By fall most skunks are fat and though not true hibernators, the animals settle down, sometimes in an occupied woodchuck burrow, and sleep for periods of varying lengths during severe weather. Occasionally several skunks of both sexes and differing ages den together. Females and younger animals remain inactive longer than males, and often sleep through the trapping season which may be one reason why skunks are plentiful.

About a year after birth the animal is mature and ready to breed. A full-grown male weighs about eight pounds and measures two or more feet in length, including an eight-inch tail, usually, but not always, white-tipped. Although a female is about one-fourth smaller than a male, there is no difference between them in coloration;

neither animal undergoes a seasonal variation in the fur—a combination of soft underfur protected by long guard hairs. If the musk glands are removed from a young animal it makes an affectionate pet, playful and a better mouser than a cat. Pet skunks have lived to be ten or twelve years old; wild skunks probably have a shorter life span.

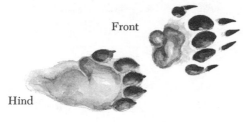

Front

Hind

½ actual size

As it sets out in the late afternoon on its ordinarily silent quest for food, the animal has few natural enemies to worry it. Only the great-horned owl preys regularly on the skunk and captured owls of this species generally have a noticeable odor of skunk. When the usual prey of badgers, bobcats, coyotes, and foxes is scarce these animals kill skunks. But for the most part a skunk goes foraging practically unmolested and in its foraging is a greater boon to agriculture than many people realize. A good example of what a striped skunk eats is the following year-round diet of a Texas animal, reported in *Texas Game and Fish*, March 1951:

Spring: insects, 96 percent; reptiles, 1.6 percent; small mammals, 2 percent; balance, small birds and vegetation.
Summer: insects, 88 percent; spiders, 4 percent; reptiles, 1.5 percent; small birds, 3.5 percent; balance, centipedes, small mammals, and vegetation.
Fall: insects, 76 percent; spiders, and so on, 24 percent.
Winter: insects, 52.3 percent; spiders, 5.3 percent; reptiles, 1.6 percent; small mammals, 18.3 percent; vegetation, 22 percent; balance, birds and millipeds.

In New York the skunk did such an effective job of destroying the hop grub, a ravenous eater like most larvae, that the first legislation to protect the animal in that State was initiated at the insistence of the hop growers. Skunks eat the eggs of snapping turtles, one of the most savage enemies of ducklings, but never eat the common toad, one of nature's most effective controls of garden insects.

Those that develop a fondness for poultry and eggs or prove troublesome around concentrations of nesting waterfowl can be box-trapped and drowned; they can also be killed by disulphide or carbon monoxide gas. But before taking such drastic measures make sure that the predators are not rats or weasels. The odor of skunks that have denned beneath floors of buildings is often annoying. Such animals can be discouraged by placing about a pound of mothballs or naphthalene in the den.

In most states skunks are protected by law except during a trapping season. If they get out of hand during the closed season a permit to trap them can be obtained from your state game department. Trapping season is the best time to rid an area of them, as the animals' fur is prime or nearly so and marketable. A skunk pelt of prime quality and with a minimum of white brings about one dollar and twenty-five cents. This fur has a durability rating of 50 to 70 per cent compared to 100 per cent for otter fur (see page 7 for other durability ratings). Today it is marketed as skunk, but in the past the fur was sold under the trade names "Alaskan Sable" and "Black Marten."

In skunk country there are several means by which you can tell if the animals are present. Odor, of course, is the easiest way, barring a glimpse of the animal itself. Pits, one to two inches deep and three to four inches across, where a skunk has dug for insects, are another indication. Look, too, for their tracks, which run somewhat diagonally in a row with the prints of the larger hindfeet outside those of the smaller forefeet; claws of the forefeet leave a drag and heel marks show, as the animal is a plantigrade—walks on its soles. Sets of all four tracks in a running gait are generally less than one foot apart. Scats, too, are another means of detecting a skunk's presence; droppings, found along trails and near dens, consist largely of chitinous insect coverings and undigested seeds of such fruits as blackberries, cherries, and strawberries. And finally, look for traces of hairs around den entrances.

The striped skunk, subject to sinus trouble and rabies, has a number of local names. "Polecat," "wood pussy," "big skunk," and "line-backed skunk" are the most familiar; the animal is frequently called *enfant du diable* by French-Canadians. The skunk's common name, however, is derived from the Algonquian Indian name "Seganku" and the scientific name, *Mephitis,* is a Latin word, meaning, "noxious vapor."

Mephitic poisoning of the air once routed an entire congregation. At the request of an asthmatic clergyman, Audubon procured the musk glands of a striped skunk. The clergyman kept the glands in a tightly corked smelling bottle; whenever an asthmatic paroxysm was upon him, he uncorked the bottle and inhaled deeply. Relief was immediate. One Sunday morning midway through his service, the clergyman, on the verge of an attack, whipped out his smelling bottle and vigorously waved it to and fro under his nose. The congregation, according to Audubon, "finding the smell too powerful for their olfactories made a hasty retreat."

In addition to the striped skunks, which include the hooded skunk (*M. macroura*), known only to the Trans-Pecos region of Texas, there are two other races of skunks in the United States. These skunks, like the striped skunks, protect themselves by discharging musk and have similar habits:

The hog-nosed skunk (*Conepatus*) has a long, piglike snout with which it roots out grubs; it is distinguished by short coarse fur, and a white back and tail often tinged with yellow. This race, the only South American skunk, extended its range into Central America, then worked its way into southeastern Arizona, southern Colorado, and southwestern Texas, where it lives in foothill country or partly timbered and brushy areas.

The spotted skunk (*Spilogale*) is our smallest species; it weighs about one and one-half pounds and is the only skunk agile enough to do some tree climbing. The animal has one white spot on the forehead and one under each ear; narrow broken white stripes give the silky fur a spotted appearance. The animal is found in mountainous country of the Southeast, the Southwest, and in the rain forests of the Northwest, and in Mexico. Sometimes the spotted skunk is called "civet cat," a name which is misleading as the little animal is not related to the civet cat of the Old World.

BADGER

Taxidea taxus

Wheezing as if troubled by asthma, the American badger shuffles along on short, powerful legs from one rodent burrow to another in search of prey. Once pocket gopher, prairie dog, or ground squirrel is scented, the low-slung badger starts boring spirally into the burrow entrance at top speed. Using its long-clawed front feet, shorter-clawed hind feet, and snoutlike nose, the badger digs in so rapidly that it sometimes disappears below soft earth in a minute and one-half. Prey rarely escapes unless its den is among rocks or has other exits.

The badger, a member of the weasel family and closely related to the wolverine, lives in plains and prairie regions of western, northern, and north-central America. It is sometimes found in mountain country or in wooded areas in which there is no heavy undergrowth.

For its home a badger either digs its own burrow or enlarges one of an animal on which it has preyed. Except when caring for young, a badger does not remain long in any one burrow. The oval entrance, eight to twelve inches in diameter, is marked by a large pile of excavated earth. You can generally see the toed-in tracks, measuring two and one-quarter inches in length, around a burrow entrance. The imprint of the long claws on the front feet, kept sharp by honing on tree trunks, usually shows; claws on hind feet rarely leave an imprint. If a badger runs, hind prints are ahead of fore tracks and sets of tracks are as much as five to six feet apart.

The animal digs a tunnel five to thirty feet long, ending in a large chamber two to six feet below the ground. The chamber contains a nest of dry grasses in which young are born. Generally three—though there may be one or five—badgers are born in May or June. The young are conceived during a monogamous mating in autumn or early winter, depending upon the whereabouts of the animals within their range. Cold weather arrests growth of the embryo for eight weeks, but once growth is resumed the embryo develops in five or six weeks to the proper stage for birth.

The eyes of a young badger, which is furred at birth, open when the animal is four to six weeks old. When it is nearly half-grown it is weaned and the mother brings it food—a routine that is continued until the offspring is two-thirds grown. At this point a young badger accompanies its mother on hunting trips, and by late summer the family disbands. Each animal then lives a solitary existence except for the mating and rearing periods, when the male occasionally helps care for the young.

An adult male measures about 25 to 30 inches from the tip of its snoutlike nose to the end of its stubby 5-inch tail and weighs about twelve to fourteen pounds. The flat, muscular body is well layered with fat and the tough, pliable skin hangs loosely—a physical characteristic that makes it difficult for any assailant to get a telling grip on the animal. Females, somewhat smaller than males, are similar in appearance. Although there is no actual seasonal variation in the long shaggy black fur tipped with white, the fur is apt to take on a brownish cast in summer.

A badger usually begins to hunt in late afternoon and continues its search for prey through the night. Sometimes the animal hunts during the day and it may, if necessary, swim to get from one hunting ground to another. In addition to many species of rodents, either freshly killed or carrion, a badger eats quantities of insects, some ground-nesting birds and their eggs, and lizards, skunks, and snakes. The animal relishes honey and digs out nests of bumblebees for honey and larvae. It preys on rabbits, which find sanctuary in deserted badger holes—used, too, by burrowing owls. If a badger kills more than enough to satisfy immediate hunger, the carcass is buried and later dug up to be eaten as needed.

During winter a badger in the extreme northern parts of the range hibernates. A more southerly animal remains active, but its appetite is not so great as in summer and it is inclined to be drowsy. A badger often goes below frost line and plugs up the tunnel behind it with a clod of earth to keep out the cold. If it brings food underground, the animal holes up for as long as the food supply lasts. Once the food is exhausted, the badger comes aboveground to hunt.

A badger has few natural enemies due to the ferocity with which it fights. Occasionally a coyote kills one and dogs frequently attack the animal. But dogs, particularly inexperienced ones, are generally worsted. Unless forced to fight the badger digs itself underground on the spot when approached, or, with head held close to the ground to protect the neck, scurries off to its burrow. If it fights the animal hisses or growls, raises its tail and secretes a musk that is less acrid than skunk musk, then tries to sink its powerful, interlocking jaws in the throat of its assailant.

Left front

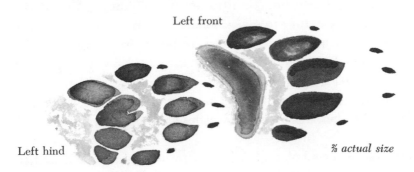

Left hind ⅔ *actual size*

Its ferocity led to the custom of badger baiting, popular in Great Britain during the first half of the nineteenth century, but banned about 1850. In this "sport" a small barrel was sunk as a retreat for one badger in a pit in which several dogs were released. The dogs were supposed to pull or draw the badger from its haven. Pit fights were held in Texas as late as the 1920's. A Burnet badger once whipped eleven dogs, including a male, white pit bulldog, which outweighed the badger by five pounds. After each fight the badger went to the man who owned it and without a whimper let its wounds be daubed with iodine.

Presumably the animal's common name is derived from *bageard*, a word of French origin, meaning "one with a badge"—no doubt a reference to its distinctive vertical black-and-white head pattern. "Badger State" is the nickname of Wisconsin and in some localities "badger" is the designation for a dealer in grain or a food peddler. A badger's tooth carried in your pocket is supposed to bring good luck at cards.

If captured young, a badger makes an amusing, playful pet, becomes domesticated in a few weeks, and according to the owner of the fighting Texas badger, anyone in the family can handle it without fear of being bitten. A captive may live to be twelve years old; the animal's life expectancy in the wild is undoubtedly less.

One way to catch a badger is to flood the burrow so that the animal has to come out for air. Remember that if you ever use this tactic to flush one, the animal will come out fighting. A second method of getting a badger is to trap one. Any strongly scented bait such as sardines or spoiled fish does the trick.

Quality badger pelts brought fifty dollars each during World War I. Now the price is four to seven dollars. The fur, formerly used to line women's coats, is used currently to point the poorer grades of fox—or other long furs dyed to simulate fox—by gluing in the white-tipped badger hairs. At one time badger fur sold for $85.00 a pound and was used in making fine shaving brushes; it is still used for artists' brushes, but synthetic bristles have largely replaced natural ones in shaving brushes.

Although badger holes are a hazard to horses and riders and the animal does some damage to ditch banks in irrigated areas while digging out prey, its enormous consumption of insects and grain-eating rodents makes the animal much more of an asset than a liability. The badger is one of nature's checks that helps to prevent overpopulation among certain other forms of wildlife.

LAND OTTER

Lutra canadensis

The lithe-bodied otter occasionally shoots rapids no experienced canoeist would attempt; it often bellywhops down a steep streambank to drop into a pool; and regularly the otter rolls through the water, surfacing and submerging in a series of dolphin-like arcs which leave a wake of silvery bubbles. In each of these pursuits, the animal seems to be having the time of its energetic, roving life.

This apparent zest for living is typical of the otter, a large, sleek brown member of the weasel family with a bullet-shaped head, well-whiskered muzzle, short legs ending in webbed feet, and a stout tapering tail which serves as a rudder. Various species and subspecies of otters live along inland and coastal waterways of every continent but Australia. In North America several forms of otters (*Lutra*) are found throughout the greater part of the continent. Only an area in the far North and parts of southern California, Nevada, Arizona, and New Mexico, and western and southwestern Texas are not included in the animal's range on this continent.

The otter dens in deserted beaver houses or tunnels, vacant muskrat tunnels, hollow logs or hollow bases of trees, and in tangles of streamside vegetation. In the flat marshes and tules of California, the animal bends together marsh plants to make a small circular enclosure for its den. Occasionally deserted woodchuck burrows serve as dens, even if located some distance from water. Such dens, usually lined with dried grasses and leaves and sticks, are temporary homes in which young are born and reared. For a permanent home the otter tunnels into a stream bank for three to five feet, making a ten-inch bore as it does so. At the end of the tunnel a fair-sized chamber is dug out, with a lining similar to those in temporary dens. Designated spots well away from dens are used for voiding and for burying wastes. Droppings are also found at spots where the otter rolls, dries itself, and deposits scent from the anal glands on tufts of grass. These "posts" attract every otter passing through the area.

A male otter is sexually mature at two years and starts to court one or more females. Courting, accompanied by a sort of chuckling sound on the part of the male, occurs during late winter or early spring, and mating takes place in the water soon after the female delivers the young conceived the previous year. After mating, a male usually stays with a single female until the cubs are born. In the North otters are born in mid-April; in the South somewhat earlier. Birth comes after a gestation period that varies from nine to twelve or more months. The usual annual litter is two or three animals; sometimes there is only one but there may be as many as four.

At birth an otter cub is covered by a silky coat of black fur, weighs less than half a pound, and is blind and toothless. A cub develops rather slowly; eyes remain sealed until the animal is five to six weeks old. At three months a cub leaves the den and plays outside with its litter mates and its mother. Then, to start weaning the cubs, the mother brings them solid food.

As soon as cubs are weaned they are taught to swim. Recalcitrant cubs are forced into the water; the mother gets such cubs on her back, swims out into the center of a pool, and dives. While cubs are learning to swim the male often joins the family group and plays with the cubs or helps with their training.

An otter family seems compatible and happy; mother and cubs comb one another's fur, frolic in the water, toss bits of clam shells into a pool, then dive in to retrieve them, and toboggan down streambanks on slides that sometimes measure as much as twenty-five feet. To get going on the slide an otter pushes off with all four feet, then quickly turns its feet backward, with the front ones held close to the sides of the body and the back ones stretched out behind. Thus, with resistance cut to a minimum, the otter shoots down the slide headfirst on its belly and drops into the water with such force that spray flies in all directions. As soon as the first otter starts down the slide, a second takes off, to be followed in rapid succession by the entire family. At the height of such activity the slide looks rather like a conveyor belt, as the animals hurtle down the bank one after another, swim back to shore, scramble up the bank, and fall into position for the next takeoff.

When a slide has been used a few times, the wet bodies of the tobogganing otters make it slick and fast—which the animals seem to enjoy thoroughly as they shoot down at ever-increasing speeds. How many slides an undisturbed otter makes is problematical. Audubon watched a pair make twenty-two slides apiece before he frightened them away by a sudden movement.

In winter otters use snow slides that shoot them into ice-free areas created by fast-moving water. After using a winter slide an otter often swims away under the ice, perhaps coming up in open water a quarter of a mile away; for the animal can submerge as long as four minutes.

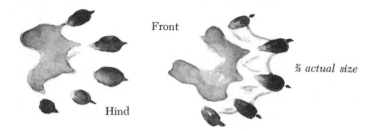

Front

⅔ *actual size*

Hind

A cub leaves the mother when it is eight months old to go its separate way. Two years after its birth, the animal is fully grown. An adult male weighs ten to thirty pounds, measures thirty to thirty-five inches in length, and has a tail of twelve to nineteen inches. A female is about one-third smaller. Both animals have the same coloration and neither has a seasonal change in the fur. If acquired as cubs, otters make fine long-lived pets—if you do not mind their somewhat doggy odor or their prank of turning a room topsy-turvy as they romp. An otter can be trained to act as a retriever, a boon to the hunter whose bird has sunk to the bottom of lake, pond, pothole, or slough.

The home range of an otter is variable. As feeding and living conditions change an otter moves; in winter the animal travels across country from one watercourse to another in search of streams with falls and rapids that remain unfrozen. Seasonal wandering of a male may add up to fifty or sixty miles. On an overland trek, an otter hurls its body forward in a bounding gait, creating a foot-wide trough or furrow in the snow in which you can see the animal's rounded tracks. Imprint of all four toes on each foot is plain but that of the fifth toe, if it shows at all, is indistinct. When an otter runs, hind tracks about 2¾ inches long by 2½ inches wide are staggered behind 2-inch square front tracks; in a running gait, hind tracks are side by side and may cover front tracks. The wavy tail drag is heavy and often diagonal to the line of travel.

Aside from man the otter has few enemies to worry about while traveling abroad; in a day's feeding the animal often covers as much as six miles. Both on land and in water it is agile enough to escape would-be predators and strong enough to fight off most of those that actually attack, including dogs. On overland trips some young otters may be killed by bobcats and coyotes. But except where the otter is trapped or hunted, as in England which has had otter-hunting since 1175, the animal seeks its prey with little chance of being preyed upon.

Of all the animal foods eaten by an otter, crayfish are the most sought. Frogs, insects, mussels, snails, snakes, turtles (mostly the soft-shell forms), shrimps and crabs, and various water plants appear in the diet. The otter catches some trout and other game fish; but most of the fishes on which the animal preys are species which compete with trout for food and which eat trout eggs. By preying on such fishes the otter helps to create more normal conditions in overstocked waters.

Trappers often complain that the otter preys on young muskrats. Undoubtedly some muskrats are taken by the animal, but the marsh-dwelling raccoon or the mink is more apt to be the predator. The otter has been accused of killing beaver, but there is little evidence to support this charge; in most areas the two fur animals live compatibly. And it should be remembered that otter predation is never prolonged in any one area as the animal is restless and wide-ranging.

A limited number of otters are trapped each season in accordance with various federal and state laws. In Michigan, for instance, they may be trapped in designated areas in the early spring—a season which also permits the taking of beaver. Otter fur, a combination of dense underfur protected by long guard hairs which "silver" the pelt, is rated as standard by the fur industry on the basis of durability (see page 7 for other fur-durability ratings). During the fur boom of 1920 an otter pelt of prime quality commanded a price of

$105.00. Today a No. 1 skin brings $10.00 to $30.00, depending upon size and condition. Finest Eastern pelts are those from Labrador; best Western ones come from Alaska. For centuries otter fur was used to trim men's clothing, but today it is used principally for women's coats and jackets.

Also known as "common otter," "land otter," and "river otter," it is a vocal animal. It snuffles like a swimmer trying to get water out of his nostrils, growls, snarls, and hisses on occasion, and at other times utters birdlike chirps and piercing whistles.

Although otters frequently live close to man's activities—even on such a place as Aberdeen Proving Ground in Maryland—and are abroad at any hour throughout the year, the animals are so retiring that few people see them, let alone hear them. By chance, Bob Hines, the wildlife artist, saw an unusual demonstration of otter behavior. While walking near a watercourse on Mattamuskeet National Wildlife Refuge in North Carolina, Hines caught sight of a pair of otters swimming along with their usual dolphinlike grace. Every so often the two animals interrupted their progress to rear up out of the water and rub noses.

SEA OTTER

Enhydra lutris

In the waters around Amchitka, one of the Aleutian Islands, you can sometimes catch a glimpse of the rare sea otter. Most likely the animal will be floating on its back, with forearms crossed over chest, flipperlike hind feet turned upward, and stout, short tail held straight out. Rising and falling with the swell of the ocean, the sea otter looks thoroughly content—as if all was right in its world of wind and water, rocky isle and rolling fog.

The broad, white-whiskered face of the sea otter appears toothless and makes the animal look rather like a quizzical old man—hence the nickname "old man of the sea." Like the land form, to which it is closely related, the sea otter is sportive. Often while floating on its back and popping bits of seafood into its mouth from a supply on its chest, the sea otter suddenly dives with a sort of forward somersault, surfaces almost immediately, and continues floating as before. As far as we know this antic is carried on for sheer fun and it is reason enough for the animal's second nickname, "child of the sea."

Forty-odd years ago survival of the sea otter did not seem probable; there were only a few hundred animals left along the Pacific coast of North America. Today, due to rigid protection, more than five thousand of them live in the waters of the Aleutian Islands area, with a herd of about four hundred in the vicinity of Amchitka—rocky, treeless, and windswept. On Amchitka's sloping beaches you can occasionally find sea otter tracks: the rounded imprints of the webbed front feet show large toe-pads, those of the seal-like hind feet, about six inches in diameter, resemble a scallop shell in appearance and form. Droppings, too, containing shell fragments of marine life, are scattered on the beaches and volcanic rocks. Although the sea otter hauls out on land from time to time, the greater part of its life is spent in the water, where it eats, sleeps, and breeds.

To study sea otters at Amchitka or on the California coast, near Carmel, where there is another herd of more than two hundred animals, you need some sort of telescopic glass for the animals are shy of man approaching in an open boat. Otters are often active a mile from shore and in the beds of brown kelp, which they frequent, the animals' heads look so remarkably like the large kelp bulbs that it is difficult to differentiate the animal from the vegetable. But with a glass of fairly strong power in hand you can watch a floating otter or pick out an animal taking its ease in a kelp bed. Frequently an otter interrupts its habitual back float to assume a position like that of a man treading water. Then bending slightly backwards the animal shades its big, black eyes with a paw and scans the ocean's surface in search of the single, large fin of the killer whale—the only sea mammal which preys on the otter. If a whale's fin is sighted, the otter flops down on its belly and strikes out for the nearest kelp bed, its powerful, flipperlike hind feet driving the animal through the water in an undulating style at about ten miles an hour.

In addition to providing sanctuary from killer whales, kelp beds are resting, sleeping, and whelping quarters for the otter. An otter at ease wraps a kelp frond—the ribbon-like variety is preferred— around its body to keep from drifting away. The animal also plays with the fronds, and, according to folk tales, even wads kelp into a ball, which is then tossed into the air and caught while the otter floats on its back.

The original range of the sea otter was the Pacific coast of North America from central California to the Aleutian Islands, as far north as the Pribilof Islands in Bering Sea, and along the coasts of North-east Asia. For more than two centuries the animal was hunted for its beautiful pelt—fine, dense, and durable. Having no fear of man then, according to report, the sea otter was easy prey for the Russian fur hunters, the *promshlenniki*, who slaughtered the animals by the thousands. It has been estimated that 150,000 sea otter pelts were carried back to the mother country by the Russians in a two-year period. After the United States purchased Alaska in 1867, the slaughter of the sea otter did not stop; adventurers of various nationalities continued taking sea otters, whose pelts were in great demand by Asiatic and European royalty, and by Chinese mandarins, who used sea-otter fur to trim their robes. At the beginning of the century otter pelts commanded a price of $500.00 to $1,000.00 and in 1910 a pelt is reported to have brought almost $2,000.00 at a London auction. Today no one knows their exact value and it is illegal to have a pelt without a permit. Finally, in 1911, when there were only a few hundred sea otters left, all killing was prohibited; this gave the small Aleutian Islands herd a chance to rebuild—a slow process as the female bears only one kit or pup a year.

Though births occur at any time throughout the year, most otter pups are born in April or May; some authorities say births are in the water; others maintain that they take place on land. At birth an otter pup weighs about three and one-half pounds, measures about seventeen inches, and has its eyes open. A newly born pup, grayer than adults, has a full set of teeth, an indication that the gestation period is fairly long. Despite its teeth a pup nurses—while the mother floats on her back—for six months and continues to nurse for the better part of a year, even after the mother feeds it bits of crabmeat and other seafood.

The female is one of the most solicitous mothers in the animal kingdom. Should danger threaten, she tucks her pup under her arm and dives, surfacing frequently so that the little animal can get air. A sea otter mother fondles and kisses her pup, but does not "spare the rod," if the pup's behavior warrants discipline. If, in being taught to swim, the young animal fails to dive under the crest of a breaking wave—correct sea-otter technique—the mother spanks the pup and in spite of its crying, keeps on spanking until a dive is executed to her satisfaction. A pup stays with its mother for some time—in fact a female often has two pups of differing ages with her.

A male has nothing to do with the raising of the pup it sired—after a courtship during which a male woos a prospective mate by nuzzling her with the tip of its nose or stroking her with forepaws. Males frolic together in kelp beds, spend endless hours floating on their backs, and squabble among themselves. During squabbles they nip and cuff one another as the spirit moves them, and squeal, bark, and growl.

A sea otter is fully grown by the time it is four years old, and some have been known to live eight or more years. An adult male weighs from twenty-five to seventy-five pounds, measures four to five feet, and has a ten-inch tail. A female is somewhat smaller. The pelage of both is similar, but among sea otters there is a distinct color variation in the fur: reddish brown, dark brown, and almost black

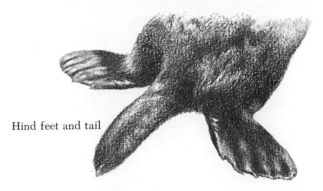

Hind feet and tail

are the shades of sea-otter fur. Silvery-gray guard hairs "luster" the fur.

Although sea otters, which live in units known as pods, are active on moonlight nights, the animals are diurnal, and usually feed three times a day, with occasional snacks between meals. The spiny sea urchin is the principal item of the diet. These marine invertebrates abound in the comparatively shallow waters around Amchitka. The sea otter can submerge four or five minutes if necessary, but most dives for food last only fifteen to thirty seconds. When the animal surfaces with a sea urchin, it rolls over on its back and uses its chest as a table, placing the sea urchin there. Bit by bit the otter pulls a large sea urchin apart (smaller sea urchins are eaten whole) and pops the morsels into its mouth. When a meal is finished, the animal delicately licks its paws.

The sea otter also eats mussels—cracking them open on the chest with a rock brought up from the same dive on which the mussel was procured—and feeds on rock oysters, scallops, sculpins, chitons, snails, limpets, flounders, and crabs. California sea otters eat abalone, prying these six- to nine-inch mussels from the rocky bottom.

Although the Japanese have kept these otters in captivity (a claim made by the Russians, too), attempts to do so here have not been successful. In 1951 biologists in the Aleutians captured thirty-five sea otters, to be moved to other coastal areas in the hope of establishing new herds. All the otters died within two days, but during the process of moving them by jeep, the reaction of one old male to being chauffeured around added an item to sea-otter lore. Whenever the jeep stopped, the otter leaned over and nipped the driver—apparently the animal's way of saying, "Keep going."

MOUNTAIN LION

Felis concolor

With a single shot you can kill a catamount, a cougar, a silver lion, a mountain screamer, a panther, a purple panther, a brown tiger, or an American lion. These are all names for the mountain lion or puma, the second largest of the cats native to the United States. Once the mountain lion, a tawny animal with a long, rounded tail and heavy, well-muscled legs, was found in all types of deer country. Today the animal is generally restricted to wilderness areas of the West and Southwest, isolated spots like the Everglades, and small areas like one in New Brunswick, where six mountain lions were recently reported.

A mature mountain lion weighs anywhere from 100 to 175 pounds and averages about 8 feet in length, including 2 feet of heavy, black-tipped tail. In the snow the tail often leaves a mark on either side of the four-toed tracks as the animal hunts over its home range, which covers many square miles and is governed by the abundance of food.

The mountain lion is primarily a night hunter. To bring down deer—the mainstay of its diet among the wild hoofed mammals—the animal waits beside a deer run or stalks its quarry. When sure of its prey the lion makes a quick dash, jumps onto the deer's withers, pulls the head down with one paw, and bites into the neck or the throat. As a rule the lion eats immediately as it likes freshly killed meat. When the animal has satisfied its hunger, the carcass is dragged to a convenient spot and covered with any type of litter—dead grasses, leaves, sticks, or pine needles. Sometimes a fresh kill is carried some distance before it is eaten and buried.

Until a kill is completely eaten or starts to decompose, the mountain lion stays in the vicinity of the latest kill; then, as the animal does not eat carrion, it moves to another area to seek new prey. No wanton killer like the timber wolf, the mountain lion takes only what it needs. Biologists have estimated that it probably kills from forty to one hundred deer a year. In areas where the mountain lion and the timber wolf have been extirpated, deer populations often become too large for their forage requirements.

With the introduction of domestic livestock into the range of the mountain lion, the animal learned that livestock was easier prey than wild animals. Colts are frequently the favorite prey of the mountain lion and our largest form of this animal has been given the scientific name *hippolestes*, horse-killer. Wherever they become stock killers mountain lions should be eliminated; otherwise they should not be killed off for they have a definite role in the predator-prey relationship in the animal community.

During its travels of as much as twenty-five miles in a single night, the animal makes scratchings or sign heaps—spots at which droppings are buried. Sooner or later these guide posts attract a female; eventually the two animals meet for a mating period that may occur at any time during the year and that usually lasts about two weeks.

Most mountain-lion kits are born in the spring, after a gestation period of a little more than ninety days. The birthplace is usually a cavern or in a dense thicket. An average litter consists of two kits, though there may be one or four. At birth a kit weighs eight to sixteen ounces and measures anywhere from eight to ten inches in length. It is well furred, but its coat is not like that of the plain ones of the parents. The pale fur is dotted with large spots of dark brown and the little tail is ringed like that of a tiger. At the end of fourteen days a kit's eyes open; at the end of three months the little animal is weaned; and by the time it is six months old the spotted coat has been replaced by one similar to an adult's.

Sometimes the mountain-lion kits stay with their mother two years. The female is solely responsible for the kit's rearing; she drives away the male, who is apt to eat the young he has sired. When a mountain-lion kit is about two months old, the mother takes it and her other young on nightly hunting trips. She teaches them the ways of a mountain lion's existence and stays with them until they are able to fend for themselves. As a result a female mates every two years, sometimes every three, and may bear young every third or fourth year during the ten or twelve years she is thought to live.

As a female and her young go out on hunting trips there are few mammals that try to prey on them. Perhaps a bear occasionally kills one or the quills of a porcupine may cause the death of one. The jaguar probably kills some mountain lions in the southern border regions of Arizona, New Mexico, and Texas, where the ranges of America's two largest cats overlap. But on the whole it is man who is the mountain lion's greatest predator.

Men hunt the mountain lion on horseback with a pack of dogs, which bring the animal to bay by treeing it. Once dogs jump a lion, the animal generally streaks over the ground for the nearest tree, up which it clambers with all possible speed. A treed animal rarely leaves its refuge, but should it jump from the first tree, it runs only a short distance before climbing another. From this perch the lion can be tumbled with a shot from a light carbine. A .30–.30 or a .32 special is sufficient to bring down a mountain lion. If the animal is shot down but not killed it may give the dogs a bad time or even claw some of them to death. If you have no aversion to eating "cat," you will discover that mountain-lion meat is not gamy and tastes something like a combination of veal and lamb.

The cry of the mountain lion has been the subject of much discussion. The animal has been reported to utter a scream that has the volume of a whistle on an old-fashioned steam locomotive or one that is similar to that of a woman in great distress. However most people who know anything about it say that, except at mating time when the animal is inclined to be extremely vociferous, these big cats utter a variety of sounds similar to those made by a house cat but of greater volume and depth. Occasionally the mountain lion, which sometimes has a melanistic or black phase, makes a reasonably good pet while still a kitten. As the animal grows older it is apt to become untrustworthy.

Down in the mesquite thickets along the Rio Grande and in the lonely mountains of southern New Mexico and Arizona live three other American cats—the jaguar, the ocelot, and the jaguarundi.

The jaguar (*F. onca*) is our largest cat. The animal is similar in appearance to a leopard; it has a deep yellow coat that is marked with black or brownish rosettelike spots. A full-grown jaguar, *El tigre* to the Mexicans, measures from six to seven feet and weighs anywhere from 175 to 250 pounds. A ground hunter, the jaguar preys mostly on the collared peccary (*Pecari angulatus*), a piglike animal which is also known as the javelina. Peccaries travel in bands frequently numbering as many as twenty-five animals and roam through the brush country of Texas and the scrub growth on the foothills and lower mountains in New Mexico and Arizona. In addition to feeding on the peccary (America's only native wild pig), the jaguar preys on deer, turkeys and other birds, turtles and other reptiles, some fish, and domestic livestock.

The second of these Border cats, the ocelot (*F. pardalis*), is about twice the size of a housecat. This animal has a pale-gray to warm-brown coat, dotted with brownish spots that are elongated on the back and flanks. A good climber and swimmer, the ocelot hunts at any hour, though it is more often out at night than during the day. Prey of the animal includes rabbits, snakes, birds, and other small wild animal life, and some poultry and young pigs and lambs. Of all our native cats this one makes the best pet.

The jaguarundi (*F. eyra*), the third of the cats in the Border area is the least-known American feline. Jaguarundis occur in two color phases: a uniform brownish-red and a solid gray. In Mexico the animal is called the "otter-cat" because it looks more like an otter than a cat and takes to the water without the usual hesitation of a cat. A full-grown jaguarundi weighs anywhere from ten to twenty pounds and measures about three to four feet. Seldom seen by man this American cat hunts through thickets for its prey—rabbits, mice, rats, and various small birds.

Another native cat is the lynx (*Lynx canadensis*), a close relative of the bobcat, but today a much rarer animal. The lynx has been retreating steadily northward, until the animal prowls only the remotest wilderness areas of upper New England and the Adirondacks and those of the Cascades and the Rocky Mountains. The lynx looks rather like an outsize tabby cat and has a bobbed tail, prominent ear tufts, and large feet. The animal's exceptionally soft fur is light gray streaked with brown. Although the staff of life for the lynx is the snowshoe hare, the animal also preys on grouse and

Bobcat

Lynx

Comparison of heads and tails

ptarmigan, songbirds and rodents. Abundance of the lynx in the North varies with the cyclic abundance of snowshoe hares.

The last of our native cats and one that has increased markedly during recent years is the bobcat (*L. rufus*). The fur of the bobcat is spotted and a light, reddish-brown in color; the tip of the animal's tail is light instead of all black like the tail of the lynx.

Also known as the wildcat, the bobcat occupies a varied habitat in middle North America from coast to coast. In forests, thickets, swamps, rocky regions, desert areas, and in mountainous country, the bobcat sleeps the day away. By night the animal, a year-round hunter, roams over a range that may be five or six square miles, inspecting every nook and cranny for possible prey.

Studies of the bobcat's food habits show that the animal prefers rabbits and such rodents as mice, rats, chipmunks, and gophers. Small birds and other small mammals and some forms of aquatic life are included in the diet, too. In the spring this cat kills fawns and in the winter it takes adult deer. To kill a deer, the bobcat jumps up and bites at the throat with its doglike teeth which are slightly ridged lengthwise. A deer rarely manages to run more than thirty feet after the initial, usually killing attack by the animal. Poultry and domestic livestock killing by the bobcat is generally the work of one that has learned such prey is easier to come by than wild prey.

The bobcat commonly dens among rocks or under a rocky ledge, less frequently in a hollow tree or stump, and in or under logs. In such a spot one to four kittens are born in the early spring, following a mating which took place in January or February. During the mat-

ing period the male announces his readiness for a mate by a horren-
dous caterwauling, which is well described by Thackeray:

A shriek and a yell
Like the devils of hell.

Once the male has mated, he goes on his way to seek another mate
if one is available. After a gestation period of about three months,
one to four young are born; two or three is the usual litter.

As a bobcat moves away from its place of birth, the animal leaves
tracks that are more rounded than those of the coyote or the dog.
The imprint of the sharp, retractable claws is never evident in the
tracks, which show a stride of eight to ten inches in a walking or
trotting gait. In addition to the bobcat's tracks, another indication
that the animal is present are the trees on which it has scratched and
sharpened its claws much as a house cat claws and scratches a tree.

By the time a bobcat is mature, a male weighs anywhere from
twelve to fourteen pounds, measures thirty to forty inches in length,
including its four- to six and one-half-inch tail. The heaviest cat on
record weighed nearly forty pounds and the known age of a captive
animal is fifteen years.

The bobcat is of such uncertain disposition that the animal does
not make a good pet. Audubon commented on the untractability
of bobcats when he wrote: "We once made an attempt at domesti-
cating one of the young of this species. Only two weeks old, it was
a most spiteful, growling and snappish little wretch, and showed no
disposition to improve its habits and manners under our kind tuition."

Bobcats like to doze in the sun: sometimes the animal uses the
limb of a tree as a perch and at other times curls up on the ground
in a berry patch or thicket. It maintains such immobility that it is
almost impossible to detect; in fact the bobcat goes about its business
in such a stealthy manner that few people are aware that they may
be in the neighborhood of North America's most numerous cat—
an animal that has been able to adapt to our civilization so well that
it is increasing in numbers and even extending its range. This increase is probably an asset in the wildlife world for the bobcat kills
deer that are sick, old or weak, and thus is one of nature's methods
to improve the deer through natural selection.

WHITE-TAILED DEER

Odocoileus virginianus

Of the three species of deer within the United States—whitetail, mule, and blacktail—the whitetail is the most numerous, the most frequently killed, and the most widespread of all our big-game animals. In various forms more than five million whitetails live in well-watered open woodlands throughout the greater part of the country, except for some areas in the West; additional herds are found in southern Canada, and south through Mexico into Central America and northern South America.

There are thought to be more whitetails now than there were in Colonial times. The present deer population is due to several factors: the many tracts of cutover timberland in brush and sprout-growth stages provide the type of habitat that the whitetail likes; fewer natural controls, such as coyotes, mountain lions, and wolves, which have been killed off in control campaigns; and the rapidity with which whitetails multiply, due to the polygamous habits of the male and the fecundity of the female. Usually a doe bears two fawns—sometimes three, occasionally four—a year, after the first year when only a single fawn is dropped.

Generally a northern whitetail is born in April or May, after a gestation period of six and one-half months. At birth a fawn is weak and unsteady on its legs; it weighs about three to five pounds, stands a foot and one-quarter at the shoulders, and has its soft, black eyes open. With its slim legs tucked under, the little animal lies quietly where it was dropped in a circular bed of matted-down grasses concealed in a thicket. In such a place the white dots of a fawn's reddish-brown coat make it appear part of the forest floor. This protective coloring and the fact that a fawn is practically odorless save most young deer from various predators, including the red fox.

For the first three or four days of its life, a fawn remains almost motionless, feeding six or seven times a day when the mother visits it. She often announces her approach with a soft bleat—the "dinner bell" for the fawn which, upon her arrival, nuzzles her warm, white belly, suckles until it is full, then drops off to sleep. This routine is continued for nearly a month, by which time a fawn is ready to accompany its mother as she goes to feed and drink in the early morning or at dusk.

During these first trips a fawn learns to use its legs in various gaits. The whitetail runs when something startles it close at hand; a trot, the whitetail's usual pace, carries the animal along at a rate of ten to twenty miles an hour; a gallop, consisting of three to four bounds, then a high curving leap of ten to twenty feet, is the gait most of us see. The whitetail's speed in a gallop is estimated at forty miles an hour. In either a trot or a gallop, the animal takes off with a whistling snort and moves with head and tail erect, the white underside of the tail or flag flashing like a semaphore as the animal streaks through the woods. The deer's sharp ears and keen nose overcome the handicap of only fair vision for detecting danger.

As a fawn moves about with its mother over well-defined, regularly used trails, the little animal's narrow-heeled, cloven hoofs leave heart-shaped prints that are miniature replicas of those made by an adult. When walking a whitetail leaves sets of prints about eighteen inches apart in which the hind prints are nearly in the prints made by the forefeet. Dew claws—imperfectly developed lateral claws— usually show in running or bounding gaits. If the adult deer comes upon a snake, the sharp, even-toed hoofs may be used to particular advantage as the deer in a frenzy jumps on the reptile, cutting it to pieces.

In September a fawn is about the size of its mother and has started to change from its dappled coat to the heavy, gray-brown winter coat. The lighter, reddish-brown coat of summer is common to all species of whitetails, with variations in the intensity of the coloration, except for the small Coues deer (*O. couesi*) of southwestern Arizona and the Big Bend country of Texas. Known locally as "fantail," "Arizona whitetail," "Sonora whitetail," or "*venado*," the Coues deer remains brownish-gray all year. Throat and underparts of all these deer are white as is the underside of the tail, flipped up at the first hint of danger; tips of the large, white-lined ears, a rim around each eye, and the cartilage of the nose are black. White hairs fringe the scent glands on the middle of the hind legs.

By the time a whitetail is fully grown the animal weighs anywhere from 50 to 300 pounds, has a tail 7 to 11 inches long, and measures up to 3¾ feet high at the shoulders. A buck, the antlered member of the family, is larger than a doe; sometimes the tips of the antlers of a mature buck are as much as 6 feet from the ground. A wild whitetail may live to be ten years old, while those that are tame or captive have lived to an age of twenty years.

¼ actual size

When a male is a year old, two little knobs appear on the forehead in front of each ear. From these knobs grow the antlers, and by August of the first year, a buck may have either single, curving spikes, which give it the name "spike-horn," or antlers may show small points, if the animal was born on an underpopulated range. These first antlers are replaced in the years to come by antlers that have numerous tines, or points, for several subsequent years.

From spring, when antler-growth starts, until September, when they begin to harden, antlers are soft and furred and fed by blood vessels. During this period when antlers are "in velvet," a buck is careful of them. Toward the latter part of the velvet stage, a buck rubs its antlers against tree trunks to scrape off the furry substance; saplings are often scarred from a buck's rubbing—a sign to look for in deer country. Occasional wallows in which there are hairs and soft summer droppings are other deer signs.

By October the antlers are hard and insensitive and remain in this condition for about four months, then they become brittle, loosen, and drop off as the animal strikes them against a low-hanging branch. As a rule a buck six or seven years old has the finest antlers; bucks older than that are apt to have poor ones—heavy beams with fewer tines. Sometimes antlers are malformed, either through injury or due to the animal's poor physical condition; occasionally a female bears antlers. Such animals as porcupines, rabbits, and squirrels gnaw on shed antlers for the calcium and other minerals contained in them.

A whitetail buck is shy, timid, and solitary. For the better part of the year, a buck keeps to himself on a home range that has a radius of four or five miles. He secretes himself in swamps and thickets when he is not moving about, and generally feeds, drinks, or goes to a salt lick at the same time each day. But during the fall rutting season, usually at its peak in November, a buck becomes bold. At this time the animal's neck swells until it is often ten inches larger than usual. On meeting in combat over a doe two bucks paw the earth, snort, and lower their antlered heads. The animals heave and push one another, often meeting head on with a mighty crash. Sometimes antlers become temporarily locked and they may even become permanently locked so that the contending bucks die of starvation. Victorious males stay with one mate for about three days before seeking another.

Except in the arid Southwest the whitetail is not gregarious, though in winter when the snow is deep the animals "yard up," as many as fifty deer concentrating in a limited area. If the yarding period is prolonged, so much browse is consumed (trees are often cropped as high as the animals can stretch) that one summer's growth does not replace what has been eaten. In such areas deer are undersized, prone to disease, and the females do not produce so many fawns as do those in areas where the numbers of wintering deer are within carrying capacity of the range. To maintain the proper numbers of wintering deer in areas where there is insufficient browse or where the animals destroy farm and garden crops to supplement their diet, heavy shooting of both does and bucks should be permitted.

Sometimes chemical repellents, though costly, are successful in stopping crop depredation by deer. More recently the inexpensive fire-cracker rope, a length of chemically treated hemp rope on which twelve firecrackers are strung, has been used to scare deer out of milo and pea fields. The rope is designed to burn slowly, with the crackers exploding about every thirty minutes.

The fire-cracker rope has been used successfully in western states to control waterfowl depredations by scaring the birds out of grain fields. For information on controlling crop depredation by deer or regulating animals that have become a nuisance in suburban areas, consult your state game commission or write the Branch of Game Management, Fish and Wildlife Service, Department of the Interior, Washington 25, D. C.

A whitetail crops and nibbles its food. Deer browsing may be differentiated from rabbit browsing in that deer pull or break off twigs, whereas rabbits cut twigs by biting. Once a deer has broken off its browse, the animal chops up the food with its twenty-four grinding teeth on the back of the jaw and, like a cow, chews and rechews its food.

The whitetail eats cedar, spruce, acorns, and apples, in fall and winter; in summer the animal browses on leaves of many kinds, grasses, mosses, and lichens, buds, berries, fruits, and mushrooms, and many aquatic plants, including pond lilies.

A deer often wades out into water until it is belly deep, to pull up great mouthfuls of water lilies, at the same time getting partial protection from deer flies, black flies, mosquitoes, and other insect pests which annoy it. The ability to swim is common to all species and subspecies of whitetails. Even the key deer (*O. v. clavium*), numbering now about one hundred animals and no larger than a collie dog, swims from Big Pine Key in Florida to nearby keys along the coast in search of food and fresh water. Buoyed up by the air-filled hairs of its coat, the whitetail swims along at a speed of about four miles an hour.

Historically the whitetail was important as a source of food and clothing for the Indians and for the Colonists, who enacted laws for the animal's conservation as early as 1646, when Rhode Islanders declared the first closed season. Currently the whitetail has an esthetic worth which cannot be accurately evaluated and an enormous economic and sporting value. In recent years hunters have paid nearly thirty-eight million dollars annually for licenses and killed almost six hundred thousand whitetails—only a fraction of the number that could and should be killed to maintain a proper balance; for when the animals are uncrowded, individual deer are larger and stronger, and herds produce larger annual crops of fawns.

MULE DEER

Odocoileus hemionus

Next in numerical importance to the whitetail is the mule deer, a stout-bodied animal with big eyes, big ears, a white rump, and a rounded white tail tipped with black. More than three million mule deer live in the West on both sides of the Rocky Mountains from Canada to Mexico. In addition there are herds of mule deer in the southern provinces of western Canada and in the northern states of Mexico.

Although more of a mountain animal than the whitetail, the mule deer is also found in cactus and sagebrush country, where it covers the ground in great bounding leaps of four or more feet, and seems to land with all four feet striking the ground at once. These leaps temporarily give the animal an elevated vantage point from which it can see pursuing enemies; they also give the mule deer the local name "jumping deer" in Manitoba.

The mule deer, more gregarious than the whitetail, is a migrator. At the end of the fall rutting season, herds of mule deer move down from elevations of seven to eight thousand feet, where the animals have browsed on aspen and pine since June, to lower regions where they winter, feeding on shrubs and grasses.

Much of the life history and behavior of the mule deer is similar to that of the whitetail, but there are differences. The mule deer runs with its tail held down, often stopping after it has gone some distance to turn around and look back, whereas a whitetail keeps on going once it has started to move. During rutting season a mule buck sometimes has a harem of three or four does, and as this deer mates later in the season than the whitetail, the twin fawns are born late in June or early in July.

The mule deer is taken by more predators than a whitetail; at fawning time black and grizzly bears, bobcats, coyotes, mountain lions, lynxes, and wolverines kill some young mule deer, and under favorable conditions the golden eagle, according to the Denver Wildlife Research Laboratory, kills both young and adults. Frequently the deer outrun these predators and sometimes the animals kill predators by kicking them to death, particularly in defense of young.

During the 1920's the mule deer was subject to the hoof-and-mouth disease and thousands of the animals died or were shot to stop the epidemic. Today the animals, a nuisance in many agricultural areas and a competitor of elk for food, have staged such a comeback that hunters kill more than 300,000 each year.

BLACK-TAILED DEER
Odocoileus columbianus

The third of the American deer is the blacktail, a smaller animal than the mule deer. The blacktail was first noticed by Lewis and Clark at the mouth of the Columbia River. This animal has shorter and broader ears than those of the mule deer and a bushier tail that is black on the outside and white underneath. Sometimes a blacktail holds its tail erect in a fashion similar to a running whitetail; at other times the tail droops rather like that of a running mule deer.

Originally classed as a distinct species but now often considered a subspecies of the mule deer, the black-tailed deer is confined to the Pacific coast from San Diego to the vicinity of Sitka in Alaska. Also known as the "coast deer," two forms of the black-tailed deer in herds numbering more than a million, are resident in the United States. In the northern part of its range the animal is the Columbian blacktail; in the lower part of the range, an area south of San Francisco Bay, the animal is called the southern blacktail. And in Alaska a third form is known as the Sitka black-tailed deer.

A characteristic of the black-tailed deer in Alaska is a vertical migration. As snow melts from higher elevations, many of the deer, particularly bucks and yearlings, climb as high as 2,500 feet. There they stay until late fall, when the deep snows force them to lower feeding grounds. By midwinter, if the snow is extremely deep, all deer may be driven to the beaches, where they eat kelp and other marine vegetation. Ordinarily their food consists of huckleberry bushes, ground dogwood, fine meadow grasses, skunk cabbage, and cedar.

In late summer or early fall, hunting the blacktail in Alaska means a climb of 2,000 feet or more, when the animals are sometimes at higher elevations than goats. Later in the fall many bucks are taken within a few hundred feet of tidewater. In Alaska more blacktails are killed each year than any other big game. The animals in the Territory and the United States are likely to maintain their numbers if their brush-range habitat is not destroyed.

White-tail   Mule   Black-tail

Comparison of heads and tails

ELK OR WAPITI

Cervus canadensis

"Heard at a little distance, and in its proper place, it is one of the grandest and most beautiful sounds in nature." So wrote Theodore Roosevelt concerning the call of the American elk or wapiti. The call or bugling of the elk starts on a low note, rises until it has a bugle-like tone, then "flats" as the animal ends with a sort of grunt or bray. The terminal note of the elk's call has given the animal the name "jackass deer" in some localities. But once heard the bugling of a bull elk during rutting season is a call of the wild never to be forgotten.

Up until the middle 1800's the bugling of elk reverberated in forested areas throughout the greater part of the country. The eastern form of the animal was exterminated by 1860; the western forms were greatly reduced as the animals were hunted by Indians and early settlers for meat and hides, for sport, and for the two upper canine teeth which were used as charms. The Indians ornamented garments with elk teeth and Audubon was presented with a garment on which fifty-six elk teeth had been sewn. Charm hunters killed thousands of animals, taking only the two upper teeth, and leaving the animals where they had been killed.

Today the distinctive call of the elk is almost exclusively confined to special areas—National Parks, National Forests, and National Wildlife Refuges—in western states, where four forms of elk live in widely differing environments: at high altitudes in the Rocky Mountains; in the dense rain forests of the Pacific coast; and out on the hot, arid plains of southern California, where the elk (*C. nannodes*) is small and pallid—far different from the Roosevelt elk, the largest of our elks and named for Theodore Roosevelt in 1897. In the East there are two small herds of introduced elk which feed in abandoned pastures on Jefferson National Forest in Virginia. Sometimes at dawn or again at dusk you can see a few of these animals as you drive along Blue Ridge Parkway. But the herds there are dying out and no plans are being made to restock them.

Outside the United States there are elk in the southern parts of the central Canadian provinces; on Afognak, one of the Aleutian Islands, where the original eight introduced animals have multiplied to more than three hundred; and in Australia, where the animals eat the bark of the pokaka tree instead of their native aspen—a nice example of an introduced species adapting itself to the forage at hand.

An indigenous North American animal, the elk was called "wapiti" by the Shawnee Indians. Wapiti, meaning "white deer," is probably a reference to the elk's light rump patch. The Indian name is far more accurate than "elk," the name given the animal by early European settlers in America, who thought it was a form of moose. Our animal, commonly though erroneously called elk by most of us, is similar to the European stag and almost the same as the Thian stag of Turkestan.

The bugling of the bull elk is loudest during the rutting season, which lasts from September through October. During this period the polygamous males fight to round up harems and a single bull sometimes gathers together thirty or more cows. Harems are maintained throughout the year and are relinquished only when a stronger bull ousts the reigning "sultan."

Fights among bulls are furious; the contending animals, necks arched, veins distended, hair on end, come together with such force that the repeated crashes of their branching antlers sound as if a company of men were fencing with bone rapiers. During fights animals accompany their pushing and straining with numerous bellows and grunts. Sooner or later the weaker of the contending animals gives way and quits the field of battle. At the end of the rutting season the victorious males and their harems leave the high altitudes, where, since May or June, they have fed on various mountain grasses and sedges, and head for lower regions, where the weather in winter is less severe and the foraging is easier.

In May and June of the following year when the elk are again back in the mountains, the females leave the herds and seek thickets in which to drop the young—born after a gestation period of about eight and one-half months. Usually there is a single calf, though sometimes a cow bears twins. At birth a calf weighs thirty to forty pounds, measures about three feet, and has a light-tan coat with white spots on the back and flanks. The little animal nurses at once, then in an hour or two gets up and takes a few wobbly steps before returning to the thicket in which it was born. Here a calf stays quietly for a week or more, waiting for each nursing period—frequently announced by a soft bark from the mother. At the end of the first week a calf runs rapidly and will eat some vegetation, though it often nurses well into the winter before being completely weaned. As soon as a calf is sufficiently strong it accompanies its mother to the highest part of the summer range. Here for several hours early in the morning and again late in the afternoon the calf, like all other members of the herd, feeds on various grasses.

¼ actual size

By August an elk calf loses most of its spots; by September its shaggy infant coat is replaced by its first adult coat, but it is not fully grown until it is four years old. A full-grown bull elk weighs 700 to 800 pounds, measures 7½ to 9½ feet in length, and stands 4½ to 5 feet at the shoulders. The antlers, huge, branched, many tined, extend far back over the shoulders in the direction of the rump patch from which dangles a tail 5 to 7 inches in length.

A bull sheds its round-horned antlers each year, late in December or during January; spike-horn bulls, whose spikes measure 8 to 15 inches in length, shed theirs in May or June. Antler growth starts again in March and April. It is in the "velvet stage," soft and furred, during the summer, and hardens by fall. During the period of antler growth a bull is thin and emaciated and stays by itself.

Cows, smaller than bulls, are hornless and weigh from 400 to 600 pounds. Both animals exchange the short summer coat, worn from May to August, for a heavier winter coat. In winter a mature elk of either sex has a dark brown head, mane, and legs, and a yellow-haired body.

As elk herds move between summer and winter ranges over fairly well-defined trails, visit mineral licks, or go to the water's edge to drink, the animals leave even-toed tracks, measuring four inches in length, that are smaller and less pointed than those of moose and similar to those made by young domestic cattle.

Other indications of elk country are saplings with broken limbs on which the animals have rubbed their antlers to scrape off the velvet and to polish them. Aspen trees on which the elk feeds are often barked—that is, the animals have gnawed off quantities of bark with the lower incisor teeth. Additional elk signs are the flat, elongated or circular chips, similar to those of domestic cattle, which the animals drop in summer and the pellet-form droppings of winter; wallows or depressions in the grass where the animals have lain down horse-fashion; and pawed snow where they have dug for browse.

At fawning time black and grizzly bears and coyotes, mountain lions, and wolves take some young elk. Today there are not so many of these predators as there used to be. Adult elk usually escape predators by taking off at a gallop which builds up to thirty-five miles an hour, or defend themselves with hard, fast blows from their hoofs; these blows can break the back of a wolf.

The elk, an excellent big-game animal generally hunted with a high-powered rifle equipped with a telescopic sight, has become a problem in some areas. Like the white-tailed deer, the elk has adapted itself so well to the fringes of civilization that it competes with domestic livestock for food and range in addition to competing with other forms of wildlife for the same essentials. According to Walter H. Kittams, park service biologist at Yellowstone National Park, forage requirements of one elk equal those of two deer, two antelopes, or two bighorn sheep.

In areas where elk exceed the carrying capacity of the range or endanger other forms of wildlife or domestic stock, remedial steps should be taken to reduce the size of the herds. But civilization's demands should never eliminate the elk and that bugling which is a true call of the wild.

MOOSE

Alces americana

From mid-September until the end of November the quiet of wilderness areas in half a dozen northern states * is broken by the crash of antlers as one bull moose fights another during the period of the rut. The crashing of antlers also resounds in the forested areas of the Canadian Provinces and in the vast, timbered stretches of Alaska. Conflicts between bull moose are preceded by low, challenging grunts. Early in the season such encounters seem more like sparring bouts than actual fights. But as the season progresses the ungainly, dark-brown animals with hand-shaped antlers and banjo-like muzzles charge one another with battering-ram force, tearing up the forest floor and trampling down bushes and saplings as they do so.

A bull moose on the offensive tries to knock its opponent sidewise. If such a maneuver is successful the challenger follows through with another thrust of its broad antlers. Such a thrust may puncture the ribs and drive one of the several short prongs on the outer edges of the antlers into a vital organ. Frequently before a challenging bull can deliver a crippling blow, the weaker animal quits the fight and, with antlers broken or hide gashed, lumbers off at a swinging trot to seek refuge in a willow thicket or swampy hideaway before starting out on another quest for a mate. Sometimes, though less frequently than with deer or caribou, the antlers of fighting bull moose interlock, and the two animals die of starvation or are killed by wolves or by a bear that has not yet settled down for its winter sleep.

A victorious bull stays for a week or ten days with the cow that it has won. Then it goes off to battle with another bull for another cow. In Alaska the Kenai moose (*A. gigas*), the largest of its kind on earth, has harems of several cows.

Bulls and cows have the same coloration; the animals are dark brown or brownish black for the most part; their muzzles are gray; and the bellies and lower legs are light brown. A cow is about twenty-five percent smaller than a bull, which weighs anywhere from nine hundred to fourteen hundred pounds. A Kenai bull moose often

* Maine, Michigan, Minnesota, Montana, Wyoming, and Idaho.

weighs as much as eighteen hundred pounds. A cow has no horns and a smaller "bell" than a bull. A bell is the growth of skin and hair which hangs from the throat and measures from four to ten inches.

During the mating period a cow often has her offspring of the previous year with her as she goes about bellowing to attract a bull. But early in May of the year following a mating, a female drives away her year-old progeny, then seeks the safety of a thicket or an island to drop her new calf. The first-born of a cow, which usually mates at two or three years of age, is a single calf; thereafter twins are the rule, with triplets a rarity.

At birth a moose calf weighs about twenty or twenty-five pounds, has its eyes open, and is covered by a woolly coat. The muzzle is black and there are dark spots over each eye. Although a calf has a bell, the high shoulder hump and overhanging upper lip of an adult are not present and there are no spots on its bay-colored coat. A calf walks a few hours after birth, but spends the first weeks of its life close to its birthplace; it is often the prey of bears or wolves, and less frequently of cougars, coyotes, or wolverines. An adult moose can usually outrun these predators or trample them to death. As soon as a calf is strong enough it travels with its mother to higher country to which the bulls have already repaired.

All summer long a cow and her calf wander along the banks of streams and the edges of lakes, feeding on such land vegetation as asters, ferns, and jewelweed, and on such floating aquatics as water lilies and duckweed or submerged water plants like burreed and duck potato. To get the floating plants a moose wades out into the water and scoops them up; to reach submerged plants the animal wades out until it is under water, then comes up with a mouthful of burreed or duck potato, blowing amid a shower of spray from its antlers. Moose also seek water to get protection from insect pests.

The moose is a good swimmer and seems to prefer to cross lakes rather than go around them. The animal swims with its head and part of the neck out of the water. When a calf, swimming with its mother, becomes tired, the little animal sometimes rests its neck on that of its mother or throws front legs over her neck and is towed.

During the summer sojourn at higher elevations the bull moose grows its new set of antlers, to replace those shed the previous De-

¼ actual size

cember. In April or May little bumps on each side of the forehead
start to swell, then enlarge until they are knobs covered with a black
fuzz and fed by the blood which flows through a network of veins.
Finally the knobs develop into antlers: spikes six to eight inches
long for a yearling; a fork-horn for a two-year old; and narrow
palmate, or hand-shaped, antlers with three or four irregular points
on the outer edges for a three-year old. By August antlers are fully
developed and white and streaked with blood. As a bull rubs and
polishes his antlers on small trees without low branches the antlers
become hard and brown. When a bull reaches maturity at twelve to
fifteen years the antler spread may be as much as five feet from tip
to tip in the case of the common moose and six feet or better for the
Kenai moose. The antlers of one Kenai moose weighed eighty-five
pounds. As a bull grows older antlers and the bell become smaller.

Movements of moose are purely local and are controlled by
weather and available food. Sometimes the moose is forced to leave
a favorite pond due to muskrats that clean out the pond lilies. As
the weather grows colder, the moose travel to lower elevations. When
the snow becomes deep, the animals "yard up" in spots protected by
stands of close-growing trees. Such spots are crisscrossed by numerous irregular paths and sometimes cover several acres. Yards are
usually occupied by a bull, a cow, and two young; older bulls tend
to be solitary. In the area of a yard the moose eat all the browse they
can reach, often "cleaning" fir trees to a height of eleven feet. Sometimes an animal straddles a sapling, "rides it down," with its heavy
body to pull off all the tenderest parts.

The staple, year-round food of the moose is the leaves and twigs
of the willow. In winters when the snow is extremely deep and
buries the willows until only the tips show, the moose has to compete with snowshoe hares for food; this competition does not occur in every winter as the abundance of snowshoe hares follows a
cyclic pattern. Moose also eat the leaves and twigs of aspens, balsams,

birches, maples, and mountain ashes; sometimes poplar bark is included in the diet. From the animal's habit of feeding on woody plants comes the Algonquin Indian name, *musee*, "wood-eater," whence comes our word "moose."

In a day's feeding the moose eats forty to fifty pounds of browse. Unchecked a moose herd can increase beyond the carrying capacity of the winter forage plants that support it. This rise in numbers results in range deterioration and starvation in severe winters.

Frequently the moose lives for eighteen or twenty years in the area in which it was born, if conditions there are favorable. As the animal moves about its territory of perhaps one square mile, it leaves cloven tracks, similar to those of an elk but larger and more pointed. The seven-inch tracks of a bull moose show a stride of three to eight feet and the imprint of the dew claws. The tracks of a bull toe out; those of a cow are inclined to be straight.

Moose feed in the early morning or late in the afternoon or early evening. As the animals feed their large ears are flapped back and forth to pick up the slightest sound that indicates danger. Even while sleeping the moose keeps its ears in constant motion and at the first hint of danger is up and away. Surprisingly the animal despite its size can slip through the woods without a sound, its head held back so that the antlers do not catch on low-hanging branches.

If you go out to observe moose remember that the animal is inclined to be belligerent. Railroaders in Alaska learned this through experience. During the winter of 1952 near Kaswitna a bull moose was being herded down the tracks of the Alaska railroad by the maintenance crew in a gas car. Progress was being made until the bull did an about-face. The operator put the car into reverse as quickly as possible. But he was not fast enough; the bull charged with such force that the animal rammed its head through the supposedly shatterproof windshield. Like a vanquished bull moose at mating time, the maintenance crew took off in their car, leaving the bull to the length of track which it considered its own territory.

The next day the same bull charged the gas car again; this time the animal broke off the bolts and hinges of the windshield support. Two days later the animal charged a locomotive; this encounter proved that an iron horse is stronger than a bellicose bull moose.

PRONGHORN (ANTELOPE)

Antilocapra americana

Early French-Canadian explorers discovered vast herds of deer-like creatures racing across or feeding on the sage-dotted prairies of the Northwest. These hollow-horned animals, with large, pointed ears and rumps like white rosettes, were pronghorns—an animal peculiar to North America, and well adapted for life on open prairie, rolling plain, or tableland.

The body hair of the pronghorn is hollow and acts as good insulation against prairie winds; the large windpipe of the animal makes for easy breathing; the large, strong leg bones permit long runs and high speeds. The large black eyes have a particularly wide angle range of vision and are so powerful that the distance the pronghorn can see is comparable to the distance a man can see with an eight-power telescope. In fact that animal's vision is such that one old guide and hunter, quoted in *Mammals of America*, was moved to comment:

What a live Antelope [pronghorn] don't see between dawn and dark isn't visible from his standpoint; and while you're a gawkin' at him thro' that 'ere glass to make out whether he's a rock or a goat, he's a countin' your cartridges and fixin's, and makin' up his mind which way he'll scoot when you disappear in the draw to sneak on 'im—and don't you forget it.

The pronghorn is not a true antelope and is the only present representative of a distinct family of ruminants alive in the Pleistocene age. Formerly the animal—known too as antelope, prongbuck, and prong-horn antelope—was so numerous that millions covered a range that included southern Alberta and Saskatchewan, the western states between the Missouri River and the Pacific Coast, and northern Mexico. Today about 200,000 pronghorns occupy only parts of their original range, with the largest herds in Montana, New Mexico, and Wyoming.

Pronghorns are gregarious; in herds of fifty to one hundred animals they feed over a somewhat circular area, whose diameter is three to four miles. Once a day the animals water. Their concentrations are determined by forage, water, protection, and competition with domestic livestock.

Late in summer mature pronghorn bucks are restless. It is their peculiar habit at this season to make sudden jumps from a standing position to the right or left. They fight among themselves, and collect females; sometimes there are as many as fifteen does in a harem. About eight months after the fall mating period the female moves a little away from the herd to give birth. The first time a female bears young she drops only a single kid; subsequently twins are born each year. In the North kids are born in late May; in the South between the end of February and the middle of March. At birth a kid weighs four to five pounds, measures sixteen to seventeen inches at the shoulder, and is paler than its mother. A male kid has little hairy spots on the forehead where the horns will grow and a black streak across the muzzle and on each side of the lower jaw. A female kid has neither of these marks which differentiate the sexes at birth.

A young pronghorn lies quietly where it is dropped for two or three days; the mother moves cautiously between her twins, hidden some distance from one another, to nurse them. By the time a kid is four days old it can outrun a man and by the time it is ten days old it can keep pace with its mother. At three weeks the little animal eats green vegetation; at three months it acquires a coat similar to that of an adult—the upperparts a rich tan, the underparts, white, and the rump patches all white.

At an early age a kid starts flashing the white rump patches which are a combination of hairs shorter in the center and longer as they radiate outward. When a pronghorn is alarmed or excited, the animal is able to flare its rump patches so that they look like great, white rosettes. Flared patches reflect so much light that another pronghorn two miles away can see the warning, and in turn warn other members of the herd as it was warned. When the rump is flared, musk is secreted from glands in the rosette, which can be detected by another pronghorn several hundred yards away. As soon as an entire herd has been alerted, it gathers at a central point, then takes off at a smooth, level gait in which there is hardly a discernible rise at each bound.

A pronghorn on the run can probably average thirty to forty

miles an hour; and it can run fifty, sixty, or even seventy miles an hour for short distances. Long runs at high speeds usually result in the sudden, complete collapse of the animal. The pronghorn generally outruns the coyote or the wolf, which kill some kids, however, and old or disabled animals. A running pronghorn neither stops for wire fences nor goes over them. A horizontal rather than a vertical leaper, the animal has learned to go under such fences or between the strands with no appreciable slackening of speed. Sometimes a strand or two is snapped as the animal passes beneath.

¼ actual size

An adult male pronghorn weighs about 100 to 140 pounds, measures 3 ½ feet from tip of nose to tip of tail and stands 3 ½ to 4 feet high at the shoulder. A male has a black streak across the muzzle, black patches on the sides of the neck, and horns that are longer than its ears; he runs with his nose pointed downward. A female is smaller than a male and usually lacks the black mask and jaw spots. Her horns are shorter than the ears, and she runs with her nose held horizontally. Both animals run with their mouths open.

Unlike deer the pronghorn has no dew or lateral claws, and it is the only animal on this continent with but two toes on each foot. The pointed hoof marks are similar to those of domestic sheep, with the imprint of the front hoofs slightly longer than those of the hind feet. The pronghorn paws away snow to get at low-growing vegetation and also paws out little pockets in the earth in which to deposit wastes.

Both males and females shed their horns and continue to shed them each year for the five to seven years that a pronghorn lives. The bucks shed theirs in the late fall; the does and young somewhat later. The horns originate from skin tissue, which covers two bony pedicals attached to the skull. From these pedicals grow the horns—a combination of black hair and tissue, which becomes hard by July and breaks off in November. Such animals as porcupines, prairie dogs, and gophers gnaw on the shed horns of pronghorns for the calcium contained in them. Sometimes the pronghorn itself gnaws on the old horns, which even in dry climates generally disintegrate within a year or two.

The pronghorn, a good swimmer, was formerly one of our most curious animals. A white handkerchief tied to a stick pushed into the ground was one way of piquing the animal's curiosity. Sooner or later the pronghorn was tolled in by the fluttering handkerchief. The animal rarely came closer than forty or fifty yards. At the slightest hint of danger, it took off after pawing the ground once or twice and snorting explosively. More wary today, the animal seldom comes in so close to investigate, and is more easily scared. It still takes off in the same manner, and then covers the ground in leaps of twelve to twenty feet, the white rump patches flashing like a heliograph to warn all members of the herd grazing in the area that danger is at hand.

Other members of the deer family in North America are the reindeer (*Rangifer tarandus*), an introduced species from the Old World, and the two forms of caribou, the barren-ground caribou (*R. arcticus*) and the woodland (*R. caribou*).

The reindeer, a clove-brown animal, was imported from Siberia. More than twelve hundred of these semidomesticated animals were brought into Alaska between 1891 and 1902. Although reindeer are not so numerous as they were some twenty years ago when there were about 600,000 in Alaska, good-sized herds still roam over the tundra from St. Michael on the south shore of Norton Sound to Barrow on the Arctic Ocean. And there are herds on the Pribilof Islands and on Nunivak, St. Lawrence, Kodiak, and Umnak.

On Nunivak Island, a national wildlife refuge in Bering Sea, reindeer share the refuge with the muskox (*Ovibos moschatus*), one-time associate of the woolly mammoth. The muskox, a brownish-black animal with broad, flat, and hollow horns, was exterminated in Alaska about a century ago. In 1930, thirty-four muskoxen were brought in from Greenland and released on Nunivak, where the herd maintains itself, and in the 1950's numbered nearly 80.

The barren-ground caribou, found in Alaska, includes two subspecies—the Grant caribou (*R. granti*) of the Alaska Peninsula and the Stone caribou (*R. stonei*) of the eastern half of the Interior and the Arctic Shelf. Caribou herds are constantly on the move in search of the slow-growing lichens or "reindeer moss," their principal winter food supply. Herds sometimes cover as much as 600 miles in search of this food.

The other species of caribou, the darker woodland animal, inhabits forested areas of Canada. Less nomadic than the barren-ground caribou, the woodland species is also less gregarious. The animals band together in winter, but in summer they travel in family groups or alone. There may be a few woodland caribou in northern Minnesota; occasionally some are seen in northern parts of eastern and central states along the Canadian Border, for these areas are the extreme southern limit of the woodland caribou's range.

BUFFALO (AMERICAN BISON)

Bison bison

In the early 1800's more than sixty million buffaloes, or American bison, roamed the continent from Great Slave Lake in north-central Canada southward into Mexico, as far east as upstate Pennsylvania, and westward to the Blue Mountains of Oregon. Most herds were on the vast central prairies and high plains on the western part of the buffaloes' range, over which the animals traveled in small herds from summer to winter feeding grounds; herds often covered two, three, or four hundred miles in these seasonal shifts.

The buffalo was the source of food, clothing, and shelter for the Plains Indians, who also used buffalo chips, the hardened droppings of the animal, for fuel. The Indians hunted the buffaloes in various ways: they stampeded entire herds over cliffs, at places like the Buffalo Jump-Off in the Yellowstone River valley, north of Gardiner, Montana; drove them into slaughter pens; or fired the prairies to put herds at their mercy. Only a fraction of the animals thus slaughtered were butchered; the rest were left to rot or for the wolves and coyotes which, with cougars and black and grizzly bears, killed some young and old animals.

Even such wasteful hunting methods did little to reduce the great herds of buffaloes. What brought about the animals' destruction was their calculated slaughter by the white man in order to subdue the Indians as the nation expanded westward and recognized the agricultural possibilities of the lands over which the animals grazed. The peoples of a fast-growing nation needed the buffaloes' habitat— a habitat that had supported relatively small numbers of men but which was to support millions as the nation's granary. By 1889 what had once been America's most numerous hoofed mammal numbered only 541 head.

One of the places within the United States on which you can see a bit of the "America-that-was" is the National Bison Range near Moiese in western Montana. From High Point on the Range I have watched individuals in a small herd of buffaloes, two thousand feet below, move ponderously in to and out from saucer-like water holes. Huge and humpbacked, the animals seemed blacker than they actually were against the fall yellowing of the prairie grasses; even at this distance their scraggly knee-hair made them appear as if they had on tattered pantalettes.

Seen nearby a buffalo is an unfriendly looking beast, with a massive, sharp-horned, shaggy, and bewhiskered head. An enormously strong animal, it is unpredictable. Though ordinarily timid and inoffensive, a buffalo may turn on horse or man without provocation. Ernest Thompson Seton, in his *Lives of Game Animals*, states that "A buffalo male or female, young or old, is a savage, treacherous animal, always a menace to man or beast, never to be trusted."

Because of the animal's unpredictability much of the Bison Range's 18,000 acres is restricted and various areas are fenced with miles of big-game fencing and are closed by heavy gates. There is an exhibition pen around which you can walk or drive to observe the buffaloes. You can also see elk, mule and white-tailed deer, pronghorn antelope, and mountain sheep on the Bison Range, established in 1908 for the preservation of the buffalo and other big game.

The buffalo is a member of the cattle family, and when Cortez saw one in 1519 in the zoo of the Aztec ruler, Montezuma, the Spanish conqueror described the buffalo as "a rare combination of several divers animals." When the first Spanish explorers reached what is now Texas and Oklahoma, they were astounded by the numbers of buffaloes, which they described as "crooked-back oxen."

Young of the bison are born in May—offspring of a pair that mated the previous July or August. Actual mating is preceded by furious fighting—seldom fatal—among males for the favors of cows. About nine to nine and one-half months after mating a cow's time is at hand; she moves a little distance from her particular herd, and gives birth to a single calf. Twins are rare, albinos so rare that in the first half of the twentieth century there were only three albinos among the five thousand buffaloes within the United States. (Big Medicine, an albino with a brow of curly black hair, could be seen on the Bison Range as recently as 1956.) Though a young buffalo nurses for nearly a year, two or three days after birth a calf is strong enough to follow the herd. In about two months the shoulder hump becomes evident and at about the same time the horns appear on the male; those of a female show somewhat later.

A buffalo is not fully mature until the animal is eight years old, but it usually mates at three years of age. Normally buffaloes live about fifteen years; some have lived as long as forty. At maturity a male averages 1,600 to 2,000 pounds, though Black Dog, an animal in the herd at the Wichita Mountains Wildlife Refuge, attained a weight of 2,800 pounds. The average mature male measures 10 to 11½ feet, stands 5½ to 6 feet at the shoulders, and has a tail of nearly 2 feet. A male has a red-brown coat, lighter on the shoulders and darker on the head, legs, and tail. A cow is lighter in color, has a less massive hump, and is less bearded. The horns of a cow are more slender and curved than those of a bull. Both animals have tufted tails and both have lighter hair in winter than in summer.

¼ actual size

Although old bulls are often solitary and three or four mature bachelors frequently herd together, buffaloes are the most gregarious of the wild cattle. They band together in small herds, actually family groups led by a cow. Within this family group the most important animal is a prime bull between four and eight years of age. Such an animal appears completely disinterested in its fellow buffaloes and everything else as it stares myopically about. To compensate for poor eyesight, a buffalo's senses of hearing and smell are acute.

In winter buffaloes stay close together; in summer they fan out over a greater area to feed. As they feed—various prairie grasses are the staple diet, though occasionally low-growing shrubs and the twigs and leaves of aspens are eaten—the animals leave tracks similar to those of domestic cattle, with a cloven hoof about 5½ inches across.

The hoof prints are often found around the bases of trees, telegraph poles, and boulders against which a buffalo rubs itself and on which it usually leaves some long, scraggly hairs. These rubbing or scratching posts are the means whereby the animal gets temporary relief from the various insects which bite and cause its skin to itch. The buffalo also rolls and wallows to relieve its itching skin. Sometimes blackbirds, cowbirds, or magpies "ride" a buffalo and feed on the mosquitoes or flies in its coat.

Although the crossing of buffalo with cattle, resulting in a hybrid known as "cattalo," and with yaks, the offspring of which is called "yakalo," was once considered promising, it has not proved commercially practical.

Saved from extermination largely through the efforts of the American Bison Society, the New York Zoological Society, and the work of Theodore Roosevelt who persuaded the Federal government to set aside areas for the buffalo's preservation, the buffalo is one of the few native animals that have appeared on our postage stamps. It is pictured on the four cent Trans-Mississippi issue of 1898 and on the thirty-five cent regular issue of 1932, and a buffalo skull is in one corner of the stamp issued in 1940 to commemorate the centennial of the Pony Express.

The animal shown on these stamps is the plains buffalo, closely related to the wood buffalo (*B. b. athabascae* Rhoads), a larger and darker species than the plains animal. Today there are wood buffaloes in Wood Buffalo Park in northern Alberta and another herd, a wild one, in the Northwest Territories.

In addition to the National Bison Range, there are several other places where you can see these representatives of the vanishing prairie. Under controlled conditions herds roam in Yellowstone National Park, Wind Cave National Park in southwestern South Dakota, at the Wichita Mountains Wildlife Refuge in southwestern Oklahoma, at Big Delta, about ninety miles southeast of Fairbanks in Alaska, and in some State Parks like Custer in South Dakota. But in studying or photographing buffaloes remember that the animals may charge you head-on if frightened.

MOUNTAIN GOAT

Oreamnos americanus

To see the whiskered, humpbacked mountain goat in the animal's own environment requires a great deal of climbing in rough, rocky territory. This white-coated animal, with daggerlike horns as black as its eyes, lips, and hoofs, lives among the crags of mountains in south-central Idaho, along the Continental Divide in western Montana, and in the snow-capped Cascade Range of southern Washington. Outside the United States there are goats in the mighty coast range of southeastern Alaska, in the Chugach and Talkeetna Mountains, and in the Copper River area; they are also distributed throughout the greater part of British Columbia, and are in the southern Yukon, too.

Our goat is not a true goat; a member of the ox family, the animal is a type of antelope and closely related to the chamois of Europe and the serow of Asia. In 1804 Lewis and Clark obtained the first skins and in 1816 M. De Blainville published the first scientific account of the animal, whose range and distribution have been little affected by civilization or over-hunting.

Although mountain goats are sought in a few accessible areas, most big-game hunters prefer animals that are easier to locate and ones that provide spectacular trophies. As a game animal the goat was held in low esteem by Theodore Roosevelt. The late President once shot a billy, which was accompanied by several nannies and their kids. After the reverberation of the President's shot had died away, one nanny ran only a short distance from the spot where the billy was dropped; she then started browsing as unconcernedly as if the calm of her mountain fastness had never been disturbed. Looking at the animal Roosevelt is said to have snorted: "The White Goat is the fool-hen among beasts of the chase!"

Except for the Dall sheep of Alaska—the only wild white sheep in the world—the mountain goat is the only other native ruminant whose coat is white all year. Sometimes it is tinged with yellow in summer, and occasionally an animal has a few brown hairs in the mane or tail.

This coat is a combination dense, fine wool protected by long, shaggy guard hairs. Such a coat makes it possible for the animal to live above timberline, where the wind is strong and icy and where snow often lies on the peaks throughout the year.

The hoofs of the goat—a sturdy creature weighing anywhere from one hundred and fifty to three hundred pounds—are so formed that the animal is more sure-footed than the mountain sheep. The sole of the toe acts like a suction cup, for it is concave, and the clefts between toes open towards the front. Thus equipped the animal moves around sure-footedly on a home range that is usually about five miles in diameter.

Generally the male goat is solitary; for long periods it stands stiffly on a table rock, apparently studying the countryside with its yellow eyes. Frequently the goat assumes a position that distinguishes it from all other horned mammals by sitting down on its haunches for minutes at a time, to watch something that has aroused its curiosity.

Although capable of ten- or twelve-foot leaps, the animal does not make the spectacular jumps of the mountain sheep. The goat often gets from ledge to ledge by standing on its hind feet, and placing the forefeet on the ledge above. Then in a manner somewhat akin to shinnying it slowly and carefully inches itself up the face of the ledge and over the edge and onto the higher shelf. As the animal moves over its range at a plodding gait it leaves squarish tracks which show cloven hoofs. Other signs of goat are depressions in the dust or snow where the animal has slept or rested, piles of shed wool, and the rather deer-like droppings.

In November both billy and nanny goats become restless; the glands behind the horns exude an oil that is presumably for the purpose of attracting a mate. The males fight among themselves, sometimes inflicting fatal wounds with their sharp horns which curve backward slightly, and measure about nine inches. About six months after a mating—during late April, May, or June—the kids are born. Usually there is only one, but twins are not uncommon.

Shortly after birth the woolly kid stands up and begins to nurse. When it finishes the first meal a kid may frisk about for a little while in the stiff-legged manner peculiar to the goat. The mother keeps her offspring hidden for a few days; she returns to the "nursery" frequently to feed the little animal, which bleats plaintively if hungry. (Though usually silent, adults grunt upon occasion.) In a short time the nanny and her kid join a band composed of other mothers and their offspring, young females, and young billies.

⅓ actual size

Individual bands browse on a single mountain slope for days at a time, feeding on grasses and weedy plants. In winter the animals eat woody growths and in Glacier National Park the diet includes hemlock, douglas fir, and alpine fir. Sometimes individual goats or small herds come down into wooded areas to visit mineral licks; at other times they cross mountain valleys, swimming if necessary, to get to another mountain. A feeding herd is generally watched over by a sentinel; this animal stands in one spot, feet planted far apart, and keeps a sharp lookout for danger. The goat, however, depends more on its keen sense of smell to detect danger than it does on vision or hearing.

As goats move over their territories the animals have few predators to worry them. Sometimes bears, coyotes, and wolves kill an animal below timberline, and the golden eagle is reported to take many kids. Probably the chief predators are the cougar and the lynx. The goat puts up a good fight if cornered. It can kill a black bear or a grizzly by thrusts of the horns in the heart, lungs, or belly. Some goats are killed by rock and snow slides and some die of pneumonia or succumb to a big-game disease, known as necrotic stomatitis, but many die of old age, when the animal is ten to twelve years old.

At one time the Indians of southern British Columbia killed a great many goats for the fine under wool. This was spun into blankets with the quality of cashmere, known as Chilkat robes. Although these robes are still manufactured, their production is now limited; the Department of Trade and Commerce permits only a certain number of goats to be taken each year.

Mountain goats are live-trapped to restock old ranges, particularly in Montana, and to furnish stock for new areas. The goats are rendered helpless to each other and to their handlers by having short pieces of garden hose looped and cemented over the horns. Then the animals are blindfolded and their feet are tied before they are taken out of the mountains. Once out of the mountains the animals may be loaded into a plane and flown to a new area, where they are packed into the mountains on horses, and then freed.

Releases have been made in isolated mountain ranges east of the Divide—territory never before occupied by mountain goats. The fourteen nannies and the seven billies released in April 1941 and April 1943 in the Crazy Mountains are responsible for a herd of more than two hundred and fifty animals by 1952 when an aerial count was taken.

During the 1930's several goats escaped from Custer State Park in South Dakota. These animals made their way to the region around Harney Peak, with an elevation of 7,242 feet, in the Black Hills. By 1939 there were twenty-three goats at Harney, and by 1949 three hundred animals were estimated for the area—which had never been mountain-goat territory before. So it appears that the animal is able to adapt to new environments and when at liberty to do so seeks one that is not likely to be affected by the spread of civilization.

BIGHORN SHEEP

Ovis canadensis

Rocky Mountain National Park in north-central Colorado is one of the places within the United States where you can sometimes catch a glimpse of the bighorn or Rocky Mountain sheep. Occasionally a small band of these curly horned animals with gray-brown coats stations itself on a crag near Milner Pass, some 10,000 feet above sea level on Trail Ridge Road, the transcontinental link in the Park. On this lookout the bighorns stand quietly, gazing out across the deep forested canyons and the snowy gorges, their great golden eyes seeming to take in every detail of the habitat.

In 1800 the bighorn was so numerous that its numbers have been estimated at 2,000,000. Due to poor range conditions, the introduction of domestic sheep (whose diseases the wild sheep are prone to), populations too large for existing ranges, over-hunting, and possibly some predation, the numbers of bighorns decreased as the years went by. In 1954 there were slightly more than 19,000 of these animals according to the big-game inventory compiled by the U. S. Fish and Wildlife Service. Colorado has the greatest number; about five thousand of these members of the ox family live among the crags and peaks of that state, with the largest and best-known herd in the Tarryall Mountains.

Various races of bighorn sheep, including the desert form, and two northern species inhabit an extensive range. In Alaska and parts of the Yukon there is the Dall mountain sheep (*O. dalli*)—the only wild white sheep in existence. A little less than half the estimated population of these more lightly built animals live in the remote Brooks Range north of the Arctic Circle. In the south-central Yukon and parts of British Columbia the Stone or black sheep (*O. d. stonei*) lives at elevations of 6,500 feet. And in the mountain regions of nine western states,* the Mexican states of Chihuahua and Baja California five types of bighorns occupy diverse habitats.

* Arizona, California, Colorado, New Mexico, Oregon, South Dakota, Texas, Utah, and Wyoming.

At elevations "up among the eagles" rams of the mountain species start fighting among themselves in November for mates. Snorting and grunting the rams charge one another, reared-up and running forward on their hind legs. With no perceptible pause they then drop to all fours, to meet head on with a resounding crash of their heavy hollow horns. Broken horns or splintered horn tips are never renewed. Some fights are accompanied by a great deal of kicking with the sharp, black hoofs, and occasionally one ram butts another over a cliff. By the time the two months' mating season is over rams are sometimes as battered and bruised as overworked prizefighters. Some rams acquire harems, others are content with a single mate.

About six months after mating the ewe is ready to drop her lamb. In the North a lamb may be born in May, early June, or even later in Alaska; in the South a lamb is born in March or early April. When her time is at hand the ewe moves away from the herd; she seeks a spot protected from the elements and with only one approach for the cougar or the wolverine—or the lynx and the wolf, which prey on bighorns when unusually hungry. The spot to which the ewe retires is also protected from the swooping attack of the golden eagle, a killer of some lambs.

Once in a while twins are born, but usually the ewe has only a single lamb. Shortly after birth the long, pale-brown coat of the lamb is dry and it stands on unsteady legs to nurse. For the first week the ewe barely leaves her offspring, feeding it at least once an hour and ever on the alert for danger. At the end of a week the ewe and her lamb join a band of bighorns composed of other ewes, their young, and some yearlings. Rams usually stay in groups by themselves, though some old males are solitary.

By the time a lamb is a month old the little animal feeds on various mountain grasses, herbs, and some woody plants. Foods vary according to the growths native to each area in which the animals live. The desert bighorn eats such shrubs as mountain mahogany, acacia, and various kinds of cacti, which supply the necessary moisture in climates where the animal may drink water only once every three or four days. In the far North the Dall mountain sheep feeds almost entirely on alpine grasses, though sometimes the animal eats alder, birch, and cottonwood.

By the time winter is at hand a lamb weighs nearly eighty pounds
—about half the weight of its mother—and has lost its woolly coat.
The young animal has acquired a body coat of fine hair, which is
protected by dense outer hairs about two and one-half inches long.
With the acquisition of this coat the cream-colored rump patch—
a distinguishing mark of the adult—shows clearly.

⅓ actual size

For the first two years of its life the horns of a ram are similar to
the small, backward curving horns of the ewe. But by the time a ram
is five years old the horns have grown until they reach the bottom
of the downward swing. When a ram is six or seven years old the
horns form the better part of a circle. Sometimes the circle is completed, with the tips of the horns continuing up past the nose as
far as the eyes.

Although fable has it that the bighorn lands on its horns after
plunging down an almost perpendicular slope, this is not so in fact.
The animal drops down the side of a mountain in a zigzag manner,
its concave, sharply edged hoofs acting as suction cups on even the
slightest kind of foothold. It also scales mountain sides in a series of
bouncing leaps, especially when a predator is at hand, for the bighorn likes to keep a position above any foe.

As the animals feed, one acts as a sentinel. This guard scans the
countryside to detect any sign of danger, depending more on its keen
vision than on its senses of smell and hearing to warn if trouble is
at hand. At a hint of danger all members of the band take off after
the leader, generally a ewe, and do not stop their flight until they
have climbed as high as they can go, or have passed around to the
other side of the mountain. The bighorn swims well, and often
plunges into deep rivers or lakes to move from a summer feeding
ground to a wintering area.

The home range of a band of bighorns is marked by feeding and
resting areas and spots where the animals bed down during darkness.

The bighorn sleeps through the night, then gets up early in the morning to feed. Around ten o'clock it is ready to lie down and chew its cud. By noon the animal feeds again, then rests during the afternoon, to feed for a third time from late afternoon until early evening, when it beds down in a protected spot. Although lambs and ewes call to one another during the summer in the manner of domestic sheep, the bighorn is usually a silent animal. Danger is sometimes announced by uttering a sort of snorting sneeze, and angry rams grind their teeth.

If you ever visit bighorn country, you will find that the ranges of these animals, usually not more than a circular area of about a mile in radius, are well marked by numerous deep and narrow trails. The wide-spaced tracks show the cloven hoofs of this animal, whose progenitors are believed to have reached North America from Asia in the mid-Pleistocene age by way of the land bridge across Bering Strait.

In addition to Rocky Mountain National Park, other areas in which you can sometimes see the bighorn are: Glacier National Park, Montana; Grand Teton National Park, Wyoming; Challis National Forest, Idaho; Chugach National Forest, Alaska; Cabeza Prieta Game Range, Arizona (desert bighorn); and San Andres National Wildlife Refuge, New Mexico.

AMPHIBIANS
and
REPTILES

POISONOUS SNAKES

Crotalidae and *Elapidae*

S nakes belong to a class of cold-blooded, lung-breathing verte-
brates known as Reptiles—a word derived from a Latin verb
meaning "to crawl." Short-legged or legless, reptiles are classified in
the animal kingdom above the amphibians and below the birds and
the mammals. In the Mesozoic era, 205 to 135 million years ago, they
dominated the land, sea, and air. Today, the age of mammals, reptiles
are represented by comparatively few species, which have a distinguishing characteristic in common—they abandon their young to
circumstance.

The clean, cold body of a snake is covered either by smooth scales
or scales that are keeled—that is, ridged. Those on the belly are
more than a mere protective coat. The large, transverse belly scales
are attached to the free end of each rib by a small muscle. Pressure
from the ribs raises individual scales, and this action pulls the snake
over the surface of the ground. To move about a snake must be on
terrain that is somewhat rough; on a smooth ground surface or on
glass it is as helpless as a turtle on its back.

As the snake slithers over the ground at a rate of no more than a
quarter of a mile an hour—the speed of a hunting whip snake, our
fastest-moving species—the creature constantly throws out and
withdraws its forked tongue through a notch in the lower jaw. The
tongue is flicked this way and that during its outside intervals. Contrary to popular belief the snake's tongue is not used to sting, but
as an aid to the sense of smell.

The tongue itself does not detect odors, but the moist and delicate
tips pick up traces of chemicals and transport them to the Jacobson's
organs—two small cavities in the upper part of the mouth lined with
sensory cells and capable of receiving odors. The forked tip touches
objects lightly, and is then withdrawn. In this way the snake learns
of its surroundings. It does not, as was formerly believed, hear with
its tongue. There are no external ear openings, so the snake has to

depend on ground vibrations received when it is coiled to warn of the approach of other animals, which it sees clearly at close range.

Some snakes have eyes in which the pupils are vertical, in others the pupils are round. But no snakes have movable eyelids; their eyes are covered by hard eyecaps which have the appearance of transparent plastic. These eyecaps prevent injury as the snake burrows in gritty soil or glides through the brush; they give the creature's eyes their fixed glittering expression which has led to the mistaken belief that the snake has a hypnotic stare. Eyecaps are shed each time the snake sheds its skin. Shedding takes place about three times a year, after the animal sluffs off its skin for the first time about two weeks after birth.

Among our one hundred and thirty-odd species of snakes are two groups that are poisonous. One group (the *Crotalidae*) includes the copperhead (the highland moccasin), the cottonmouth (the water moccasin), and the various species of rattlesnakes. Known as pit vipers these animals have deep pits on each side of the somewhat triangular head between the eyes and the nostrils. The pits, sufficiently large to be seen at a reasonably safe distance, are one means of differentiating poisonous snakes from those that are non-poisonous. Pits act as locators of warm-blooded prey; if one is covered by wax the pit viper misses its target.

The largest poisonous snake in North America is the eastern diamondback rattler (*Crotalus adamanteus*), an olive or grayish-green animal with diamond-shaped markings edged with yellow on its back, and a dull yellow underside. This species ranks second to none among the known deadly snakes of the world.

Adults of this southeastern coastal species often measure five feet; the record length is seven feet, three inches. Although the western diamondback (*C. atrox*) is usually somewhat smaller than its eastern counterpart, one was caught that measured seven feet, five inches.

The large rattlers and the pygmy or dwarf rattlers are viviparous or live-bearing. The eastern diamondback has seven to eighteen young at a time; the average number is nine or ten. This species mates toward the end of its hibernation, and the young are born during late summer or in the fall.

A newly born rattler has a little round button on its tail tip. This button is lost the first time the young snake sheds its skin—probably about two weeks after birth—and is replaced by a permanent button. From then on, each time the rattler sheds its skin a new segment or rattle is added, and the button is pushed farther back from the end of the tail. The number of rattles on a rattlesnake's tail is not a reliable indicator of age. If all rattles were kept intact they might be a reasonably good way to tell how old a snake is, but rattles break off or wear out through use between sheddings.

After the first shedding of its skin the young rattler is able to produce a slight buzzing sound by vibrating its tail. An adult has a rattle composed of a jointed string of loosely interlocked segments. When these thin dry hollow segments are vibrated from side to side, they produce a whir or buzz—a sound that can be heard at a considerable distance and one that means danger. The whir or the buzz made by the rattle caused early American colonists to report that the New World had "serpents with bells on their tails." Some non-poisonous snakes vibrate their tails; among dry leaves the sound is similar to that made by an angry rattler.

Although a captive Pacific rattlesnake lived twenty years, it is doubtful that wild ones reach any such age. The chances for survival of young rattlesnakes are not great. Independent from the time they are born, few diamondbacks live past the first winter. Hawks, skunks, and snake-eating snakes kill many and hogs and deer stamp numbers of them to death. Others starve, many freeze, and still others succumb to intense heat.

The body temperature of the diamondback and other snakes is maintained by movements to and from warm places. Too much heat, however, kills; a desert rattler (*C. cerastes*)—known, too, as the sidewinder and the horned rattler—died seven minutes after it was placed on warm sand in the sun, although the air temperature was only 96° F.

Like most wild creatures the rattlesnake rarely looks for trouble. But if someone or something goes beyond the "critical distance," the point at which any animal fights when surprised, endangered, or cornered, then the rattlesnake strikes. Even a young rattler is able to strike and inflict painful wounds as soon as it is born. The strike is a maneuver of jet-speed in which an S-shaped curve of the front

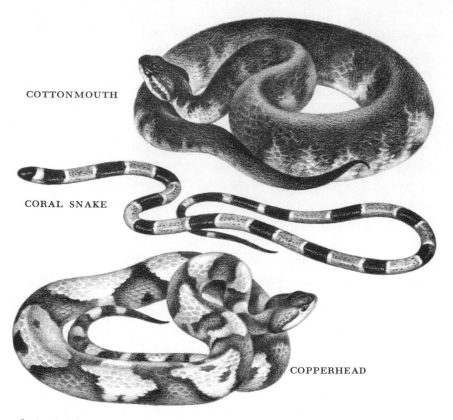

COTTONMOUTH

CORAL SNAKE

COPPERHEAD

of the body is straightened out. The snake that has its tail braced against a solid object strikes its full length; otherwise a strike is about one-third to one-half of the creature's length. And a rattler can and does strike more than once—from any position, in any direction—even in the water, where it swims with head and tail held high.

Glands in the sides of the head behind the ears contain the venom of pit vipers—the rattlesnake, the copperhead, and the cotton-mouth moccasin. A duct or canal runs from each gland to the base of the curved, hollow fang, where there is an opening leading into the canal of each fang. Similar to hypodermic needles, fangs are attached to movable bones on the upper jaw. They are folded against the roof of the mouth when the jaws are closed and covered by sheaths of white flesh from which the tips protrude. As the snake's jaws open the fangs automatically spring forward. (Fangs are replaced every few months.)

When the pit viper bites, muscles in the glands force out the venom—primarily hemotoxic, it damages the red blood cells and ruptures capillary walls of a victim. The bite of a poisonous snake usually punctures the skin, whereas that of a non-poisonous snake generally makes the skin look bruised.

The chief prey of the eastern diamondback rattler is the cottontail rabbit. The snake strikes its prey so rapidly that an observer hardly sees anything but the results; the rabbit bounds forward, rolls on its side, kicks convulsively, and dies. The food of all snakes is bolted whole and consumed head first. Such feeding is possible because the jaws of a snake are so constructed that it can open its mouth until it is like a large scoop. Snakes in general are infrequent feeders, and many like the eastern diamondback spend the day coiled in some protected spot and hunt in the late afternoon or at night.

The other group of poisonous snakes are the coral snakes (*Elapidae*), small-headed, brilliantly colored members of the cobra family, and distinguished by black snouts. The snout is one way of differentiating these poisonous snakes from the harmless scarlet snake and the scarlet king snake which, while similar in appearance to coral snakes, have red or yellow heads. The coral snake is restricted to the Southeast, the Gulf states, and a part of Arizona. It is our smallest dangerous snake, and in its largest form, the Arizona species, measures no more than 19½ inches. The coral snake is oviparous, that is, it lays eggs; clutches vary from two to twelve eggs.

Although there are some sections of the country in which there are no poisonous snakes, every state has one or more of these reptiles within its boundaries. To make sure of the distribution of poisonous snakes, it is wise to use range maps. Such maps are contained in *Field Book of Snakes of the United States and Canada*, by K. P. Schmidt and D. D. Davis, G. P. Putnam's Sons, New York.

When walking in snake country, watch where you put your feet, stand behind logs or stones that you tilt up, do not climb without first making sure that a possible handhold is not occupied by a sunning snake, and, finally, leave snakes alone if you encounter them. Snakes try to escape if given a chance. Proper clothing, too, often prevents a snake bite from being serious. Leather boots with loose tops are the best footwear; heavy socks give added protection; and trousers worn outside the boots often cause a snake to strike short.

The bite of any poisonous snake is serious, but that of the coral snake is exceedingly serious due to the nature of the venom. It is neurotoxic and irritates and paralyzes the nerves, and a minute amount can kill a man.

One or more snake-bite kits for applying first-aid treatment and a few packages of antivenin should be carried on outdoor trips on which you are likely to encounter venomous snakes. First aid treatment for a bite includes a one-quarter-inch deep cross cut through the fang puncture, so that the venom can be drawn out, and a tourniquet above the bite—that is, between the bite and the heart. The tourniquet should be tight enough to retard the spread of the poison through the blood stream, but not so tight as to cut off circulation entirely. The tourniquet should be loosened every few minutes, and should be moved ahead of the swelling as it increases. If you have a snake-bite kit, use the contents, following the directions, and administer ACTH. Then without undue exertion start for the doctor or hospital.

Experts believe that more than seventy-five percent of the snake bites in this country would not cause death even if given no special care. But with prompt treatment the chances of death from snake bite are perhaps less than two percent for a healthy adult.

On the control of snakes, the Missouri Conservation Commission says:

Poisonous snakes have no place around human habitation and even the presence of non-poisonous ones is often objectionable. There are no really effective means of eliminating snakes completely but it is possible to discourage them around homes by the same means found effective for control of all animal pests—destruction of their food and shelter. Disorderly piles of boards, fence posts, dump heaps, slabs of roofing paper. corrugated iron sheeting, burlap, slabs of bark, piles of rock, etc., all provide hiding places for snakes and their prey. Removal of these attractions and general tidying up are the best ways of keeping the premises free of reptiles. Loose chinks in the masonry of building attract rodents which in turn attract snakes; proper upkeep of the masonry will further discourage these unwanted guests.

NON-POISONOUS SNAKES

Boidae and *Colubridae*

The Sac-Fox Indians believed that the first clap of spring thunder ended the hibernation of snakes. Perhaps the source of their belief was the behavior of the garter snake, one of the first reptiles to come out of hibernation. Even in March this non-poisonous species is abroad, seeking the sun, its first meal, and a mate.

The garter snake is one of the most familiar reptiles in the United States; there is at least one form in every state, with the eastern garter snake (*Thamnophis sirtalis sirtalis*) having the greatest distribution. You will find it from southern Canada to the Gulf of Mexico and westward to the Great Plains. Usually no more than thirty inches in length, this reptile may have a ground color that is brown, green, olive, or blackish. Three yellowish or greenish stripes run the entire length of its slender body, and there are generally two rows of black dots between the stripes.

If the weather is warm the garter snake is often abroad late in the fall. At this time these snakes congregate in large numbers in an area suitable for hibernation, often on the south side of a rocky hill. During the warmest period of the day they sun themselves, but as soon as the air cools they retire into crevices or burrows, which may be three or more feet in depth. When the weather becomes really cold they remain in their chosen places of hibernation. In the spring before it is warm the garter snake mates. Like the ugly looking water snake (*Natrix sipedon*)—found in most ponds, swamps, or streams east of the Mississippi—the garter snake has minute sensory organs on the chin. At mating time the male rubs these organs along the back of the female, while passing his body over hers.

In August the female brings forth anywhere from twenty to fifty young. The little reptiles are independent immediately; they start feeding on earthworms—their chief diet until they hibernate for the first time. Like all the numerous striped snakes, the garter feeds on frogs, toads, fishes, but continues to eat worms all through its life. Its feeding habits, therefore, are not beneficial to the farmer.

In spite of the glands near the base of the tail which secrete a musky fluid when the snake is alarmed, the garter snake makes an interesting pet; it soon becomes tame, and does not attempt to nip you or discharge its musk.

In addition to the garter snake, often found in city parks, the little DeKay's snake (*Storeria dekayi*) is one that you are apt to see— particularly if you are crossing a trash-strewn lot or field or walking near an old stone wall. Named in honor of James E. DeKay, an early zoologist of New York, this foot-long snake is chestnut or grayish brown in color, and has keeled scales. Like the garter snake, DeKay's is one of the first of our reptiles to appear in the spring. Look for it then on flat rocks or bare patches of earth in almost any area east of the Rocky Mountains.

But in summer this species is not so readily seen; then it secretes itself in a protected spot during the day, coming out to hunt in early morning or late afternoon. Prey includes worms, snails, soft-bodied larvae of various insects, and some of the smaller salamanders. In turn DeKay's snake is preyed upon by hawks, owls, skunks, snake-eating snakes, and house cats. In spite of these predators and man, who kills numbers of them, this snake maintains itself.

In midsummer the female gives birth to ten or twenty snakelets; they are about the size of an old-fashioned wooden toothpick, but grow rapidly on their diet of insect larvae, and soon measure four or five inches in length. By fall those that have survived are in condition to hibernate, and seek a crevice or burrow to spend the winter.

Two of our non-poisonous, egg-laying species, the bull and the pilot black snake, are excellent controls of vermin. Like many other snakes these two feed to a considerable extent upon destructive mice, rats, other rodents, and injurious insects. To the farmer the value of a bull snake has been estimated at $3.75 a year.

The bull snake (*Pituophis catenifer sayi*), a constrictor, is one of the four largest snakes in the country; it often grows to a length of eight feet. The ground color of this animal is orange or reddish yellow and the dark yellow head has a brown or black band across the top in front of the eyes. Over its range between the Mississippi River and the Rocky Mountains from southwestern Canada to Mexico, the bull snake eats quantities of grain-destroying rodents, as well as full-grown rabbits and some birds and eggs.

The female bull snake lays eggs that are yellowish white and about as large as those of a chicken. Like all oviparous snakes the female seeks a place to lay her eggs that will aid in their incubation. A half hollow log in which there is decaying wood is a good spot. Here the eggs are laid in a heap by the female, which glides away as soon as the last one is deposited. In this natural incubator the eggs hatch within several weeks, and for a short time after the snakelets come out of the shells they feed on the yolks of the eggs from which they emerged. When the young snakes have shed their skins for the first time, they are ready to go their separate ways; those fortunate enough to escape predators are soon ready to hibernate—a five or six months' period of dormancy when the animals are insensible.

The other great destroyer of rodents is the pilot black snake (*Elaphe obsoleta obsoleta*); it is also known as the "mountain black snake" and the "black chicken snake." A reptile with a broad head and a white chin and throat, this species is such a shiny black that it has an anthracite sheen. In rocky, hilly, or mountainous country as well as meadowland from southern New England to Florida, and as far west as Texas and Illinois, the pilot black snake seeks its prey. Primarily a night hunter the animal tracks down such warm-blooded prey as mice, rabbits, rats, ground squirrels, and birds. It also preys on frogs, lizards, and some other snakes. Although a constrictor it does not kill frogs by squeezing, but swallows them alive.

An oviparous species the pilot black snake deposits its eggs, measuring two inches long by an inch in diameter, in hollow stumps or in windfalls. In such natural incubators the eggs hatch; young pilot black snakes are a pale gray, a color that is replaced by the black of adults in the second summer.

Although the pilot black snake is tamable, care should be taken in handling one. If frightened it might entwine itself around your neck, and, as the strength of a constrictor of this size is considerable, the experience is not worth risking.

One of our largest snakes is the indigo or gopher snake (*Drymarchon corais couperi*). Shiny and blue black, this reptile sometimes measures more than seven feet. It inhabits sandy regions in the Southeast, the Gulf States, and parts of Texas, and is one of the few snakes to which there is no general aversion. It is considered a friend

PILOT BLACK SNAKE

HOG-NOSED SN. KE

DE KAY'S SNAKE

GOPHER OR INDIGO SNAKE

of the farmer, for it consumes quantities of mice and rats. The diet of warm-blooded prey is supplemented by frogs and lizards, and some eggs; in captivity the indigo snake eats small fishes. This species is gentle and easily tamed, and is the snake often used by those who practice "snake-charming."

Another of our useful snakes is the yellowish-brown corn snake (*Elaphe guttata*), whose stout body is marked by somewhat square crimson patches bordered by black. Also known as the "red chicken snake," the "mouse snake," and the "scarlet racer," this reptile frequents cornfields during late summer. The corn snake is a tree-climber; in the spring when nestling birds are plentiful it climbs to get its prey. However the young birds it destroys are more than compensated for by the numbers of rats and mice it kills during the hours when it hunts—early morning or late afternoon.

The hog-nosed snakes (*Heterodon*) have a number of local names. Depending upon the section of the country, these thick-bodied reptiles with hog-like snouts are called "flat-headed adders," "spreading adders," "sand vipers," "blowing vipers," and "puff adders."

A characteristic of this snake is to hold its head high, then take a deep breath, which is expelled with such a sharp hiss that it can be heard for several yards. While hissing the reptile strikes as if it meant business, but the strikes are nothing more than a device to frighten. If the hiss and the feint do not achieve the desired effect, the hog-nosed snake goes into the next part of its act—a realistic shamming of death. It suddenly opens its mouth and contorts its body as if seized by a convulsion. The "convulsions" diminish until only the tip of the tail wriggles. About then the snake flips over on its back, and becomes limp. Once it makes sure that danger has passed, it flips back on its belly and glides off. If something startles it while making a getaway, the animal immediately "plays dead" again.

For the first few weeks in captivity the hog-nosed snake may flatten its head and hiss fiercely when approached, but it soon discards such behavior and becomes a good pet. Percy A. Morris, author of *They Hop and Crawl*, once caught a hog-nosed snake at the edge of a meadow. Carrying it in one hand, he continued on across the meadow, saw a small frog, stooped down and picked it up with his free hand. As he went on with his walk, the hog-nosed snake reached out, relieved Mr. Morris of the frog, and swallowed it.

The common fear and dislike of snakes has hindered recognition of their value—particularly the value of the harmless species as rodent controls. According to the reports of various herpetologists and such institutions as the American Museum of Natural History, most of the snakes killed are non-poisonous. This indiscriminate killing is unfortunate in view of the function that these reptiles serve. As Doris M. Cochran of the U. S. National Museum said in "Our Snake Friends and Foes," *National Geographic* magazine, September 1954:

Perhaps one day, more schooled in natural history, we shall be able to view the serpent clan with less fear and greater objectivity and even refrain from murdering its members on sight. It should not take too much reflection to recognize that the snake, like the often despised hawk, owl, fox, and weasel, has a vital and logical role to play in the maintenance of Nature's delicate balance.

BOX TURTLE

Terrapene carolina

As it shambles along over the dry leaves of the forest floor, the rustling of the dark-brown box turtle is sometimes startling. But noisy as the animal might be in these surroundings there is no cause for alarm; the box turtle or box tortoise is one of the gentlest members of the animal kingdom. And of all the wildlife you are likely to encounter in your back yard, on a country walk, or in a berry patch the box turtle is unique.

Nature has provided the box turtle with a shell fortress, which can be rendered impregnable by a kind of drawbridge arrangement at either end. The upper shell, known as the carapace, is arched and globular, and flecked with yellow. The bright yellow lower shell, known as the plastron, is hinged near the middle. This divides the shell into two movable lobes, so that when danger threatens, the box turtle can withdraw its head, limbs, and tail, and close the two lobes so tightly that not even the edge of a piece of paper can be inserted.

Occasionally the box turtle has a little difficulty in shutting the plastron tightly. The creature loves wild strawberries and may gorge on them to such an extent that it becomes too fat to be confined within its own shell. If it manages to withdraw the head and fore-limbs, then the rear limbs and tail pop out between the carapace and the plastron at the back; on the other hand if it manages to get its stumpy hind legs and short tail inside, then the head and forelegs pop out.

To feed on strawberries, other fruits, mushrooms, garden lettuce, grubs, worms, and insects, the box turtle employs a scissors technique. Toothless but with the edges of the sharp jaws covered by horny tissues and with the lower one fitting closely inside the upper, the animal shears off bits of food. These particles are swallowed whole. When it wants a drink, the box turtle wades into water until it is partially submerged, then extends its neck and opens its mouth, letting the water flow in.

The box turtle is a great wanderer; in the East the animal roams over its chosen territory from New England to Georgia, and west to Illinois and Michigan; in the Gulf States from Florida to Texas, another form (*T. major*), with long yellow lines on the upper shell instead of spots, mogs along in true turtle style; and from Illinois to the Rocky Mountains and south to Arizona the western box turtle (*T. ornata*) ambles over rather open or arid areas.

Somewhere in its travels the red-eyed male runs across the yellow-eyed female. For a while he is content to follow her around, but soon begins to court her by gentle nips on the head and legs. If these advances do not bring the desired response, the male puts his fore-feet on her back so that she cannot amble off. Once the mating is consummated, the two animals go their separate ways.

At the approach of cold weather the box turtle seeks a spot where the soil is dry and loose, and digs well below the frost line. For almost six months the animal remains dormant—in a state of deep sleep, like that of a hibernating woodchuck, when the metabolic rate practically ceases. Some time in April the box turtle emerges from its earthen winter quarters, and soon thereafter the female is ready to drop her eggs.

The female scoops out a shallow hole in the ground, then drops anywhere from four to eight white eggs, whose shape is elliptical. Each egg is covered with loose soil as it is deposited, and the entire clutch is carefully covered after the last egg has been released. Most eggs of the box turtle hatch in late September or October. Upon hatching the young turtle is about the size of a quarter. It digs itself to the surface. For the first few days the little creature hides, subsisting on the egg yolk which is still attached to the under shell. When this has been consumed, it starts foraging; the first food is probably small earthworms. Soon it is eating a variety of foods, including the flesh of dead mice or rabbits, for the box turtle is practically omnivorous.

During the first few years of its life the turtle keeps as well concealed as possible; before the shell hardens completely, skunks and other flesh-eating animals prey on it. But by the time it is five or six years old, the shell is so hard that the turtle feels free to wander at will over the well-established routes of its territory.

The animal may occupy the same territory for twenty, thirty, or forty years. Exceptionally long-lived ones reach fifty years, and one, according to William Bridges in his *Zoo Expeditions*, was at least 129 years old. Sets of dated initials on the under shell of a box turtle discovered in New England helped to determine the age of this animal.

One tortoise (generally the term used for land turtles) has set something of a record in the way of longevity. This animal was presented by Captain John Cook to the king of Tongatabu in 1777. How old the animal was when Cook made the presentation is not known, but for more than a century and three-quarters this gift tortoise, named the King of Malila, has been strolling around the compound built for it in 1777 by a former ruler of the Tonga Islands.

SNAPPING TURTLE

Chelydra serpentina

Along the eastern seaboard commercial fishermen frequently augment their incomes from April to September by catching turtles to sell to seafood packing plants. The turtles caught and processed for eventual soups and stews are snapping turtles—savage creatures that hatch from round white eggs so elastic that they bounce.

In early summer the female snappers leave slow-moving muddy streams and rivers or lakes, ponds, and marshes to deposit their eggs on land. Throughout the better part of the country east of the Rocky Mountains, from Canada to Mexico, these large, web-footed creatures with beaked jaws scoop out depressions in the soft earth in which to lay about a dozen eggs. The female lowers herself into the hole she has excavated, then wriggles around until the earth has fallen over her. She remains hidden until she has deposited the last egg. Then, emerging from the "nest" at such a sharp angle that the earth falls back over the eggs, she heads for water to remain there until the following year.

At birth the young snapper is black, but by the time it reaches maturity the upper shell is a dark brown and the under shell is dull

yellow. The snapping turtle spends so much time half-buried in the mud on the bottom of its chosen home that the upper shell often becomes encrusted with moss. Adult snappers weigh from twenty to fifty pounds, and among the numerous fresh-water turtles of the eastern and central States it is second only in size to the alligator snapper (*Macrochelys temminckii*)—an inhabitant of waters flowing into the Gulf of Mexico. The alligator snapping turtle, a retiring but savage reptile, sometimes weighs as much as one hundred and fifty pounds.

Occasionally the snapper catches its prey on a stream bank, but it usually seizes its victims in the water and always eats them there. Fishes, frogs, young muskrats, goslings, and ducklings are taken by the snapper, which strikes with the rapidity and accuracy of a snake. Fishes and frogs are chopped to pieces by the beaked jaws; the young of waterfowl and muskrats are seized from beneath as they swim, and dragged to the bottom, where they are torn apart by the large nails of the webbed feet.

The snapping turtle is dangerous to handle; the only safe way to pick one up is by the tail. Then the creature should be held well away from the body, for it can bend its head backward or sideways, and snap with such force that it can shear off a finger. If the snapper locks its jaws on part of the body proper it hangs on. A Virginia trapper once had a snapper latch onto the small of the back. Although there is an old saying that the snapper only lets go when it thunders, the trapper did not wait for a storm to prove the truth of the saw. He lay flat on his back; this position bent the turtle's neck backward forcing the animal to release its pincer-like grip.

If you want snapping turtles for soup or stew it is better to buy the meat in city markets than to go snapper trapping yourself. Handling them is a risky business best left to professionals—though bare-handed turtle-hunting, known as "noodlin'," is a popular sport in West Virginia.

PAINTED TURTLES

Chrysemys

In almost every state east of the Rocky Mountains you can find some form of the painted turtle. This typical small pond species is distinguished by bright red and yellow concentric rings on the marginal edges of the lustrous olive, brown, or black shell.

Often several of these thoroughly aquatic turtles bask together in the sun on a partially submerged log. At your approach they plop helter-skelter into the water, and swim to the safety of the mud and vegetation at the bottom.

The painted turtle eats aquatic insects and their larvae, fishes and their eggs, snails, salamanders, tadpoles, and water plants. Its fondness for fish makes the painted turtle a problem pet in an aquarium; it swims after the fishes, and bites at their tails and fines. If the fishes are not too large it overpowers and eats them. The largest painted turtle, the western (*Chrysemys bellii bellii*), makes a long-lived pet; one lived ten years. These animals learn to take such foods as chopped raw beef, chopped fish, and earthworms from your fingers. But they always submerge to eat.

One of the first species to hibernate, the painted turtle buries itself deep in the mud early in the fall. Perhaps because it begins its hibernation so early, this turtle is one of the first to appear in the spring. It does not announce its appearance by vocalizing of any kind, most turtles only squeak or make sort of a sighing sound.

Only one turtle lets you know it is around. The dark-brown wood turtle (*Clemmys insculpta*) of the Northeastern and Middle Atlantic states announces its presence with a whistling call. This call has sufficient volume to be heard thirty or forty feet away.

HORNED TOAD

Phrynosoma cornutum

Late in the sixteenth century Philip II of Spain sent Francesco Hernandez to Mexico to collect natural curiosities. Among the many New World specimens Hernandez secured or saw, and later described in his natural history of 1628, were the flat-bodied horned "toad" and the poisonous gila monster. Both these lizards are familiar to the traveler in the West and Southwest.

The gray or brown horned toad is a funny little creature about six inches in length, with a short tail and short legs. The large head has a crown of sharp spines, and there are bony ridges over the eyes, which give the animal a wide-awake appearance. The body is covered by scales, some of which are large and sharp-pointed.

During the late afternoon the horned toad hunts on the ground for ants, beetles, caterpillars, grasshoppers, and weevils. It catches its prey in the same way the American toad does (possibly the reason it was called the horned toad). It flicks out its tongue, to which the prey adheres because of a sticky substance, and then returns the tongue and prey to its mouth.

At night or on overcast days the horned toad often digs itself into the sand until it is covered. Sometimes it does not bury itself completely, but leaves its head out.

Although most lizards do not bring forth live young, this species does. Anywhere from six to twelve are born at a time; the little creatures look like adults, but do not appear nearly so rough. Young horned toads are active at once and, like the young of all other reptiles and amphibians, are able to take care of themselves.

The horned toad is distinguished by a peculiar trait. When something excites or startles it, the animal raises its head, the eyes bulge, and then twin jets of blood spurt from the eyes or eyelids. This defense measure—if it is one—lasts about a second. Afterwards, the animal keeps its eyes closed and remains quiet for a short time.

This lizard makes an interesting, long-lived pet. A roomy cage in which the floor is sanded and placed to get sunshine for the better part of the day is the right kind of home for a captive horned toad. Food should be mealworms, ants, flies, and other small insects. To give the animal a drink, immerse a lettuce leaf or any leafy salad green in water. Do not shake off the drops, but put the leaf in the cage so that the horned toad can lap the drops from the edges.

Probably the best-known horned toad in the country was "Old Rip" of Eastland in north-central Texas. Old Rip was sealed in the cornerstone of the Eastland courthouse in 1897. Thirty-one years later, February 28, 1928, the stone in which he had been placed was opened. Dusty and limp at first, Old Rip quickly revived in fresh air. And his story of thirty-one years without a drink received nationwide newspaper coverage—second in space, so Texans claim, only to that received by Lindbergh, who made his nonstop flight to Paris in May of that year.

Old Rip was displayed in a goldfish bowl in Eastland when he was not on tour, and his likeness appeared on some sixteen thousand postcards. On January 20, 1929, he died, and his preserved body is on display in a marble and stone tomb in Eastland's present courthouse.

GILA MONSTER
Heloderma suspectum

The gila monster inhabits the deserts of southern Arizona, Nevada, Utah, and westerly New Mexico, and is one of the two poisonous lizards in the western hemisphere. The stout body of the gila monster is covered by tubercles, small knoblike prominences. The head and the body are strikingly marked with black and another color, which may be salmon, pale pink, yellow, pale yellow, or sometimes white. The pattern of these color combinations looks like Indian beadwork—an illusion enhanced by the beadlike knobs of the skin.

Two sacs embedded in its lower jaw contain the poison that is as aromatic as the rootstalks of calamus or sweet flag and as toxic as the venom of the rattlesnake or the moccasin. The venom is injected through grooved teeth in the back of the jaw. If the gila bites with only the front teeth, little or no poison is injected into the wound, but when the animal lies on its back to bite and hangs on, the venom flows into the wound. The poison has enough potency to kill frogs, mice, and rabbits.

Cases on record in which people have been bitten by the gila indicate that painful and extensive local swelling results. The only fatality on record from a gila bite, according to the *Arizona Wildlife-Sportsman* (September 1952), was in 1930. However, anyone unfortunate enough to be bitten should use the treatment prescribed for venomous snake bites. Poisonous effects have also been combated effectively by applications of ice—a treatment used for scorpion stings.

The regular food of the gila is centipedes, insects, worms, lizards' and snakes' eggs, and small rodents. The huge tail is used as a farmer uses a silo. The tail apparently acts as a storage place for fats, so that in periods when food is scarce the animal utilizes its accumulated fat. The gila with a thick round tail can live several months without eating, or sustain itself during extremely hot weather when it buries itself deep in the sand.

In late July or early August the female deposits from six to twelve large, soft-shelled eggs in a shallow hole scooped out in moist sand. She covers the clutch by scraping sand over them. About a month later the eggs hatch, and the young gilas emerge. They look like adults in every way, except that the coloring is more vivid and their length is only four inches. As adults they will measure a foot and one half, or occasionally two feet.

Although the gila is dangerous in the wild state, it soon becomes docile in captivity, and even likes to have its beadlike back scratched. Captive gilas are exceedingly fond of eggs, preferably served beaten to a froth. To eat this food from a shallow pan, the animals lap it up with their long flat tongues, then raise their heads so that the fluid runs down their throats.

SIX-LINED LIZARD OR RACE RUNNER

Cnemidophorus sexlineatus

Of all our lizards the one known as the six-lined lizard or race runner has the widest distribution. This dark-brown species, with six bright yellow stripes running from head to tail, inhabits dry areas from the Middle Atlantic States to Florida, and west to Arizona, then north to Nebraska. It is also found in the Mississippi Valley as far north as Lake Michigan.

This is a terrestrial species, and covers the ground at such speeds that it is almost impossible to follow with the eye. The front legs are shorter than those of the back, which may account for its peculiar, jerky gait, and also its ability to rear up and run along on its hind legs. The long, tapering tail is held straight out behind to aid in balance. As the striped lizard moves about on its sandy habitat or often along the edges of dirt roads, the animal searches for insects, its principal diet. But if it happens to locate the nest of a small, ground-nesting bird, the animal cracks the shells with a snap or two of its strong jaws, and laps up the whites and the yolks.

Unlike the American chameleon (*Anolis carolinensis*)—a lizard distinguished by its ability to change color—the race runner cannot assume various hues. Therefore it does not make so interesting a pet as the chameleon, whose color changes are influenced by light, temperature, and excitement—not by placing the creature on variously colored backgrounds.

AMERICAN TOAD

Bufo americanus

Cold-blooded and back-boned, amphibians evolved some 230,-000,000 years ago. In the rock formation known as the Supai formation in the Grand Canyon region are the tracks of some of these first amphibians—fat, sluggish creatures that "pottered," as Thomas Huxley said, "with much belly and little leg, like Falstaff in his old age." Huxley's "potterers" occupy a position in the animal kingdom midway between the fishes and the reptiles.

The term "amphibian" derives from the Greek word "amphi," meaning double, and "bios," meaning life. And that is exactly the kind of lives frogs, toads, salamanders, and newts lead. These creatures hatch from eggs deposited in water, undergo a water-breathing stage as tadpoles, then through changes in form and structure—metamorphosis—they become air-breathing animals. Some continue to live in water; others adopt a primarily terrestrial life. One of these land-dwellers is the toad.

During its active season from April until fall the common toad devours thousands of May beetles, caterpillars, flies, grasshoppers, grubs, and slugs. The animal's enormous consumption of garden and crop pests makes the toad worth about $20.00 a year to argiculturists. (In France the toad is so highly regarded as an aid in controlling insect pests that gardeners buy it for release in gardens.)

The squat brown toad with its rough, warty skin is well equipped to catch insects of all kinds. The long tongue, attached by its tip to the front of the jaws, is covered with a sticky secretion. The toad hops as close as possible without alarming its intended prey, then sits still, cocking its head first one way and then another. When the toad has its prey lined up, it flicks out the entire length of its tongue. The animal manages its tongue with the accuracy of a drover handling a snake whip, and rarely misses its target. The struck insect sticks to the tongue and is thrown back into the mouth. The toad secures its prey so rapidly that the action is almost impossible to follow.

The toad does most of its hunting in the early evening or during the night, after spending the day in a moist, sheltered spot. But once the sun had gone down, the animal comes out of hiding and hops over its territory in search of food; its progress is not distinguished by the long leaps of the frog, for the toad's hind legs are shorter than those of the frog. As the animal moves about, such birds as crows, hawks, and owls prey on it, as well as skunks and snakes.

Although the toad cannot fight predators, the animal does have a defense measure. Behind each eye are two large swellings, known as the parotoid glands. These glands secrete a white, acrid fluid, which the toad emits when in danger or great pain. Skunks that have caught toads are reported to rub their catches over the ground to get rid of the secretion, and dogs that have attacked a toad rarely attack a second one. The toad has another fluid which it secretes when handled. This is watery, colorless, and harmless, and does not cause warts, as many people believe.

Soon after coming out of hibernation the toads foregather in large numbers in ponds and marshes to deposit their eggs. For a few days they lead an aquatic existence; they paddle about to the accompaniment of the singing of the male toads. The females lay strings of eggs beneath the surface of the water. Three to ten days later, depending on the air and water temperatures, the eggs hatch. For the next nine weeks the little toads are in the tadpole stage, but by the middle of July they have lost their tails, have developed legs, and are air-breathing creatures.

Less than half an inch long, the young toads may be found along the edges of ponds and lakes in which they were hatched. At first they stay in hiding near the water, coming out only when the dew is heavy or if there is a shower. But when they have become conditioned to land life, they hop off to find individual territories on which they remain, except for the brief spring interlude each year in water.

In 1953 scientists at the University of Natal, South Africa, discovered that two species of toads related to our American toad changed their skins as frequently as every three or four days. (Some sluggards among other species under observation, however, took as long as nine days.) The molted skins are eaten. And still more recently, scientists at the University of California discovered that the foot-long Colorado toad can squirt its poison twelve feet and devours rats and mice. Such discoveries indicate how much there is still to learn about the wildlife that may be right in our own back yards.

SPRING PEEPER
Hyla crucifer

On a warm spring night prairie pond, woods pool, or marshland is loud with the shrill but sweet song of the peeper—a little frog distinguished by a rough cross on its ash-gray or dark-brown back.

The music of the peeper has a tonal quality like that of distantly heard pipes: four two-toned notes, "Pe-ep, pe-ep, pe-ep, pe-ep," then a pause, after which the four notes are repeated. The second trilling is at a pitch higher than the tone we designate as middle C. To hear the song of the peeper on a night when a marsh is washed with moonlight creates the impression of the primeval—as if you were transported back in time to the period when the world was a vast bog filled with sound as the calls of our first amphibians broke the quiet of the earth in the morning of time.

A cold snap stills the treble voices of the peepers. But if you hear them once in the spring, you can be sure that you will hear them again on their range, anywhere from Canada to Florida, and west to Arkansas and Michigan.

The one-inch peeper, infrequently seen, often heard, belongs to the family of tree toads. On the tips of its fingers and toes are adhesive discs; these enable it to climb and cling to marsh plants. It is almost impossible to locate during the day, but comparatively easy to find at night. With its music as a guide and a flashlight to turn on the spot from which the peeper sings, you are likely to see one clinging to a reed, riding on a floating twig, or sitting on the leaf of a May apple or mandrake.

Once you have located the peeper, you will witness a remarkable performance. The animal assumes a singing stance by rearing back

on its haunches and, in this position, it inflates the white throat, which swells and swells until it looks like a glistening bubble. Then, with the mouth closed, *Hyla crucifer* voices its eerie, swampland song. When the performance is over the throat deflates until a bag of loose skin is left under the chin.

In the early spring the female attaches her eggs to the underwater parts of the stems of plants or lets them float free on the bottom of a pond. Eggs hatch quickly, and for about seven weeks the peeper is in the tadpole stage. By June it has developed into a full-fledged frog, whose over-all size is about that of a honeybee.

Quiet during the summer, the peeper spends most of its time either on the ground hunting for tiny insects of all kinds, or perched in low bushes. When the first frosts rime the leaves and grasses with crystal the peeper buries itself deep under mosses and leaves—not to be heard again until the following year when it announces the advent of spring, the clear, vibrant notes seeming to pipe dogtooth violets, trilliums, and lady slippers up through the carpet of humus on the forest floor.

BULLFROG

Rana catesbiana

The dusky green bullfrog is the biggest and most aquatic of our frogs. This large-headed creature sometimes measures as much as nine inches in length, and has long powerful hind legs and fully webbed feet. Although the male has ears larger than the eyes, those of the female are about the same size as her eyes. Both have green heads, great bulging eyes, white lower jaws, and yellow undersides.

The female is usually larger than the male. Some tubercles, little knobs, roughen the comparatively smooth skin.

Probably better known by sound than by sight, the male bullfrog booms its "Jug-O-Rum" from every pond, pothole, and marshy area east of the Rocky Mountains, and from some sections of the country where it has been introduced. Perched on a snag, the male slowly inflates the internal vocal sacs, which act as resonating organs, then begins its deep-pitched croaking. The sound this frog utters has enough volume to be heard half a mile away. Although the female does not call like the male, she has a piercing squeak when injured or frightened, a sound which is uttered with the mouth wide open. Both sexes give forth with what has been described as a loud "yarp" when startled. The bullfrog generally sounds off in this manner immediately before diving into the water with a loud splash.

One of the last amphibians to rouse from hibernation, the bullfrog does not appear in the quiet parts of ponds until the middle of May. Soon after it emerges from the mud, moist crevice, or hole in which it has passed the winter, the male starts a courting interlude which lasts until July.

Depending upon what part of the range she is in, the female lays jellylike sheets of eggs from February to June. Sometimes a complement of eggs floating upon the surface of a stagnant pool contains 20,000 to 25,000 eggs and covers five square feet.

If the weather is warm eggs may hatch in four days, but if it is cold it may take three weeks. The larval or tadpole stage—when the little creatures have tails—often lasts two or three years. During this prolonged metamorphosis, the "frog" changes from a fish-like creature to a four-legged, tail-less creature with lungs, whose life expectancy may be as much as sixteen years.

In the first stage of its life, the bullfrog eats algae and decaying vegetation. As a juvenile it eats water insects, larvae, and other small living animal matter. As an adult it preys on crayfish, fishes, mice, and salamanders, and other frogs.

Giant water bugs prey on the bullfrog in its early tadpole stage, and such fishes as bass and pike, water birds, and water snakes include the bullfrog in their diets from the time it is hatched until it is fully mature, when opossums, raccoons, and skunks kill it.

The bullfrog escapes some predators by closing its nostrils and sinking to the bottom of a pond, where it lies safe among the roots of pond lilies. The animal can submerge for some time; oxygen is absorbed from the water through the skin.

Man also preys on the bullfrog; the milky white flesh of the hind legs is excellent in both texture and flavor; it tastes like the white meat of chicken. In 1953 the Federal Government estimated the annual catch at about 171,000 pounds, worth approximately $46,000.

The bullfrog is easily caught by tying a piece of brightly colored cloth—preferably red by tradition—on a fishhook at the end of a line attached to a long pole. The gaily "baited" hook is then dangled in front of the frog. This lure is so enticing that a frog often leaps several inches to get it.

One of the best places in the country for frogging is in Florida's vast Everglades. Frogging here is done from air-thrust boats; a two-hour trip, under the direction of an expert frogger, costs ten dollars.

A common species of the Everglades area is the green frog (*Rana clamitans*), also known as the spring frog, the pond frog, the bronze frog, and the screaming frog. This last name derives from its staccato honk. W. Frank Blair, Associate Professor of Zoology at the University of Texas, and a colleague, David Pettus, have made tape recordings of the calls of twenty-seven different frogs and toads. The two men have learned that each species has a call distinctly its own. The Sonoran spadefoot toad (*Scaphiopus couchi*) of the Southwest and Mexico, sounds like a baaing lamb; the barking frog of Texas (*Eleutherodactylus latrans*) has a call somewhat like the yapping of a dog, and the Colorado toad (*Bufo alvarius*) has what these scientists describe as the low-pitched croak of a sick crow.

When the recordings of these voices are run through a machine named Sona-Graph, the call of the narrow-mouthed toad (*Gastrophyne carolinensis*) registers as layers of wave-like lines; that of the green frog looks like intermittent squiggles that grow closer together as the calls increase. The call of the spring peepers, considered the only cheerful frog call by the two zoologists, registers on the tape as a parade of barber poles—symbols for the music that announces that spring is about to come to the land once more.

TIGER SALAMANDER

Ambystoma tigrinum

SPOTTED NEWT

Triturus viridescens

Eye of newt, and toe of frog,
Wool of bat, and tongue of dog.
                    ACT IV, SCENE I, *Macbeth*

The newt, whose eye was one of the ingredients in the witches' brew, is frequently referred to as a Tailed Amphibian. The spotted newt, also known as the pond newt and the red eft, lives in wooded areas in the eastern half of the United States, in parts of the West, and in Canada.

A true amphibian, the newt has two distinct stages in its double life. It hatches in the water, then comes ashore for two or three years. As a land creature the newt measures anywhere from one to three inches and is distinguished by its brilliant coloring. The slender body is brick- or orange-red on the upper side and marked by rows of black-ringed vermilion spots. The underside is a paler hue and dotted with black spots.

On overcast days or at night the newt scurries around on short legs which, like the tail, are regenerated if lost. On bright days the animal remains hidden under stones or logs. And in winter it hibernates under the thick carpet of leaves that covers the floor of the woods.

At the end of its land sojourn the newt is about three and one-half inches in length. It returns to the water, where it undergoes a radical change in appearance. The color on the upper side becomes olive-green, whereas that on the belly is yellow. The spots remain unchanged.

The female lays her eggs during the aquatic part of her life. Early in the spring she attaches them, singly, to water plants. When the baby newt emerges from the egg, it is greenish-brown and has easily seen gills that look like little plumes. During the three months of its tadpole stage, the newt develops lungs and acquires its land color. When this has been accomplished, it comes out on land, where it feeds on insects, snails, and worms. (In water its prey is aquatic insects, their larvae, and other tadpoles.) After its land cycle, the newt spends the rest of its life in the water. But now that it has become an air-breathing animal, the newt must rise to the surface every so often, for it seems to be a law of evolution that a structure (the gills in this instance) once lost can never be regained.

Another tailed amphibian is the salamander, which is most abundant in the eastern United States. All told there are more than one hundred species and subspecies of salamanders, whose shapes, sizes, and colors are varied. They all have one characteristic in common: their skin is smooth and moist—perhaps the reason for the belief that they could pass through fire unharmed, and assuredly the reason for the name, which is Greek for "fire animal."

Among North American salamanders the tiger salamander (*Ambystoma tigrinum*) has the widest distribution. Except for New England, where it is rare, you will find this species in moist places everywhere in the country east of the Pacific coast states.

Seven or eight inches in length the tiger salamander—harmless and beneficial like nearly all amphibians—has a thick body, whose color is rusty black or brown. Large yellow spots and crescent-shaped markings pattern the body, and a yellow patch colors the throat. The underside is gray.

Early in April the tiger salamander breeds in cold springs or spring-fed ponds. The female attaches clusters of eggs to the submerged parts of aquatic plants. Eggs hatch in about two weeks, and after an aquatic larval stage similar to that of the newt, the tiger salamander emerges from the water to live on land. On sunny days it stays under a stone or a log, coming out at night to prey on insects, snails, and worms.

In Mexico the tiger salamander completes its life cycle in the larval stage: it attains maturity, breeds, retains its gills, and never leaves the water. Mexicans call this permanent larval form "axolotl." The animal was described by Francesco Hernandez in 1628 as "a kind of Mexican fish with soft skin and four feet like those of lizards." The first specimens of the axolotl were brought from Mexico to Europe by Alexander von Humboldt after an expedition to Central and South America and Cuba in 1779–1804, and were described by Georges de Cuvier, the zoologist and geologist, who founded the sciences of comparative anatomy and palaeontology. If a pond in which the axolotl lives dries up, the animal is capable of undergoing a transformation in which it develops the necessary characteristics for living on land.

The largest North American salamander is the Congo "eel" or "snake" (*Amphiuma means*), a brownish-black amphibian that reaches a length of two and one-half to three feet and bears a superficial resemblance both to the eel and the snake. And the largest known species, the giant salamander (*Megalobactrachus japonicus*) of China and Japan, reaches a length of six feet.

APPENDIX

SUGGESTED READING

Animals and Man, by G. S. CANSDALE. 200 pp., illus., index. Frederick A. Praeger, New York, 1953.

Animal Facts and Fallacies, by OSMOND P. BRELAND. 268 pp., index. Harper & Brothers, New York, 1948.

Animal Legends, by MAURICE BURTON. 215 pp., illus., index. Frederick Muller, Ltd., London, 1955.

Audubon's Animals, The Quadrapeds of North America, compiled and edited by ALICE FORD. 222 pp., illus., index. The Studio Publications, Inc., in association with Thomas Y. Crowell Company, New York, 1951.

Canadian Spring, by FLORENCE PAGE JAQUES. 216 pp., illus. Harper & Brothers, New York and London, 1947.

Cooking Wild Game, Meat from Forest, Field, and Stream, and how to prepare it for the table—432 recipes, by FRANK G. ASHBROOK and EDNA N. SATER. Foreword by Jay N. Darling. 358 pp., illus., index. Orange Judd Publishing Company, New York, 1945.

Ernest Thompson Seton's America, Selections from the Writings of the Artist-Naturalist, edited by FARIDA WILEY. 413 pp., illus. with drawings by Seton, index. The Devin-Adair Company, New York, 1954.

A Field Guide to Animal Tracks, by OLAUS J. MURIE. 374 pp., illus. by author, index. Houghton Mifflin Company, The Riverside Press, Cambridge, 1954. (Peterson Field Guide Series.)

A Field Guide to the Mammals, by WILLIAM HENRY BURT and RICHARD PHILIP GROSSENHEIDER. 200 pp., illus., index. Houghton Mifflin Company, Boston, 1954. (Peterson Field Guide Series.)

The Golden Treasury of Natural History (juvenile), by BERTHA MORRIS PARKER. 216 pp., illus., index. Simon and Schuster, New York, 1952.

Green Treasury. A Journey Through The World's Great Nature Writing, with introduction and interpretive comments by EDWIN WAY TEALE. 615 pp., illus. Dodd, Mead & Company, New York, 1952.

John Burroughs' America, Selections From The Writings Of The Hudson River Naturalist, edited with an introduction by FARIDA A. WILEY. 203 pp., illus., index. The Devin-Adair Company, New York, 1951.

The Natural History of Mammals, by FRANCOIS BOURLIERE. 363 pp., illus., index. Alfred A. Knopf, New York, 1954.

Nature Roundup, by ROBERT E. PINKERTON. 256 pp., illus., index. Harper & Brothers, New York, 1955.

Nature's Ways, How Nature Takes Care Of Its Own, by ROY CHAPMAN ANDREWS. 206 pp., illus., index. Crown Publishers, Inc., and Creative Bookmaking Guild, Inc., New York, 1951.

North American Birds of Prey, by ALEXANDER SPRUNT, JR. 240 pp., illus., index. Harper & Brothers in cooperation with the National Audubon Society, New York, 1955.

Our Animal Neighbors, by ALAN DEVOE with MARY BERRY DEVOE 279 pp., illus. McGraw-Hill Book Company, Inc., New York, 1953.

Our Wildlife Legacy, by DURWOOD L. ALLEN. 422 pp., illus., index. Funk and Wagnalls Company, New York, 1954.

The Reptiles of North America, by RAYMOND L. DITMARS. 476 pp., illus., index. Doubleday & Company, Inc., Garden City, New York, 1949.

The Strange World of Nature, by BERNARD GOOCH. 160 pp., illus., index. Thomas Y. Crowell Company, New York, 1950.

They Hop and Crawl, by PERCY A. MORRIS. 253 pp., illus., index. The Ronald Press Company, New York, 1945.

Ways of Mammals, In Fact and Fancy, by CLIFFORD B. MOORE. 273 pp., index. The Ronald Press Company, New York, 1953.

The World of Natural History (as revealed in The American Museum of Natural History), by John Richard Saunders. 320 pp., illus., index. Sheridan House, New York, 1952.

The World We Live In, by the Editorial Staff of *Life* and Lincoln Barnett. 304 pp., illus., index. Time Incorporated, New York, 1955.

WHERE TO GO TO SEE WILDLIFE

The following publications are guides to Federal areas supporting wildlife; some list species likely to be seen:

National-Forest Vacations, United States Department of Agriculture, Forest Service. 60 pp., illus. Lists all National Forests, their locations, and wildlife resources. For sale by the Superintendent of Documents, U. S. Government Printing Office, Washington 25, D. C. Price, 25 cents.

Areas Administered by the National Park Service, United States Department of the Interior, National Park Service, 52 pp., index. Lists all National Parks, their locations, and outstanding characteristics including wildlife. Obtainable from National Parks Service, U. S. Department of the Interior, Washington 25, D. C.

List of National Wildlife Refuges, United States Department of the Interior, Fish and Wildlife Service. Wildlife Leaflet 372. Lists all National Wildlife Refuges, their locations, type of refuge, and its wildlife. Obtainable from Fish and Wildlife Service, U. S. Department of the Interior, Washington 25, D. C.

Visiting National Wildlife Refuges, Refuge Leaflet 1, United States Department of the Interior. 8 pp., illus., locator map of 73 refuges. For sale by the Superintendent of Documents, U. S. Government Printing Office, Washington 25, D. C. Price, 10 cents.

National Audubon Society Nature Camps and Tours: Consult your local Audubon Society or write National Audubon Society Headquarters, 1130 Fifth Avenue, New York 28, N. Y.

Frog calls, 285
Frogging, 285
Frogs, 282–285
  Bullfrog, 283 f.
  Peeper, spring, 282
  Other species, 285
Fur-durability ratings, 7

Gaufre, 62
Geomyidae, 60 ff.
George VI, King, 177
Gila monster, 276 f.
Glacier National Park, 135, 147, 246,
  252
Glaucomys sabrinus, 91
        volans, 88 ff.
Goat, mountain, 243 ff.
Grand Teton National Park, 252
Great Plains, 55
Great Smoky National Park, 146
Ground squirrels, 59
Gulo luscus, 182

Hares, 28–38
  Arctic, 32 ff.
  European, 38
  Jack rabbits, 34 ff.
  Varying, 28 ff.
Hearn, John E., quoted, 129
"Hedgehog," 118
Heloderma suspectum, 276 f.
Hernandez, Francesco, quoted, 275, 288
Heterodon, 265 f.
Hibernation, 45, 53
Hines, Bob, 200
Hippolestes, 208
Hornaday, William Temple, 13
Horned toad, 274 f.
Horse-killer, 208
Hudson's Bay Company, 135, 167
Humboldt, Alexander von, 288
Hyla crucifer, 282

Indian Service, 59
Introduced species, 38, 99, 112, 122

"Jackass deer," 223
"Jackass hare," 36
Jaguar, 209
Jaguarundi, 210
James I, King, 90
Javelina, 210
"Jumping deer," 219

Kendall, George Wilkins, quoted, 58
Key deer, 218
Kittams, Walter H., quoted, 226

Land Management, Bureau of, 59
Le siffleur, 51
Lepus americanus, 28 ff.
    arcticus, 32 ff.
    californicus, 34 ff.
    europeus, 38
    othus, 32 ff.
    townsendii, 34 ff.
Lewis and Clark Expedition, 147, 244
Little chief hare, 27
Lizards, 274–278
  Gila monster, 276 f.
  Horned toad, 274 f.
  Race runner, or six-lined lizard, 278
Long, Stephen H., expedition, 9, 127
Lutra canadensis, 195 ff.
Lycanthropy, 135
Lynx, 210
Lynx canadensis, 210
    rufus, 211 f.

Macrochelys temminckii, 271
Marmot, hoary, 50 ff.
        yellow-bellied, 51
Marmota caligata, 50 ff.
        flaviventris, 51
        monax, 44 ff.
Marsh hare, 106
Marsh-management tools, 109, 123
Marsh rat, 106
Marsupial, 4
Marten, 166 ff.
Martes americana, 166 ff.
        pennanti, 170 ff.
Mast, 80, 81
Mattamuskeet National Wildlife
      Refuge, 200
Megalobactrachus japonicus, 289
Melanism, 82
Mephitis macroura, 189
        mephitis, 183 ff.
Mice, 94–99
  House, 99
  Meadow, 96
  White-footed, 94 ff.
Michtom, Morris, 146
Microtus pennsylvanicus, 96
Milner Pass, 249
Miner's cat, 159
Mink, 178 ff.
Mink ranching, 181
Moles, 13
Molossidae, 17
Monroe, Hugh, 135
Moose, 227 ff.
Mountain beaver, 173
Mountain lion, 206 ff.